AN ILLUSTRATED REFERENCE ON

HEAVEN

PARADISE

AND THE AFTERLIFE

HEAVEN

THE INSIDE STORY FROM THE BIBLE

AN ILLUSTRATED REFERENCE ON

HEAVEN

PARADISE

AND THE AFTERLIFE

HEAVEN

THE INSIDE STORY FROM THE BIBLE

ED STRAUSS

BARBOUR BOOKS

An Imprint of Barbour Publishing, Inc.

Print ISBN 978-1-63058-344-6

Published by Barbour Books, an imprint of Barbour Publishing, Inc., P.O. Box 719, Uhrichsville, Ohio 44683, www.barbourbooks.com

Our mission is to publish and distribute inspirational products offering exceptional value and biblical encouragement to the masses.

Member of the
Evangelical Christian
Publishers Association

Printed in China.

CONTENTS

INTRODUCTION

In 2012, I wrote *What the Bible Says about Heaven* as a brief treatise on the wonderful hope we have as Christians. Its purpose was to give biblical insights about Heaven, supplemented by inspiring quotes from great men and women of God, in order to help readers become aware of the reality of the bright new world we look forward to and foster an eternal perspective.

This present volume is intended as a more definitive reference book. As such, it takes a detailed look at what the Bible says about Heaven and its myriad inhabitants, as well as the many objects, structures, and places that are a reality in the heavenly realm.

This book also examines the history of God's revelations about Sheol and Paradise and shows how our doctrines of the afterlife sprang from the many truths scattered throughout the ancient scriptures. It also explores the three historic stages of Heaven: (a) Abraham's Bosom, the place to which Old Testament saints went; (b) the heavenly city, New Jerusalem, to which Christians have gone for the past two thousand years; and (c) the coming kingdom, the New Heaven and the New Earth, where believers of all ages will one day live.

We have dedicated a chapter to examining the influence that Greek philosophers are said to have had on Jewish concepts of Heaven and Hell. Rather than the Jews borrowing from the Greeks (as is commonly supposed), the Greeks were most probably inspired by the ancient Jewish scriptures.

This book will also examine several misconceptions about Heaven that persist in the public perception, even among Bible-believing Christians. And since a flurry of books have come out in recent years describing near-death experiences and supposed visits to Heaven, this volume will also briefly examine these claims.

The apostle Paul tells us that our heavenly Father has enabled us "to share in the inheritance of his holy people in the kingdom of light. For he has rescued us from the dominion of darkness and brought us into the kingdom of the Son he loves" (Colossians 1:12–13 NIV). Therefore, any meaningful discussion of Christ's kingdom of light must include a description of the dark domain from which we were saved. This is integral to understanding the afterlife and appreciating the tremendous value of our salvation.

Some concepts in this book may seem new or unusual; however, I urge you not to dismiss them just because you've never heard them before. Most are the consensus opinions of serious evangelical scholars who have studied the Bible in depth. And though at times I present some new concepts for you to ponder, I trust you will see that they, too, are grounded in scripture and worth serious consideration.

Ed Strauss

1 THE AFTERLIFE AND PARADISE

THE HEBREWS AND HEAVEN

If you browse Jewish websites discussing Heaven and Hell, one thing you'll notice is the belief that the Bible gives scarcely any information about the afterlife. The reason for this, the commentators explain, is that God probably wants us to focus on living *this* life. Christians may wonder, with the fullness of the New Testament in mind, how anyone could imagine a lack of biblical information about the afterlife. But we must remember that the Jewish scriptures consist of only the books from Genesis to Malachi.

Nevertheless, doesn't the Old Testament contain scores of verses that speak of God in Heaven? And didn't more than half a dozen Jewish prophets have visions of God on His throne, surrounded by His heavenly entourage? And what about the accounts of Enoch and Elijah being carried up to Heaven? And doesn't Isaiah 14:9–11 show the dark side of the afterlife, depicting departed kings speaking to new arrivals in Hell?

We will carefully consider all these questions. In the process, we'll learn that the Law and the Prophets contain myriad scattered pieces of the puzzle, which, when viewed together, give us a fascinating big picture of the spiritual world and the world to come—*Gan Eden*, as Jewish scholars call it, the eternal Garden of Eden.

In the first century of the Common Era, a majority of Jews believed in spirits that survive death. As Luke writes, "The Sadducees say that there is no resurrection, and that there are neither angels nor spirits, but the Pharisees believe all these things" (Acts 23:8 NIV). The Sadducees, however, argued that any descriptions of spirits conscious in an afterlife were mere metaphors, and that actual reality was found in verses such as Ecclesiastes 9:5—"For the living know they will die; but the dead know nothing, and they have no more reward"—and Psalm 6:5 (NIV): "Among the dead no one proclaims your name. Who praises you from the grave?" (See also Job 7:7–10; Ecclesiastes 9:10; Isaiah 38:18.)

Job seems to agree with this perspective: "As the cloud disappears and vanishes away, so he who goes down to the grave does

▶ Artist Phillip Medhurst's depiction of Enoch being taken to Heaven without experiencing death (1582–1583).

Rembrandt (1606–1669) depicts the "angel of the LORD" calling to Abraham from Heaven to prevent Abraham from sacrificing his son.

not come up" (Job 7:9). This present life is ghostlike enough—"but a breath" (Job 7:7 NIV). As David writes, "You have made my days a mere handbreadth; the span of my years is as nothing before you. Everyone is but a breath, even those who seem secure. Surely everyone goes around like a mere phantom" (Psalm 39:5–6 NIV).

Although mortals are described throughout the pages of the Old Testament as flickering shadows moving swiftly across the face of the earth—mere breaths (Psalm 144:4)—God Himself is described as an immortal, spiritual being whose "years are throughout all generations" (Psalm 102:24). So where does *He* live?

GOD AND ANGELS IN HEAVEN

In the Hebrew scriptures, God is repeatedly called "the creator of heaven *and* earth" and the "God of heaven *and* earth." But this only says that He created everything and owns it all. The first indication that He actually *dwells* in the heavens is found in Genesis 24:7, where Abraham refers to "the LORD God of heaven."

A century later (ca. 1930 BC), when Jacob was fleeing from his brother, Esau, he spent the night near Bethel and had a dream "in which he saw a stairway resting on the earth, with its top reaching to heaven, and the angels of God were ascending and descending on it. There above it stood the LORD" (Genesis 28:12–13 NIV).

Around 1400 BC, Moses wrote, "Look down from Your holy habitation, from heaven, and bless Your people Israel" (Deuteronomy 26:15 NASB). Written four centuries later, Psalm 115 declares: "Our God is in the heavens; He does whatever He pleases," and "The heavens are the heavens of the LORD, but the earth He has given to the sons of men" (vv. 3, 16 NASB). Though these mentions of God's heavenly abode are not numerous in the Hebrew scriptures, they nevertheless convey a consistent biblical view over a period of many centuries.

Further, we're told in Genesis 21:17 that "the angel of God called to Hagar out of heaven"; and when Abraham was about to sacrifice Isaac, "the angel of the LORD called to him from heaven" (Genesis

▶ A NASA image shows the formation of a nebula—gas, dust, and other matter that eventually form stars. This illustrates the unimaginable concept of God "heaving up things" to create the universe.

22:11 NASB). These angelic appearances, when combined with Jacob's vision of angels on the staircase to Heaven, and God Himself at the top of the stairs, show that very early in Hebrew culture, spiritual beings called angels were understood to dwell with God in a blessed, unseen realm. Though the Hebrews were unable to determine a precise location for this heavenly realm, they were certain it was above and separate from the earth.

In the book of Isaiah, we find this enigmatic statement: "Thus says the Lord: 'Heaven is My throne, and earth is My footstool'" (Isaiah 66:1). But King Solomon realized that even the heavens weren't spacious enough for God's abode: "Behold, heaven and the heaven of heavens cannot contain You" (1 Kings 8:27). This brings us to a foundational question: What exactly does the Bible mean when it says "heaven" or "the heavens"?

"HEAVED UP THINGS"

Whenever the Old Testament refers to "the heavens," it's usually not referring to the place where God lives; instead, "the heavens" refers to the vault of the sky where birds fly (Genesis 1:20), or the highest heavens where the stars are (Genesis 1:14; Deuteronomy 10:14). The Hebrew words translated as "heavens" are *shamayim* and *shemayin*, which literally mean "heaved up things." The English word *heaven* derives from the word *heave*. To heave something is to throw it purposefully and with great force—imagery that evokes the creation of the universe.

> **FAR-OUT THEORETICAL MUSINGS**
> Some physicists say that when the big bang occurred, the expansion happened at different speeds, causing an almost infinite number of "multiverses" to come into being, like bubbles in the space-time fabric. They speculate that separate universes formed, very likely with different laws governing their matter and energy.

There was a powerful, instantaneous spreading out of all primordial light and matter—a big bang moment, if you will—in which God "created the heavens and stretched them out" (Isaiah 42:5), heaving them out from a single point in space and time. Isaiah also speaks of God as the One who "stretches out the heavens like a curtain, and spreads them out like a tent to dwell in" (Isaiah 40:22). Scientists tell us that the universe is still spreading out.

But even this immense physical universe, no matter how much it expands, cannot contain God. And because He and the heavenly host existed before the creation of the physical heavens, it's apparent that the spiritual realm existed before time began.

So what are the heavens? The sky where birds fly is the first Heaven; the highest heavens, where the stars are, is the second Heaven; and the spiritual dimension, where God dwells, is the third Heaven. In the New Testament, Paul writes, "I was caught up to the third heaven. . . . I was caught up to paradise" (2 Corinthians 12:2, 4 NLT). Paul also refers to the heavenly city as "the Jerusalem above" (Galatians 4:26). So Heaven, in some sense, is definitely above us.

HEAVEN IN THE CLOUDS?

Many people have the idea that Heaven is an indefinite dreamscape of cumulus clouds, where we will float around weightlessly, on fluffy clouds, playing harps. They envision Heaven as a copy of the atmospheric heavens. They have likely come to this conclusion by misinterpreting verses about Jesus Christ's return to earth.

▶ A picture of clouds, which is where those who trust Jesus will meet Him before He leads them to Heaven.

"They will see the Son of Man coming on the clouds of heaven" (Matthew 24:30 NLT).

"Behold, he cometh with clouds; and every eye shall see him" (Revelation 1:7 KJV).

"Then we who are alive and remain shall be caught up together with them in the clouds to meet the Lord in the air" (1 Thessalonians 4:17).

These verses indicate that when Jesus returns, He will appear above the earth in the atmospheric heavens, and those who are alive in that day will be caught up to meet Him "in the clouds. . .in the air." But that's not our *destination*. That's simply where we will rendezvous with Jesus, in plain sight of the astonished world. Once we have joined Him, *that's* when Jesus will take us to Heaven.

HEAVEN IN ANOTHER DIMENSION

For centuries, the prevailing scientific view has been that the universe consists of four dimensions: *height, width, length*, and *time*. Together, these are known as *space-time*. Christians believe there is a fifth dimension, a spiritual dimension, that can't be perceived with our five senses because it is above and beyond the plane of physical matter. But within the realm of science, the temporal world comprises all there is to reality.

In the late 1960s, as scientists continued in their efforts to understand how the universe works, they were forced to the astonishing conclusion that reality consists of no fewer than *twenty-six* dimensions, containing unphysical particle states, all coexisting within the four-dimensional physical realm. This theory (called bosonic string theory) was later revised (by what is called m-theory) to include only eleven dimensions—the four space-time dimensions we all recognize and seven others that are "rolled up" at the subatomic level.

Some physicists have suggested that the matter and energy that make up our visible universe account for only 4 percent of all matter and energy. They postulate that theoretical forms of unseen "dark matter" make up the other 96 percent of our universe and account for its missing mass. The fact that this unphysical matter is undetectable (except by gravitational lensing) doesn't bother them. It makes sense mathematically, seems to explain a mystery of the universe, and is therefore accepted.

Other physicists, however, reject the existence of dark matter. They propose that hypothetical "gravitons" produce gravity in another, unseen dimension, and a small amount of it leaks into our reality from there.

As fantastic as these hypotheses sound, some of the world's most intelligent thinkers take them very seriously. All this to say that science has come a long way since the days when it was believed we live in a four-dimensional universe and that a spiritual dimension couldn't exist.

HEAVEN IS NOT FAR OFF

Heaven refers not only to the heavenly dimension, but also specifically to the New Jerusalem, the city of God that exists within this dimension. It is the eternal place where God dwells, "the city of the living God, the heavenly Jerusalem" (Hebrews 12:22). The apostle John writes, "I saw the holy city, new Jerusalem. . . . And I heard a loud voice from the throne, saying, 'Behold, the tabernacle of God'" (Revelation 21:2–3 NASB).

Many Christians believe that Heaven is somewhere among the stars, a fantastic distance away from us in the Milky Way galaxy. Job asked, "Is not God in the height of heaven?" (Job 22:12). Yes, He is. But how high up and how far out there?

Other Christians believe that the heavenly city is beyond the most distant galaxy, at the uttermost edge of the universe. Some people who claim to have visited Heaven describe traveling an immense distance past all the stars and finally arriving there. Others describe an almost instant arrival. This was the apostle John's experience. He saw a door open, heard a voice say, "Come up here, and. . .at once. . .there before me was a throne in heaven" (Revelation 4:1–2 NIV, emphasis added).

The scriptures don't say that Heaven is far off. Paul said that God

▶ Though the opening of Heaven is often described as having gates, and the apostle John described a door opening, other scriptures describe it as a tear in space and time.

"is not far from any one of us. For in him we live and move and exist" (Acts 17:27–28 NLT). Solomon said that "heaven and the heaven of heavens cannot contain Him" (2 Chronicles 2:6), which hints that God is not a *physical* distance away from us. He inhabits a timeless spiritual dimension outside of, but coexisting with, our present space-time continuum. "For thus says the High and Lofty One Who inhabits eternity, whose name is Holy: 'I dwell in the high and holy place'" (Isaiah 57:15). So where is this "high and holy place" beyond space and time? In modern terms, we'd say that Heaven is in another dimension. As Randy Alcorn asks in his book titled *Heaven*, "Is it possible that Heaven itself is but inches away from us?"[1]

Scriptures such as 2 Kings 7:2 and Malachi 3:10 refer to God's opening up "the windows of heaven." Some people believe these are literally windows and that the inhabitants of Heaven can look through them and watch us here on earth. Though this is entirely plausible, if it's true, it's probably only a secondary meaning.

The Hebrew word for "windows" in these verses is *arubbah*, which does mean "window," but scholars say a more precise meaning is "crevices." In other words, God creates crevices (or openings) in the heavens. Isaiah exclaims to God, "Oh, that You would rend the heavens! That You would come down!" (Isaiah 64:1). In other words, "God, create a tear in the space-time fabric and come through from the heavenly dimension." That's precisely what God has done at times. "He opened the heavens and came down" (Psalm 18:9 NLT).

Ezekiel writes, "In my thirtieth year. . .while I was among the exiles by the Kebar River, the heavens were opened and I saw visions of God" (Ezekiel 1:1 NIV). Consider also the time when Jesus was baptized in the Jordan River: "When He had been baptized, Jesus came up immediately from the water; and behold, the heavens were opened to Him, and He saw the Spirit of God descending like a dove and alighting upon Him" (Matthew 3:16).

WHEN DID GOD CREATE HEAVEN?

Has Heaven always existed? God has always existed, and it's difficult to imagine Him dwelling for endless ages in utter nothingness. Of course, God existed before anything He created, even His heavenly surroundings. But even if Heaven hasn't *always* existed, it has existed for eons longer than we can begin to fathom.

From the earliest mentions, every time a prophet had a vision of God, He was seated on His throne in Heaven, often surrounded by cherubim, seraphim, and angels (Exodus 24:9–10; Isaiah 6:1–2; Ezekiel 1:4–5, 26–28; Daniel 7:9–14; Revelation 4:2–5). Also, sometime before our earth came into being, God created millions of angels. When He "laid the earth's foundation. . .all the angels shouted for joy" (Job 38:4, 7 NIV). These celestial hosts, together with the cherubim and seraphim surrounding God's throne, already existed—and they weren't simply drifting in a void before physical matter was formed. We can therefore safely conclude that Heaven

▶ The Karlskirche church fresco by Johann Michael Rottmayr (1656–1730), depicting angels and cherubim that the Bible says were present before the creation of the universe.

and the spiritual dimension existed before the creation of the physical universe.

PREPARING HEAVENLY PLACES

Now we must ask: Has Heaven always existed *as it presently is*? As we shall see, the reason this question is important is that before Jesus ascended to Heaven, Old Testament believers didn't go to Heaven when they died. Instead, their spirits went to the unseen state of Sheol under the earth. The obvious question is *why*? Was Heaven at that point not ready for the spirits of departed humans?

Jesus told His disciples, "In My Father's house are many mansions; if it were not so, I would have told you. I go to prepare a place for you. And if I go and prepare a place for you, I will come again and receive you to Myself; that where I am, there you may be also" (John 14:2–3).

The common interpretation of "I go to prepare a place for you" is that Jesus meant that our habitations in Heaven weren't built yet. And according to folk theology, we "send up the building materials" for our mansions by doing good deeds. You might also hear Christians say, "Jesus has been building our heavenly mansions for the past two thousand years. So imagine how wonderful they'll be!" One could be forgiven for imagining vast areas of the heavenly city as busy construction zones. But is this actually the case? Was Heaven smaller previously, and has it since sprawled out into celestial suburbs to accommodate us?

> **MAKE READY FOR US**
>
> At the final Passover, Jesus' disciples asked Him, "Where do You want us to go and prepare, that You may eat the Passover?" He told them to go into the city and that a wealthy man would show them a large upper room, *already* furnished and prepared. Jesus said to "make ready for us" there (Mark 14:12–16). In the same way, Jesus is making Heaven ready for us.

Note that Jesus spoke in the *present* tense when He said, "In My Father's house *are* many mansions." These many mansions (literally, *dwellings*) already existed two thousand years ago. Jesus didn't have to hurry to Heaven to start building. Rather, He promised to "prepare" already-existing dwellings. The heavenly city, with its many dwellings, was already in place. Jesus simply had to make them ready for us.

However, *before* Jesus' day, Heaven was indeed "under construction," and this seems to be one reason why the Old Testament saints went to Sheol instead. The main reason, however, was that Jesus had not yet been incarnated and had not yet died for our sins to open the way to Heaven. There is only one way to enter the Father's presence: through Jesus (John 14:6).

Around 750 BC, the prophet Amos declared: "The Lord, the LORD Almighty. . .builds his lofty palace in the heavens and sets its foundation on the earth" (Amos 9:5–6 NIV). Because this verse stipulates that God "*builds* [present tense] his lofty palace in the heavens," it appears that during the Old Testament era—right up until Jesus' day—Heaven was still being prepared for God's people.

In AD 55, however, when Paul wrote to the church in Corinth, Heaven was both built and prepared. Paul writes, "Eye has not seen, nor ear heard, nor have entered into the heart of man the things which God *has prepared* for those who love Him" (1 Corinthians 2:9, emphasis added). And the writer of Hebrews says that God "has prepared a city for them" (Hebrews 11:16).

HEAVEN AT THE DAWN OF TIME

To get an idea of what Heaven was like at the beginning of time, we must look at what the Bible says about Satan's rebellion. We aren't told the precise time of this event, but many believe it happened before the creation of the earth. Very likely, however, it happened shortly *after* God formed the physical Creation. God made the angels, including the devil, before making the earth, yet after this, "God saw *all* that He had made, and behold, it was *very good*" (Genesis 1:31 NASB, emphasis added). This seems to indicate that Satan hadn't yet fallen from his original state. Also, the Bible specifies that Satan walked "in Eden, the garden of God," at which time he was still "perfect in [his] ways" (Ezekiel 28:13, 15). So every indication is that he rebelled sometime

▶ Artist Thomas Cole's (1801–1848) perspective of what Paradise looked like at creation, before the fall of Satan.

after the creation of Adam and Eve.

Satan was originally an exalted cherub named Lucifer (literally, *Day Star* or *Light-bearer*), and he had a throne and a position of great majesty and authority. But he was envious of God and aspired to be worshipped in His place. In the following passage, the prophet Isaiah describes the devil's fall: "How you are fallen from heaven, O Lucifer, son of the morning! . . . For you have said in your heart: 'I will ascend into heaven, I will exalt my throne above the stars of God; I will also sit on the mount of the congregation on the farthest sides of the north; I will ascend above the heights of the clouds, I will be like the Most High.' Yet you shall be brought down to Sheol, to the lowest depths of the Pit" (Isaiah 14:12–15).

Ezekiel also describes Lucifer's fall, saying: "You were in Eden, the garden of God; every precious stone was your covering: the ruby, the topaz and the diamond; the beryl, the onyx and the jasper; the lapis lazuli, the turquoise and the emerald; and the gold, the workmanship of your settings and sockets, was in you. On the day that you were created they were prepared. You were the anointed cherub who covers, and I placed you there. You were on the holy mountain of God; you walked in the midst of the stones of fire. . . . And you sinned; therefore I have cast you as profane from the mountain of God. And I have destroyed you, O covering cherub, from the midst of the stones of fire" (Ezekiel 28:13–14, 16 NASB).

For now, we won't focus on Satan's rebellion. The purpose of quoting these passages is to gain an idea of what Heaven was like at Creation. The first thing that stands out is that Heaven is called "the holy mountain of God" and "the mount of the congregation." As we shall soon see, it was also called "the mountain of the LORD's house" (Isaiah 2:2; Micah 4:1).

THE SHAPE OF GOD'S CITY, NEW JERUSALEM

The apostle John tells us, "The city was laid out like a square, as long as it was wide. He [the angel who talked with me] measured the city with the rod and found it to be 12,000 stadia [1,400 miles] in length, and as wide and high as it is long" (Revelation 21:16 NIV). Some people believe this means that the heavenly city is one enormous cube, and this is a possibility. After all, the Holy of Holies inside the earthly Temple was also a perfect cube (1 Kings 6:20). However, some scholars believe that the consistency of the dimensions should not be understood as a literal description of the *shape* of the heavenly city.

If we even think about it at all, we might imagine Heaven as an enormous, shining, many-spired city spread out on one level, similar to modern cities. Some might visualize it as covering a vast area with God's dwelling in the center—perhaps with His abode somewhat elevated, just as the palaces of many ancient kings rose on lofty citadels overlooking the rest of the royal city.

▶ Mount Everest, the tallest mountain in the world, reaching upward for 5½ miles. The book of Daniel describes the heavenly city as a huge mountain that fills the whole earth.

There is a third alternative, however: the persistent image throughout the Old Testament is that God's dwelling is shaped like a mountain. In addition to the imagery in Ezekiel, the prophet Daniel depicts the kingdom of God as "a huge mountain [that] filled the whole earth" (Daniel 2:35 NIV), and Zechariah calls it "the Mountain of the LORD of hosts, the Holy Mountain" (Zechariah 8:3). The writer of Hebrews states, "For you have not come to a mountain that can be touched [referring to Mount Sinai]. . . . But you have come to Mount Zion and to the city of the living God, the heavenly Jerusalem" (Hebrews 12:18, 22 NASB).

But what about Revelation 21:16, which seems to describe God's city as a cube? Notice that when John first describes the New Jerusalem as "laid out like a square, as long as it was wide," he doesn't include the *height* of the city in his initial statement. John is informing us that the *base* is a square. Later, he states that its length and width and height were each 1,400 miles. But if we consider statements elsewhere in scripture that depict Heaven as a great mountain, it would suggest the city is 1,400 miles high at its *peak*. It could well be said that God's "lofty palace" (Amos 9:6 NIV) is a multilevel, many-spired citadel of golden crystal, towering far higher than any terrestrial mountain. Notice also the reference to "stones of fire" in Ezekiel 28:14, 16. The entire city is composed of gemstones of unearthly, resplendent beauty, glowing with inner light. This dovetails with John's description of "the Holy City, Jerusalem, coming down out of heaven from God. It shone with the glory of God, and its brilliance was like that of a very precious jewel, like a jasper, clear as crystal. . . . The wall was made of jasper, and the city of pure gold, as pure as glass. . . . The great street of the city was of gold, as pure as transparent glass" (Revelation 21:10–11, 18, 21 NIV).

Revelation 21:10 says that at the end of time, the 1,400-mile high heavenly city will come down out of Heaven to earth, utterly dwarfing the mountains. (Mount Everest stands only five and a half miles high.) This event is described by Isaiah as well: "And it shall come to pass in the last days, that the mountain of the LORD's house

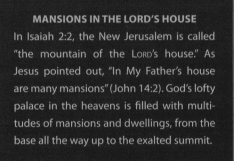

MANSIONS IN THE LORD'S HOUSE
In Isaiah 2:2, the New Jerusalem is called "the mountain of the LORD's house." As Jesus pointed out, "In My Father's house are many mansions" (John 14:2). God's lofty palace in the heavens is filled with multitudes of mansions and dwellings, from the base all the way up to the exalted summit.

shall be established in the top of the mountains, and shall be exalted above the hills; and all nations shall flow unto it" (Isaiah 2:2 KJV).

Does the *shape* of the heavenly city really matter? Perhaps not. The most important thing is that God lives there, that our names are written in the Lamb's Book of Life, and that we're destined to go there. In the meantime, however, it can be fascinating to examine scripture to try to get an idea of what our eternal home will be like.

GOD DWELLING ON A MOUNTAINTOP

In both the Bible and in other literature of the ancient world, God and other gods are described repeatedly as dwelling on mountains. Almost all ancient peoples envisioned God, or their gods, as dwelling

This print from the Phillip Medhurst Collection of Bible illustrations shows Moses receiving the 10 Commandments on Mount Sinai. God revealed His glory throughout the Bible on the tops of mountains, which are shadows of the true mountain of the Lord in Heaven.

on the tops of mountains. The ancient Greeks, for example, originally thought that Zeus and his quarreling offspring dwelled on the summit of Mount Olympus. Later, as they became aware that Olympus was merely a mountain, they theorized that the actual dwelling place of the gods was a mountain in the spiritual realm.

The Canaanites believed that El, the Creator God, ruled seventy lesser gods on top of Mount Zaphon, which rises along the seacoast on the border of Turkey and Syria. (Mount Zaphon is named in Psalm 48:2 and Isaiah 14:13 in the New International Version.) In addition, the Canaanites worshipped their gods on "high places" and every high hill throughout the land. So did the idolatrous Israelites after them. In the words of the prophet Hosea, "They offer sacrifices on the mountaintops, and burn incense on the hills" (Hosea 4:13).

The Sumerians lived on the plains along the Tigris and Euphrates rivers, with no mountains nearby. Instead, they built mountain-shaped temples, called ziggurats, and their priests worshipped and sacrificed to their gods on the summits of these temples.

The true God also manifested Himself on a mountaintop. When the Israelites were in the Sinai desert, they journeyed to "Horeb, the mountain of God" (1 Kings 19:8; Exodus 4:27), also called Mount Sinai and "the mountain of the LORD" (Numbers 10:33). "The LORD descended to the top of Mount Sinai and called Moses to the top of the mountain. . . . The glory of the LORD looked like a consuming fire on the top of the mountain" (Exodus 19:20; 24:17 NIV).

Later, Mount Moriah (also

THE MEANING OF "HELL"

Why is *Sheol* translated as "hell" in our English Bibles? The fault is not with the translators, but with the meaning read into the word *hell* in later centuries. According to the *Dictionary of Word Origins* and other sources, the English word *hell* (from the ancient Indo-Aryan word *kel*, to "conceal") originally meant "a hidden place; a covered place." To "hell potatoes" was to bury them underground or store them in a cellar. (Our English word *cellar* and the German *keller* also come from *kel*.) To "go to hell" originally meant to be dead and buried. So when "hell" was used to describe Sheol, it didn't mean a place of eternal torment. It was simply the "unseen state" under the earth.

called Mount Zion, though it is only a small hill) became known as the mountain of God, especially after the Temple was built there. It was called "the mount of the house of the LORD" (2 Chronicles 33:15) and "His holy mountain" (Psalm 48:1). The Bible states that "the LORD of hosts will reign on Mount Zion and in Jerusalem" (Isaiah 24:23), but Mount Horeb and Mount Zion are both symbols of the *true* mountain of the Lord, pale shadows of the heavenly Mount Zion above.

God dwells in New Jerusalem (Revelation 21:2–3), but where exactly in the city does He dwell? As you might have guessed, His throne room is on the very *top* of the mount of assembly. That's why the devil wanted to set *his* throne on the summit. He said, "I will sit enthroned on the mount of assembly, on the utmost heights. . . . I will make myself like the Most High" (Isaiah 14:13–14 NIV).

HEBREW *SHEOL* AND ENGLISH *HELL*

Although the Hebrews firmly believed that God and His angels lived in a heavenly realm above, they didn't think that anyone—even the departed righteous—went to be with them when they died. Instead, their spirits went to Sheol, under the earth. So now that we've had a look at Heaven, the abode of God, let's investigate what Sheol was like.

In our modern English Bibles, the Hebrew word *Sheol* is normally translated as "the grave" or "hell." The King James Version translates *Sheol* as "grave" thirty-one times, "hell" another thirty-one times, and "the pit" three times. Thus we read, "The wicked shall be turned intov hell [*Sheol*], and all the nations that forget God" (Psalm 9:17 KJV). But the same word is translated differently in Genesis 37:35, when the patriarch Jacob grieves for his son Joseph: "He refused to be comforted; and he said, For I will go down into the grave [*Sheol*] unto my son mourning" (Genesis 37:35 KJV).

The ancient Hebrews didn't think of Sheol as a place of infernal heat or torment. According to *Young's Analytical Concordance*, Sheol simply means "the unseen state." It was the abode of the dead, both the righteous and the unrighteous.

SHEOL, THE SHADOWY REALM

According to the ancient book of Job, Sheol was the underworld, the realm of darkness where the dead dwelled. Job lived about 1600 BC in the land of Uz, apparently to the east of Canaan, and he believed in the God of Abraham. Job gives the earliest descriptions of the shadowy realm of Sheol.

▶ Friedrich Wilhelm Schadow's (1789–1862) concept of Jacob's reaction to hearing of his son Joseph's death.

While suffering, Job wished that he had died, declaring that then "I would have lain still and been quiet, I would have been asleep; then I would have been at rest with kings and counselors of the earth. . . . There the wicked cease from troubling, and there the weary are at rest. There the prisoners rest together; they do not hear the voice of the oppressor. The small and great are there, and the servant is free from his master" (Job 3:13–14, 17–19).

The Hebrews understood the grave to be a place where "the dead

▶ A photograph of the Jewish cemetery in Jerusalem at the base of the Mount of Olives.

do not know anything" (Ecclesiastes 9:5 NASB). The sons of Korah asked, "Shall Your lovingkindness be declared in the grave? Or Your faithfulness in the place of destruction? Shall Your wonders be known in the dark? And Your righteousness in the land of forgetfulness?" (Psalm 88:11–12). For many, this sounds as if we simply cease to exist in the grave.

With Isaiah 14:9–11 in view, however, we see Sheol as the place where the spirits of kings (mentioned above in Job) are stirred up to greet recent arrivals to their dismal realm. But Job didn't yet have the benefit of this later revelation. Instead, Job says, "I leave—never to return—for the land of darkness and utter gloom. It is a land as dark as midnight, a land of gloom and confusion, where even the light is dark as midnight" (Job 10:21–22 NLT).

These verses might seem to describe the finality of death—and that's how the Sadducees, centuries later, understood them. But these same passages were understood by a majority of Jews to describe a literal dark, gloomy place where the spirits of the deceased continued to exist in a shadowy, futile existence.

THE ANCIENT BABYLONIAN CONCEPT

The Hebrews' concept of the afterlife was similar to that of the ancient Sumerians, from the land of Ur—which was Abraham's place of origin (Genesis 11:31). Ancient Mesopotamian tablets refer to the afterlife as "the house of darkness." It was a dark, dismal netherworld, where a person would spend eternity in a bleak existence as a *gidim* (ghost). In the myth titled "The Descent of Ishtar to the Underworld," the goddess visits *kurnugia* ("the land of no return"), where the dead live in darkness, eat clay, and are clothed with wings like birds.

The Sumerians believed this gloomy afterlife was beneath our world. It was also referred to as *Irkallu*, which means "the great below," and it was the final destination of the rich and the poor, the righteous and the unrighteous.

THE ANCIENT GREEKS AND HADES

The early Greeks also believed in a nondescript netherworld where all the dead—righteous and unrighteous—went. They called it Hades, and it was a misty and gloomy abode of the dead, roughly equivalent to the Hebrew concept of Sheol. Much later, Greek philosophers came up with a highly developed theology of mortals being judged in the afterlife—either rewarded in Elysium for righteousness or punished in Tartarus for unrighteousness; but in their early history, the Greeks believed that almost all spirits were consigned to a dismal Hades.

A few ancient Greeks believed that death was the end, the total extinguishing of life, but most imagined a continuing, shadowy existence in Hades. In Samuel Butler's translation of *The Odyssey*, Homer describes the pathetic, witless condition of souls in Hades:

THE HOUSE OF HADES
Although Homer refers repeatedly to the underworld in both *The Odyssey* and *The Iliad*, he doesn't call it Hades, but "the house of Hades"—in other words, the domain of the god Hades (Pluto). In *The Odyssey*, for example, he writes: "Thus did they converse in the house of Hades deep down within the bowels of the earth."

"Then Mercury. . . roused the ghosts and led them, while they followed whining and gibbering behind him. As bats fly squealing in the hollow

The ancient Greek god c
the underworld, Hade
whose name eventu
ally became associate
with a dark and gloom
netherworld where a
of the dead went, bot
righteous and wicked.

of some great cave, when one of them has fallen out of the cluster in which they hang, even so did the ghosts whine and squeal as Mercury... led them down into the dark abode of death."[2]

Homer describes a murky world full of witless shadows that couldn't even think coherent thoughts. This is even more miserable than Job's image of "a land of gloom and confusion, where even the light is dark as midnight" (Job 10:22 NLT). Also, Homer didn't believe that the spirit was a continuation of a person's life surviving the death of the body. Rather, he thought it was merely the quickly fading breath that escaped a dying man.

PROMISES OF A RESURRECTION

Though the Jews generally had a grim view of the afterlife, a bright star of hope—the glorious promise of a bodily resurrection—shone, and continued to grow brighter, down through the centuries.

At the beginning of the book of Job, Job glumly states, "As the cloud disappears and vanishes away, so he who goes down to the grave does not come up" (Job 7:9). Yet later Job triumphantly declares, "I know that my Redeemer lives, and He shall stand at last on the earth; and after my skin is destroyed, this I know, that in my flesh I shall see God, whom I shall see for myself, and my eyes shall behold, and not another. How my heart yearns within me!" (Job 19:25–27).

So the hope of a resurrection was able to break through the gloomy darkness, and the hearts of God's people began to yearn for a new and glorious life after death—on this same physical earth. As the centuries unfolded, God continued to give tantalizing clues about a resurrection, such as these prophetic words in the prayer of Samuel's mother, Hannah: "The LORD brings death and makes alive; he brings down to the grave and raises up" (1 Samuel 2:6 NIV). Now, some have reasoned that Hannah was merely saying that God brings sicknesses that *almost* take people to the grave, but that He then raises them up from their deathbeds. But the obvious meaning that God will raise people from the grave is the correct one.

Around 1000 BC, David prophesied, "Therefore my heart is glad,

▶ The concept of a resurrection appeared very early on in scripture; even Job knew his Redeemer lived and one day he would see Him. This stained glass art at the Saint Peter and Paul Cathedral in Saint Petersburg, Russia, illustrates one artist's idea of Jesus' resurrection.

and my glory rejoices; my flesh also will rest in hope. For You will not leave my soul in Sheol" (Psalm 16:9–10). Not only does this passage speak of the general hope of resurrection for mankind, but it is a specific prophecy about the resurrection of the Messiah, Jesus Christ (see Acts 2:25–31.)

Later, the sons of Korah, musicians appointed by David (1 Chronicles 6:31–33), said, "God will redeem my soul from the power of the grave, for He shall receive me" (Psalm 49:15). This revelation also gives us a hope of resurrection, but the following declaration by Hosea (ca. 720 BC) is even clearer: "I will ransom them from the power of the grave [*Sheol*]; I will redeem them from death. O Death, I will be your plagues! O Grave [*Sheol*], I will be your destruction!" (Hosea 13:14).

About 700 BC, the prophet Isaiah added: "Your dead shall live; together with my dead body they shall arise. Awake and sing, you who dwell in dust; for your dew is like the dew of herbs, and the earth shall cast out the dead" (Isaiah 26:19).

Finally, in 530 BC, Daniel stated: "Multitudes who sleep in the dust of the earth will awake: some to everlasting life, others to shame and everlasting contempt. Those who are wise will shine like the brightness of the heavens, and those who lead many to righteousness, like the stars forever and ever" (Daniel 12:2–3 NIV).

Belief in the resurrection of the dead steadily developed over the centuries. In New Testament times, the Pharisees believed that the resurrection would happen in the physical world—a world transformed into a glorious Garden of Eden.

GAN EDEN

The Jews referred to the garden mentioned in Genesis as "the lower Gan Eden." They referred to the coming paradise on earth as "the higher Gan Eden," which they also called the "Garden of Righteousness." However, sometimes when the rabbis spoke of Gan Eden, they were referring to a joyous celestial afterlife— the opposite of Gehenna—*not* a physical location.

THE EXISTENCE OF THE SPIRIT

We see that two separate threads are steadily woven throughout the fabric of the scriptures. The first thread is that something spiritual survives after the body dies, and it lives on in an unseen state. (The Hebrew word translated as "spirit" is *ruach*, which literally means "spirit" or "wind.") The second thread is that although death seems like the end of a person's physical body, God will one day raise people back to life.

Let's look at how concepts of the eternal human spirit developed over the centuries.

Many people believe that Genesis 2:7 describes the moment when God gave Adam, the first man, a spirit: "The LORD God formed man of the dust of the ground, and breathed into his nostrils the breath of life; and man became a living being." However, the Hebrew word translated as "breath" here is *neshama* (breath), not *ruach* (spirit). So a straightforward reading of Genesis 2:7 would be that God started Adam breathing. However, God also clearly gave Adam an eternal spirit, because Zechariah says that the Lord "forms the spirit of man within him" (Zechariah 12:1).

From the earliest times, people have believed in spirits—for the simple fact that they sometimes *saw* them. As Job's friend Eliphaz said (ca. 1600 BC), "Amid disquieting dreams in the night, when deep sleep falls on people, fear and trembling seized me and made all my bones shake. A spirit glided past my face, and the hair on my body stood on end. It stopped, but I could not tell what it was" (Job 4:13–16 NIV).

People have also seen angels in human form from the dawn of antiquity and have known that these beings dwell in an invisible realm. If spiritual beings called angels exist, and disembodied spirits exist, it is logical to conclude that human beings also have spirits that survive death—eternal spirits formed within us from some enduring spiritual substance. This then leads us to the question: Where do human spirits *go* after the body dies? Around 1450 BC, Moses wrote, "The days of our lives are seventy years. . . . For it is soon cut off, and we fly away" (Psalm 90:10). The image here is of the spirit flying away after the death of the body. Around 950 BC, Solomon asked, "Who knows if the human spirit rises upward and if the spirit of the animal goes down into the earth?" (Ecclesiastes 3:21 NIV). Though these passages don't make it clear *where* the human spirit goes, they are evidence that man *has* a spirit and that this spirit survives death. God told Adam, "Dust you are, and to dust you shall return" (Genesis 3:19), but Solomon adds, "Then the dust will return to the earth, and the spirit will return to God who gave it" (Ecclesiastes 12:7 NLT).

As we shall see, "returning to God" doesn't imply that we go directly to join God in His heavenly city. Rather, it means we enter the spiritual world, Sheol, the unseen state.

SAUL AND THE SPIRIT OF SAMUEL

Isaiah prophesied of the people of David's city, "You shall be brought down, you shall speak out of the ground; your speech shall be low, out of the dust; your voice shall be like a medium's, out of the ground; and your speech shall whisper out of the dust" (Isaiah 29:4). As early as the days of Moses (ca. 1400 BC), people communicated with the dead, which is why God specifically commanded: "There shall not be found among you anyone who. . .casts a spell, or a medium, or a spiritist, or one who calls up the dead. For whoever does these things is detestable to the LORD" (Deuteronomy 18:10–12 NASB). The spirits of the dead *could* be "called up," but it was forbidden.

From the earliest times, angels have emerged from the celestial realm and communicated with the living, but the same has not been so for departed humans. Samuel appeared after his death, but the circumstances surrounding his appearance were truly exceptional. About 1040 BC, just before a battle with the Philistines, King Saul went to a medium at Endor, seeking to "bring up" the spirit of Samuel.

"Then the woman asked, 'Whom shall I bring up for you?' 'Bring up Samuel,' he said. When the woman saw Samuel, she cried out at the top of her voice and said to Saul, 'Why have you deceived me? You are Saul!' The king said to her, 'Don't be afraid. What do you see?'

The woman said, 'I see a ghostly figure coming up out of the earth.' 'What does he look like?' he asked. 'An old man wearing a robe is coming up,' she said. Then Saul knew it was Samuel, and he bowed down and prostrated himself with his face to the ground.

"Samuel said to Saul, 'Why have you disturbed me by bringing me up?' 'I am in great distress,' Saul said. 'The Philistines are fighting against me, and God has departed from me. He no longer answers me, either by prophets or by dreams. So I have called on you to tell me what to do.' Samuel said, 'Why do you consult me, now that the LORD has departed from you and become your enemy? . . . The LORD will deliver both Israel and you into the hands of the Philistines, and tomorrow you and your sons will be with me'" (1 Samuel 28:11–16, 19 NIV).

▶ King Saul visited a medium in hopes of bringing up Samuel's spirit, portrayed in the painting *Witch of Endor* by Nikolai Ge (1831–1894).

THE INSIDE STORY FROM THE BIBLE

A number of things are evident from this episode. First, despite the fact that most modern mediums *fake* contacting the dead, spirits definitely exist in an afterlife, and certain people can summon them. That's why the Lord made prohibitions against this. And there's an even greater danger: demons can easily masquerade as departed human spirits. So "contacting the dead" is to be strictly avoided. It's clear that in *this* instance, God allowed Samuel to appear.

> **BELIEF IN SPIRITS**
> Though the scriptures don't offer many details, in Saul's day (ca. 1040 BC), there was a widespread belief among the Hebrews in disembodied spirits and the afterlife, just as there is today.

A BETTER AFTERLIFE

It is also evident from this incident that even the righteous prophet Samuel—esteemed by Jeremiah as the greatest man of God since Moses (Jeremiah 15:1)—was not in the heavenly city with God, but had been "brought up" from a realm under the ground. He was someplace in Sheol, the realm of the dead.

In the ancient world, the prevailing belief was that the righteous and unrighteous were huddled indiscriminately in the netherworld. But the Hebrews reasoned that even though the righteous were in Sheol, surely God would reward the just and they would be in a *better* part of Sheol. As Abraham once said in reference to the destruction of Sodom, "Far be it from you to do such a thing. . .treating the righteous and the wicked alike. Far be it from you! Will not the Judge of all the earth do right?" (Genesis 18:25 NIV).

As early as 950 BC, Solomon revealed that Sheol was divided into different chambers: "Her house is the way to Sheol, descending to the chambers [plural] of death" (Proverbs 7:27 NASB). Over the centuries, this line of thought eventually led to the belief in a separate location called Abraham's Bosom (Luke 16:22). Like Sheol, it too was under the earth, part of the realm of spirits, but was a much better place.

When the spirit of Samuel was summoned, he asked, "Why have

▶ *The Three Patriarchs in Paradise*, a Russian eighteenth-century icon, showing Abraham, Isaac, and Jacob alive in a lush garden.

you disturbed me by bringing me up?" (1 Samuel 28:15). The Hebrew word for "disturbed" is *ragaz*, which means "to give trouble, to cause to be angry." If Samuel had been lost in a dark, dismal region of Sheol for years, he would have been grateful for a temporary respite. Instead, he found it upsetting to be drawn away from a pleasant realm. He wasn't happy to leave there, even briefly.

There are other hints of a place of bliss in the afterlife. When Jacob was dying, he told his sons, "I am about to be gathered to my people. Bury me with my fathers" (Genesis 49:29 NIV). Now, it could be argued that "gathered to his people" was just a poetic description. Or that it refers to Jacob's physical remains being interred in the same burial place as his ancestors. After all, Abraham and Isaac, along with Sarah, Rebekah, and Leah, were already buried in that cave.

But that wouldn't explain the use of the same statement many years earlier, when only Sarah was buried there. The scripture says, "Abraham breathed his last and died in a good old age, an old man and full of years, and was gathered to his people" (Genesis 25:8). With the benefit of hindsight, it's easy to see that Abraham was *literally* "gathered to his people" who had died before him and now dwelled in the spirit realm.

But if the Old Testament saints didn't go to the dark, gloomy section of the underworld, why did Job state, "I leave—never to return—for the land of darkness and utter gloom. It is a land as dark as midnight, a land of gloom and confusion, where even the light is dark as midnight" (Job 10:21–22 NLT)? The answer is that although the gloomy section of Sheol existed, Job was mistaken in thinking *he* was headed there. He had suffered for months (Job 7:3, 5) and had been—or so he thought—abandoned by God (Job 30:16–21). If he had suffered in this life, how much more in the next? Clearly, Job had given in to despair: "I know you will bring me down to death, to the place appointed for all the living. . . . When I hoped for good, evil came; when I looked for light, then came darkness" (Job 30:23, 26 NIV).

PARADISE: ABRAHAM'S BOSOM

The idea of the existence of a bright, paradisiacal part of Sheol for righteous believers isn't emphasized in the Old Testament, but it shows up fully developed in the New Testament in Jesus' story of Lazarus in Abraham's Bosom. Most theologians, therefore, conclude that this doctrine blossomed in the intertestamental period between 300 and 100 BC. I propose that its existence was realized centuries earlier.

Jesus said, "Now there was a rich man, and he habitually dressed in purple and fine linen, joyously living in splendor every day. And a poor man named Lazarus was laid at his gate, covered with sores,

This painting by Fyodor Bronnikov (1827–1902) shows poor Lazarus at the rich man's gate, covered in sores, who was carried to Abraham's Bosom at his death.

and longing to be fed with the crumbs which were falling from the rich man's table; besides, even the dogs were coming and licking his sores. Now the poor man died and was carried away by the angels to Abraham's bosom; and the rich man also died and was buried. In Hades he lifted up his eyes, being in torment, and saw Abraham far away and Lazarus in his bosom. And he cried out and said, 'Father Abraham, have mercy on me, and send Lazarus so that he may dip the tip of his finger in water and cool off my tongue, for I am in agony in this flame.' But Abraham said, 'Child, remember that during your life you received your good things, and likewise Lazarus bad things; but now he is being comforted here, and you are in agony. And besides all this, between us and you there is a great chasm fixed, so that those who wish to come over from here to you will not be able,

and that none may cross over from there to us'" (Luke 16:19–26 NASB).

The rich man was in Sheol— here called by its Greek name, Hades—and Lazarus was "far away" in another place above, and the rich man had to "lift up his eyes" to see it. What was this realm in which Lazarus rested against Abraham's bosom? Many Bible scholars conclude that it was Paradise. Here's why:

A TRUE STORY

Many Christians accept the account of Samuel's appearance as a sober, historical event, but regard Christ's account of Lazarus as a parable, a mere story. But the Son of God preexisted both Abraham and Samuel in Heaven and remembered things He'd seen there. Jesus assured us, for example, that there were many mansions there (John 14:2). So it's likely that Jesus had witnessed the conversation between Abraham and the rich man. In all of Jesus' parables, no person has a name; yet Lazarus the beggar is named, suggesting the account is not merely a parable.

When Jesus was dying on the cross, the penitent thief said to Him, "Lord, remember me when You come into Your kingdom." And Jesus said to him, "Assuredly, I say to you, today you will be with Me in Paradise" (Luke 23:42–43).

Jesus died and went to Paradise with the thief that day, Friday. Two days *later*, Sunday morning, Jesus told Mary Magdalene in the garden, "Do not hold on to me, for I have not yet ascended to the Father"

(John 20:17 NIV). Jesus hadn't yet seen His Father, yet He had been in Paradise two days earlier, so *this* Paradise can't refer to the heavenly city where God dwells. Since Jesus had "descended into the lower parts of the earth" (Ephesians 4:9), the Paradise He went to with the thief was beneath the earth.

We tend to think of Abraham's Bosom as the actual name of the place Lazarus went, because he was "carried by the angels to Abraham's bosom," but the meaning is brought out by the following verse, in which the rich man "saw Abraham far away and Lazarus in his bosom" (Luke 16:23 NASB). Lying "in his bosom" most likely means he was reclining at a banqueting table with his head resting against Abraham's chest, just as the apostle John leaned against Jesus at the Last Supper: "Now there was leaning on Jesus' bosom one of His disciples, whom Jesus loved" (John 13:23). In life, the wealthy man had worn luxurious clothing and enjoyed lavish banquets every day, while the destitute, diseased beggar huddled in his gateway. On earth, Lazarus had been starving, desperate for even the scraps from the rich man's table; but now he was comforted and feasting with Abraham. Meanwhile, the rich man, who had fared sumptuously during his earthly life, was now desperate for a single drop of water. How the tables had turned!

The ancient treatise "Discourse to the Greeks concerning Hades," which is often attributed to the Jewish historian Josephus, but was more likely written by the Christian theologian Hippolytus of Rome (AD 170–235), nonetheless makes for fascinating reading. It gives us a glimpse of the early Christians' understanding of Abraham's Bosom, referring to it as "a region of light, in which the just have dwelt from the beginning of the world. . .while they wait for that rest and eternal new life in heaven, which is to succeed this region. This place we call The Bosom of Abraham."

CARRIED AWAY TO HEAVEN?

Now that we've established that Old Testament saints went to a region of Sheol known as Abraham's Bosom, or Paradise, let's consider Enoch and Elijah, since it's commonly believed that both men were taken directly to Heaven to be with God. If so, they would have been exceptions, because every other godly man and woman went to Abraham's Bosom.

"And Enoch walked with God: and he was not; for God took him" (Genesis 5:24 KJV). The New Testament adds, "By faith Enoch was taken away so that he did not see death, 'and was not found, because God had taken him'" (Hebrews 11:5). But to where was Enoch taken? Many people assume he went directly into the presence of God, because "God took him." But as we've seen, even the phrase "the spirit will return to God who gave it" (Ecclesiastes 12:7 NLT) refers to our entry into the spiritual world of Sheol, the unseen state; it doesn't mean we immediately go to the city where God dwells.

The King James Version gives intriguing wording for Hebrews 11:5: "By faith Enoch was translated that he should not see death; and was not found, because God had translated him: for before his translation he had this testimony, that he pleased God." The word *translate* sounds as if Enoch's mortal body was

▶ A stained glass panel of Elijah in the chariot of fire, displayed at St. Aignan Church in Chartres, France.

changed into an immortal body—thousands of years before the Rapture and resurrection. That's very likely what happened.

The Greek word *metathesis*, rendered "translated" (in the first instance), means "a putting over, translation." The Greek word *metatithemi* (in the other two instances) means "to transpose, translate." *Transpose* means "to transfer to a different place," and *translate* means "to move from one place or condition to another." The writer of the New Testament book Hebrews uses these words, because when Jewish scribes a couple of centuries earlier translated Genesis 5:24 from the Hebrew language into Greek (creating the Septuagint), they used the Greek verb *metatithem* to render the phrase "God took him."

Then there was Elijah. One day as he and Elisha "were going along and talking, behold, there appeared a chariot of fire and horses of fire which separated the two of them. And Elijah went up by a whirlwind to heaven" (2 Kings 2:11 NASB). The Hebrew word used for "heaven" here is *shamayim*, "heaved up things"—normally referring to the physical heavens. In other words, Elijah was picked up off the ground and taken into the sky, before he then disappeared into the heavenly dimension.

THOUGHTS FROM THE APOCRYPHA

The apocryphal book of Sirach (ca. 200–175 BC), while not part of the Protestant biblical canon, gives a clear idea of the thinking of the Jews in the centuries before Jesus. Sirach 44:16 states that "Enoch pleased God and was translated into paradise that he may give repentance to the nations."

Christians today assume that Elijah and Enoch were caught up to Heaven itself, the eternal city where God dwells, but even if it were true for these two men, everyone else—including great men such as Samuel and Abraham—went to Paradise (Abraham's Bosom) when they died. But there's good reason to believe that Elijah and Enoch were transported to Paradise as well, joining the rest of the departed righteous, instead of going directly to God. That is because people can only enter the Father's presence through Jesus' blood—and in Enoch's and Elijah's day, He hadn't yet died. The way wasn't open yet (Hebrews 9:8).

APPEARANCE OF MOSES AND ELIJAH

Samuel wasn't the only Old Testament saint to reappear in the world of the living. Moses and Elijah appeared to Jesus and three of His disciples on the Mount of Transfiguration. "As he [Jesus] was praying, the appearance of his face changed, and his clothes became as bright as a flash of lightning. Two men, Moses and Elijah, appeared in glorious splendor, talking with Jesus. They spoke about his departure, which he was about to bring to fulfillment at Jerusalem" (Luke 9:29–31 NIV).

This brief passage brings out a number of important facts. First, this experience happened around September, in AD 29, some seven months *before* Jesus' resurrection. At this time, the righteous of all past ages were still dwelling in Abraham's Bosom. As we have seen, it can't be argued that Elijah and Moses had been dwelling with God in the heavenly city, because Jesus hadn't yet died and opened the way to Heaven. Like Abraham, Samuel, and all the other Old Testament saints, Elijah and Moses were dwelling in Paradise.

Nevertheless, note that both Moses and Elijah "appeared in glorious splendor." The two men were not pale, weak ghosts, mere shadows of their former, earthly selves (like the spirits in Hades), but were glowing with the power and life of God. (The disciples saw not only Jesus in all His glory, but Moses and Elijah in their full glory, too.) To contain such glorified men, Paradise itself must be a region of "glorious splendor," even though the spirits there were not in God's city. Small wonder that Samuel was disturbed to be called away from such a place.

Note the contrast between the story of the rich man and Lazarus and that of Moses and Elijah at the Transfiguration: While on earth, the rich man had "habitually dressed in purple and fine linen, joyously living in splendor every day" (Luke 16:19 NASB). Now, in Paradise, it is the righteous who enjoy "glorious splendor." This is why David writes, "Do not be afraid when one becomes rich, when the glory of his house is increased; for when he dies he shall carry nothing away; his glory shall not descend after him" (Psalm 49:16–17).

▶ Francesco Zuccarelli's (1702–1788), *Landscape with Transfiguration* depicting Elijah, Moses, and Jesus in their full, glorious splendor.

Another point: Moses and Elijah were able to knowledgeably discuss events that wouldn't happen for another seven months—acts of which they had not been aware while they were alive. Samuel, also, when he appeared to Saul, had knowledge of future events (1 Samuel 28:19). Where had they learned these things? In Paradise, obviously. This shows us that the Old Testament saints, in addition to enjoying comfort and feasting with Abraham in Paradise (Abraham's Bosom), continued to learn and became wiser; and they had ongoing access to God in prayer, from whom Moses, Samuel, and Elijah received prophetic knowledge of future earthly events.

FURTHER THOUGHTS ON PARADISE

Just how glorious was Paradise? The Greek word *paradeisos* comes from a Persian word meaning "a walled enclosure." In the ancient Avestan dialect, the language of the Persian Zoroastrian scriptures, it appears as *pairidaêza*. By the sixth century BC, it had become the Akkadian loan-word *pardesu* ("domain"), and came to mean walled estates, well-tended royal gardens, and game parks. The Aramaic *pardaysa* means "royal park," and the Hebrew word *pardes* likewise means a royal park, an orchard, or a fruit garden.

The term first appeared in Greek around 380 BC as *paradeisos*, which refers to "a park for animals." Around 280 BC, *paradeisos* was used in the Septuagint to describe the Garden of Eden in Genesis 2:8 and Ezekiel 28:13. So when Jesus said to the thief on the cross, "Assuredly, I say to you, today you will be with Me in Paradise" (Luke 23:43), He was referring to a beautiful royal garden or orchard filled with exotic animals and glorious saints—whether He said it in Hebrew (*pardes*), Aramaic (*pardaysa*), or Greek (*paradeisos*).

Jesus described Lazarus as lying against Abraham's bosom, feasting, and this fits well with the image of Paradise as an enclosed orchard with an abundance of delicious food. This may also give us a glimpse of the idyllic activities of its inhabitants. "The LORD God planted a garden eastward in Eden, and. . .made every tree grow that is pleasant to the sight and good for food. . . . Then the LORD God took the man and put him in the garden of Eden to tend and keep it" (Genesis 2:8–9, 15). Adam tended the trees and gardens in Eden and ate from them. Were the Old Testament saints tending the orchards and gardens and vineyards of Paradise?

THE FOUNDATIONS OF HEAVEN

It's possible that Paradise (Abraham's Bosom) and Heaven (the city of God) are very near one another. You'll recall that Jacob had a dream "in which he saw a stairway resting on the earth, with its top reaching to heaven, and the angels of God were ascending and descending on it. There above it stood the LORD" (Genesis 28:12–13 NIV). This

▶ Sunset in an apple orchard in the middle of spring. Jesus described Paradise as a beautiful royal garden/orchard filled with exotic animals and glorious saints.

stairway was not a ladder, as the King James Version states, but rather a staircase, like the broad steps flanking the sides of a Sumerian ziggurat. And note that the base of the steps—the foundation of the structure—was "resting on the earth."

When Jacob saw it, he said, "How awesome is this place! This is none other than the house of God, and this is the gate of heaven" (Genesis 28:17 NASB). He therefore "called the name of that place Bethel [House of God]" (Genesis 28:19 NASB). Now compare Jacob's vision to Amos's declaration: "The Lord, the LORD Almighty. . .builds his lofty palace in the heavens and sets its foundation *on the earth*"

(Amos 9:6 NIV, emphasis added).

As pointed out earlier, Heaven is not physically distant from earth. And from the above verses, it appears to be *very near* this world, though separated from it in another dimension. Though some people may believe that the New Jerusalem is billions of light-years away from our planet, to believe that is to believe the opposite of what scripture states.

One distinct possibility is that the 1,400-mile-high city of New Jerusalem, existing in the spiritual dimension, towers a "lofty" height above the earth, but its foundation—as in Jacob's vision and Amos's declaration—rests in the same place as the earth, except in another dimension. The angels ascended the steps to the celestial city and Jesus ascended up to Heaven (Acts 1:9), but neither had that far to go: Jacob saw the Lord Himself standing at the *top* of the steps, and Jesus vanished

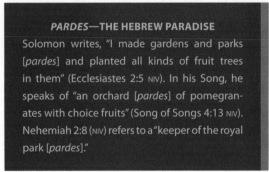

> ### PARDES—THE HEBREW PARADISE
> Solomon writes, "I made gardens and parks [*pardes*] and planted all kinds of fruit trees in them" (Ecclesiastes 2:5 NIV). In his Song, he speaks of "an orchard [*pardes*] of pomegranates with choice fruits" (Song of Songs 4:13 NIV). Nehemiah 2:8 (NIV) refers to a "keeper of the royal park [*pardes*]."

from sight before He was too distant. These verses, while certainly not conclusive proof, nevertheless provide evidence that Heaven is *near*—not a vast distance away.

WAITING FOR THE CITY

The spirits of the righteous Old Testament saints went to Paradise when their physical bodies died. They were unable to enter Heaven— the heavenly city, New Jerusalem—at that time. However, Paradise is definitely a *part* of God's celestial realm and may very well be just outside the holy city. Is there any basis for such a suggestion?

Well, there's a fascinating parallel between the "Mountain of God," New Jerusalem in Heaven, and the earthly Mount Horeb, the "mountain of God," in the Sinai desert (1 Kings 19:8). Mount Horeb is an awe-inspiring, imposing mass of rock rising above the surrounding plains. When the Israelites came out of Egypt, they camped around the base of this mountain but were not permitted to walk upon or touch the mountain itself—because the Lord was there. God told Moses, "The LORD will come down on Mount Sinai in the sight of all the people. You shall set bounds for the people all around, saying, 'Beware that you do not go up on the mountain or touch the border of it'" (Exodus 19:11–12 NASB).

> **THE MOUNTAIN AND THE GARDEN**
>
> In Ezekiel 28:13, 16, the heavenly realms are called not only "the mountain of God," but also "Eden, the garden of God," indicating that the heavenly city (filled with amazing architecture and buildings) is not all there is to God's celestial realm, but that the greater "heavenly country" is also filled with trees, parks, gardens, and animals. The Garden of Eden that once existed on earth was only a pale shadow of the heavenly Paradise.

Could it be that, in the same way, the mountain of God, the city where God dwells, rises above the glorious hills and plains of Paradise in the celestial realm? Possibly, just as millions of Israelites camped at the foot of the earthly mountain of God, the Old Testament saints dwelled in Paradise below the eternal mountain of God, whose light illuminated their realm. Remember, the only restriction we're aware of is that they weren't allowed to *enter* the city.

In the future, "the gates of it [the city] shall not be shut at all" (Revelation 21:25 KJV); but in that time, entry *was* restricted. Bounds had been set, just as Moses set bounds around the base of Mount Horeb. Now, if Paradise were spread out below the city of God, this would explain a mysterious passage that states that Abraham and the other patriarchs were waiting for a city. How did they know there was a city they should wait for with great anticipation? Perhaps it was visible from Paradise, towering not far off.

"By faith Abraham. . .waited for the city which has foundations, whose builder and maker is God. . . . But now they desire a better, that is, a heavenly country. Therefore God is not ashamed to be called their God, for He has prepared a city for them" (Hebrews 11:8, 10, 16). After the saints died, they were in Paradise, but longed to enter the city God was preparing.

If the unrighteous are under the earth in a land of perpetual darkness, what is it like in Paradise? If it's near the city, illuminated by the glory of God, then it's a land of light.

Though it could be argued that Paradise was or is wholly separated from the heavenly city and a vast distance away, that's not a compelling conclusion. Some people think that when the Old Testament saints finally went from Abraham's Bosom into God's presence in the heavenly city, they had to make a quantum leap across the entire breadth of the known universe to get there. But the picture presented here, while admittedly based on conjecture, appears to be more scriptural.

A final thought: If this concept of Paradise is correct, then it

▶ This picture of Týn Church in the Czech Republic, Prague, shows the beauty of manmade architecture and buildings against the night sky. How much more beautiful will the heavenly city of God be!

didn't remain empty after Jesus' resurrection when He led the Old Testament saints into the heavenly city in a great triumphal procession. The gardens of Paradise still exist, and the saints can still go outside the gates of the city to enjoy them. The difference is that they now enjoy access to the heavenly city as well. So when Paul says that he was caught up to the third heaven, to Paradise, *this* location could be what he was referring to. And if Paradise actually surrounds the eternal city where the Tree of Life grows, then it is indeed in the midst of the Paradise of God (2 Corinthians 12:2, 4; Revelation 2:7).

2 : HEAVEN AND HELL, ELYSIUM AND TARTARUS

W e're about to explore a fascinating aspect of the history of Heaven and Hell. To do so, we'll take what some may think is an unnecessary detour into Greek mythology. If you're already aware of how the biblical concepts of Heaven and Hell developed in the Old Testament, or believe that a discussion of such things is unimportant, by all means skip over this chapter and dive right into chapter 3. But if you're not familiar with these things and want to enrich your understanding and faith, read on.

WHAT CAUSED THE CHANGE?

Many secular scholars assume that up until the closing verses of Malachi (ca. 433 BC), the Jewish concepts of Heaven, Sheol, and the afterlife weren't much different from the views that Jacob, Job, and the patriarchs held for the previous fifteen hundred years. But when we come to New Testament times, we see the majority of Jews—who followed the teachings of the Pharisees—embracing fully developed doctrines of immortal spirits in either Hades or Paradise and anticipating either a rapturous Heaven or a fiery Hell.

From the vantage point of Jesus' teachings in the Gospels, insights from the Epistles, and the amazing visions of Revelation, we can see that the roots of these doctrines go back to verses scattered throughout the Old Testament. Yet the Bible doesn't show us the *process* by which these many clues came together into a big picture by the first century. Even the Bible's teachings on Abraham's Bosom aren't clear from the Old Testament alone. They come into sharp focus only in light of Jesus' story about Lazarus and the rich man, and in the appearance of Moses and Elijah.

This raises the question: What caused this sudden blooming of a full theology of the afterlife? Secular scholars are practically unanimous in the view that the Jews got these ideas from the Greeks. They point out that Alexander the Great conquered Israel in 332 BC, by which time the Greeks had a highly developed theology that spirits were rewarded or punished in the afterlife. The Greeks ruled Israel for 175 years, until the Maccabees revolted. According to this theory, though the Jews stubbornly resisted Greek culture, gods, and religion, they gladly embraced Greek concepts of the afterlife.

Why else, these scholars ask, would Jesus and His apostles use the Greek word *Hades* for the unseen spiritual world, and why would Peter refer to Tartarus as the prison of the fallen angels? Why does the Elysium of the Greeks resemble the Heaven of the New Testament? The answer, these scholars insist, is that the rather dull, uninspired Jews copied the philosophical musings of the bright, imaginative Greeks. I would like to challenge this assumption. Although it's clear that a cross-pollination of concepts happened, I believe the evidence suggests that the borrowing happened in the *opposite* direction, beginning many centuries earlier.

TRADE SHIPS AND THE FLOW OF IDEAS

There's an interesting connection between the ancient Greeks and the Hebrews that goes back into the mists of antiquity; but it's obscure, so we won't dwell on it or put too much weight on it. It's that the Hebrews and certain Greeks had a common origin. The book of 1 Maccabees, though not part of the canonical scriptures, is considered by most historians to be a sober, factual account of Jewish history during the time of the Maccabees. And in 1 Maccabees, we find this communication: "Ari'us, king of the Spartans, to Oni'as the high priest, greeting. It has been found in writing concerning the Spartans and the Jews that they are brethren and are of the family of Abraham. And now that we have learned this, please write us concerning your welfare" (1 Maccabees 12:20–22 RSV). The Jewish historian Josephus also quotes this letter in his *Antiquities* (12.4.10).

▶ A Phoenician ship carved on the face of a sarcophagus, dated to AD 2. These multitudes of ships easily could have opened the flow of ideas from Israel to Greece.

Genetic tests would answer this question with certainty, but rather than suggesting that the Spartans (as an entire people group) were descended from Abraham, it seems more plausible to conclude that this letter hints at the presence of Israelite expatriates in Sparta—possibly from the dispersion of 722 BC, when Samaria fell; or from 605–586 BC, when Jerusalem was under attack by the Babylonians.

In any case, the ancient Greeks were skilled seafarers and engaged in widespread trade around the Mediterranean basin, and by the 600s BC, Greek colonies were found from Asia Minor to Italy, Sicily, North Africa, and even southern Spain. Well-traveled trade routes would have allowed Israelite merchants to easily make their way to Greece, facilitating the flow of religious concepts. There was no need to wait for Alexander's armies to show up in Jerusalem. Consider that (ca. 775 BC) the Hebrew prophet Jonah went to the Israelite port of Joppa, where he found a number of international seafaring vessels, and boarded a trading ship bound for distant Tarshish (Jonah 1:3).

Several decades after Jonah, between 701 and 681 BC, Isaiah wrote his prophecies—some of which have direct bearing on the subject of Heaven. This was during the same historical period when the two earliest known Greek poets were active: Homer was writing *The Odyssey* and *The Iliad*, and Hesiod was writing *Theogony*, a description of the Greek gods and the beginning of the cosmos.

TARSHISH IS TARTESSUS

The area referred to as Tarshish in the Bible was Tartessus, a kingdom rich in metals, on the River Tartessus, west of modern Gibraltar in southwestern Spain. The Phoenicians had a mining colony there, named Gadir. When the Bible speaks of "the ships of Tarshish" (Isaiah 23:1, 14), it refers to Phoenician ships that sailed to the western end of the known world.

Around this time, a multitude of Phoenician merchant ships from Tyre, just north of Israel, plied the Mediterranean. Isaiah writes, "Your traders crossed the sea, sailing over deep waters" (Isaiah 23:2 NLT). New ideas could very easily have gone from Israel to Greece. The Phoenicians even sold Israelites there as slaves: "Also the people of Judah and the people of Jerusalem you have sold to the Greeks" (Joel 3:6).

HOMER AND HESIOD

Most modern scholars place the time of Homer and Hesiod in about the seventh to eighth centuries BC. Oliver Taplin, an expert on ancient Greece, states in *The Oxford History of the Classical World* that the consensus of modern researchers is that Homer dates between 750 and 650 BC. If Homer wrote his major works in his later years, he would have committed them to writing sometime *after* Isaiah's prophecies (ca. 701–681 BC).

Homer based his accounts on historical events that had occurred earlier, such as the destruction of Troy in 1188 BC, and it's widely believed that many of the verses came down in oral form to his day. He then committed them to writing, edited them, elaborated on them, and introduced his own views.

A painting by Jean-Baptiste Auguste Leloir (1809–1892) of Homer, who may have borrowed his ideas of the afterlife from biblical concepts of Heaven and Hell, which were spoken of centuries before.

Now, to answer to our original question: though it may seem as if Jewish concepts of the afterlife remained unchanged from Moses to Malachi, and suddenly and inexplicably bloomed into fully developed concepts of Heaven and Hell in the New Testament, this is actually not the case. As noted in the first chapter, from the days that Saul encountered the spirit of Samuel (1010 BC) and Solomon wrote Proverbs (950 BC), the concept of a *better place* in the afterlife, distinct from the general realm of dismal Sheol, was already emerging. Between 701and 681 BC, Isaiah took this fascinating conversation much further.

GREEK POETS AND PARADISE

The oldest known Greek literary sources are Homer's two epic poems, *The Iliad* and *The Odyssey*, which focus on the Trojan War and its aftermath; in addition, there are two works by Homer's contemporary, Hesiod: *Works and Days* and *Theogony* (an account of the genesis of the world and the gods). *Theogony* was the first written Greek mythical cosmogony (a theory of the origins of the universe). The Greeks are known to have drawn ideas from the Hittites, Hurrians, Phoenicians, and Sumerians, and as we shall see, some of their imagery for Elysium (Paradise) and Tartarus (Hell) was borrowed from the Hebrew scriptures. The earliest parts pertinent to our discussion describe Eden, the Garden of God:

Genesis states: "The LORD God had not sent rain upon the earth, and there was no man to cultivate the ground. But a mist used to rise from the earth and water the whole surface of the ground. . . . The LORD God planted a garden toward the east, in Eden; and there He placed the man whom He had formed. Out of the ground the LORD God caused to grow every tree that is pleasing to the sight and good for food; the tree of life also in the midst of the garden, and the tree of the knowledge of good and evil" (Genesis 2:5–6, 8–9 NASB).

Compare the Hebrew description of Eden, the Garden of God on earth, to Elysium (the Greek equivalent of Paradise). In *The Odyssey*, Homer writes: "As for your own end, Menelaus. . .the gods will take you to the Elysian plain, which is at the ends of the world. There fair-haired Rhadamanthus reigns, and men lead an easier life than anywhere else in the world, for in Elysium there falls not rain, nor hail, nor snow, but Oceanus breathes ever with a West wind that sings softly from the sea, and gives fresh life to all men" (*Odyssey*, 4:560–565).

Homer was the first Greek writer to mention Elysium, and his

▶ The Greeks and Romans identified Elysium with the Canary Islands, supposedly a place untouched by sorrow, where it never rained and life was easy. It is seen here in a beautiful picture of Alojera, La Gomera.

description of that well-watered land where it *never rained* and where life was easy seems to be borrowed directly from Genesis. The main difference is that the Bible places Paradise in the Tigris-Euphrates region in the east, whereas Homer placed it in the Atlantic Ocean, just beyond the western edge of the known earth.

The Greek poet Hesiod (700–650 BC) refers to the islands of the happy dead, also located in the western ocean at the end of the earth. In *Works and Days*, he calls Elysium "the islands of the blessed," saying, "They live untouched by sorrow in the islands of the blessed along the shore of deep swirling Ocean, happy heroes for whom the grain-giving earth bears honey-sweet fruit flourishing thrice a year."

HOMER AND GENESIS

Ever since Moses put the Genesis stories into writing (ca. 1440 BC), some eight hundred years before Homer, the Hebrew account of the beginning has been on record. It's easy to envision Hebrew travelers carrying these stories to Greece in the early centuries.

The Greeks and Romans knew of the existence of the Canary Islands just beyond the Straits of Gibraltar, and they identified Elysium with them. Plutarch (AD 46–120), a Greek historian, refers to the Canaries in his *Life of Sertorius*. Sertorius (126–73 BC), a Roman general, was told by sailors of islands a few days' sail from Spain, called "the Islands of the Blest. They enjoy moderate rains at long intervals, and winds which for the most part are soft and precipitate dews, so that the islands not only have a rich soil which is excellent for plowing and planting, but also produce a natural fruit that is plentiful and wholesome enough to feed, without toil or trouble, a leisured folk. . . . Therefore a firm belief has made its way, even to the Barbarians, that here is the Elysian Field and the abode of the blessed, of which Homer sang."

The Greek poet Pindar (522–443 BC) described a single Isle of the Blessed, where the spirits of the departed good enjoyed music and recreation in shady parks. But *all* this imaginative speculation by Greeks began with Homer about 650 BC—and his imagery was apparently lifted from the pages of Genesis.

A SURREAL PARADISE

To the Greeks, the great waters of Oceanus (the Atlantic Ocean), where the physical world ended and the spiritual world began, were something of a twilight zone—and this allowed them to vacillate between thinking of Elysium as an actual physical location and as belonging to the spiritual realm.

THE GARDEN OF THE HESPERIDES

There are more parallels between Genesis and early Greek legends. Biblical imagery also depicts Satan, the serpent, entwined around the tree of the knowledge of good and evil—beside the tree of life in the Garden of Eden. Genesis states: "The tree of life also [was] in the midst of the garden, and the tree of the knowledge of good and evil. . . . Now the serpent was more crafty than any beast of the field which the LORD God had made. And he said to the woman, 'Indeed, has God said, "You shall not eat from any tree of the garden"?'" (Genesis 2:9; 3:1 NASB).

The Sicilian Greek poet Stesichorus (640–555 BC), in his poem *Song of Geryon*, writes of "the beautiful island of the gods, where the Hesperides have their homes of solid gold." The Hesperides, in Greek religion, were the female custodians of a tree that bore golden apples; eating this fruit gave one immortality. The tree was guarded by a serpent-like dragon named

▶ The Greeks believed the magnificent colors of the sunset were caused by the sun's reflection off golden apples that grew in the garden of Hesperides.

Ladon. This imagery was most certainly borrowed from the ancient Hebrew scriptures.

Like Elysium, the Garden of the Hesperides was located in the far west—in Tartessus, in the south of Spain. The Greeks believed, rather naively, that the colors of sunset in the west resulted from the sun's light reflecting off the golden apples. If you've ever wondered where some people get the idea that the forbidden fruit was an apple, now you know. That particular detail originated with the Greeks.

ISAIAH AND THE COMING PARADISE

Genesis 2–3 describe a paradise that had been lost. The prophet Isaiah, writing sometime around 700 BC, declared that paradise would be restored on earth. This was before Homer wrote about Elysium, the island of the blessed. This is hardly coincidental. We've already seen that the Hebrew scriptures describe a resurrection of the righteous. But where would they *live*? Not in the same drought-blighted, disease-riddled, war-ravaged lands of the past. Rather, they would live in a beautiful, transformed world. Isaiah describes it in great detail: "The wolf also shall dwell with the lamb, the leopard shall lie down with the young goat, the calf and the young lion and the fatling together; and a little child shall lead them. The cow and the bear shall graze; their young ones shall lie down together; and the lion shall eat straw like the ox. The nursing child shall play by the cobra's hole, and the weaned child shall put his hand in the viper's den. They shall not hurt nor destroy in all My holy mountain, for the earth shall be full of the knowledge of the LORD as the waters cover the sea" (Isaiah 11:6–9).

"On this mountain he will destroy the shroud that enfolds all peoples, the sheet that covers all nations; he will swallow up death forever. The Sovereign LORD will wipe away the tears from all faces. . . . Your dead will live, LORD; their bodies will rise—let those who dwell in the dust wake up and shout for joy—your dew is like the dew of the morning; the earth will give birth to her dead" (Isaiah 25:7–8; 26:19 NIV).

▶ Isaiah spoke of a future new Heaven and new Earth, full of the knowledge of the Lord and unimaginable peace. The prophet Isaiah is depicted here in Antonio Balestra's (1666–1740) painting.

This heavenly world will also be a place of blissful peace and harmony: "There shall come forth a Rod from the stem of Jesse. . . . With righteousness He shall judge the poor, and decide with equity for the meek of the earth" (Isaiah 11:1, 4). "The law will go out from Zion, the word of the LORD from Jerusalem. He will judge between the nations and will settle disputes for many peoples. They will beat their swords into plowshares and their spears into pruning hooks. Nation will not take up sword against nation, nor will they train for war anymore" (Isaiah 2:3–4 NIV).

"The LORD will comfort Zion, He will comfort all her waste places; He will make her wilderness like Eden, and her desert like the garden of the LORD" (Isaiah 51:3). "Springs will gush forth in the wilderness, and streams will water the wasteland. The parched ground will become a pool, and springs of water will satisfy the thirsty land. Marsh grass and reeds and rushes will flourish where desert jackals once lived. And a great road will go through that once deserted land. It will be named the Highway of Holiness" (Isaiah 35:6–8 NLT).

"'Behold, I create new heavens and a new earth; and the former things will not be remembered or come to mind. But be glad and rejoice forever in what I create; for behold, I create Jerusalem for rejoicing and her people for gladness. I will also rejoice in Jerusalem and be glad in My people; and there will no longer be heard in her the voice of weeping and the sound of crying. . . . The wolf and the lamb will graze together, and the lion will eat straw like the ox; and dust will be the serpent's food. They will do no evil or harm in all My holy mountain,' says the LORD" (Isaiah 65:17–19, 25 NASB). (See also Isaiah 11:1–10.)

> **JEWISH CONCEPTS OF PARADISE**
>
> By Isaiah's day, the Israelites had already been thinking for *centuries* about a better celestial realm under the earth for the spirits of the righteous. Added to this was their belief that the righteous would one day rise from the dead to immortal life in a beautiful, happy paradise on earth. It was these visions of immortal Paradise that Hebrew traders, travelers, and slaves carried to the Greece of Homer and Hesiod.

THE JEWISH "HEAVEN ON EARTH"

What did the Jews imagine life in the kingdom of God would be like? What did they visualize themselves doing? Clearly, they believed that eternal life on the earth to come would be very similar to the life they were living then—only better. And they imagined a largely pastoral, agricultural existence. This prophecy sums it up best: "In the last days. . .they will beat their swords into plowshares and their spears into pruning hooks. Nation will not take up sword against nation, nor will they train for war anymore. Everyone will sit under their own vine and under their own fig tree, and no one will make them afraid" (Micah 4:1, 3–4 NIV).

After the Messiah defeated all their enemies and there were no more wars, the Jews anticipated blacksmiths busily transforming swords into plowshares, which would then be drawn by oxen to plow their fields. Crops would be planted and harvested, grain would be threshed and ground into flour, and bread baked and eaten. In addition, spears would be transformed into pruning hooks to trim the branches of fruit trees—including orchards of olives, dates, almonds, and pomegranates.

They definitely expected to be occupied with peaceful farming. In the Bible, to sit under one's own vine and fig tree describes the security and well-earned rest that come after tending and caring for one's own land. The implicit promise is that the people will own their own fields and farms, do productive labor, and enjoy peace and plenty. And as we shall see in the next chapter, the Jews envisioned enjoying the fruits of their labor in joyful feasts—both eating and drinking while they fellowshipped with the resurrected patriarchs of all past ages. This peaceful hope of Heaven on earth will be fulfilled pretty much the way the Jews imagined it.

THE GREEKS AND THE RESURRECTION

There is a huge difference between the Jewish concept of the world to come and the Greek concept of the afterlife—that is, the belief in a bodily resurrection of *all people*. This concept was central to the Jews' hope of immortal life and became increasingly important from Isaiah's time on. They knew from the scriptures that everlasting life would be enjoyed on this physical earth, in a restored *Gan Eden* (Garden of Eden).

To the Greeks, however, the idea of a general resurrection was incredible. They believed that only a very few heroes, such as Achilles, Alcmene, Ganymede, Menelaus, and Peleus, had been physically resurrected and lived eternally in Elysium. Later, it was believed that many heroes who had fought in the Trojan War also enjoyed this reward. Around 700 BC, there was a report of a certain Aristeas of Proconnesus who alledgedly came alive from the dead.

Justin Martyr, the great defender of the Christian faith (AD 100–165), commented on these Greek stories, stating, "When we say. . .

▶ The Greeks believed only a few great heroes, such as Achilles, seen here in the painting *Death of Achilles* (1630–32), by Peter Paul Rubens had been resurrected.

Jesus Christ, our teacher, was crucified and died, and rose again, and ascended into heaven, we propose nothing different from what you believe regarding those whom you consider sons of Zeus" (1 Apology 21). As far as the Greeks believed, however, only a few rare exceptions became physically immortal. All that most people could look forward to was a dismal, eternal existence in Hades as disembodied spirits. There was no belief in a general resurrection. The Greeks were convinced that even the gods couldn't re-create flesh once it had decayed.

Luke tells us the Greeks' reaction when Paul preached to the Areopagus, the highest religious council of Athens: "When they heard of the resurrection of the dead, some mocked" (Acts 17:32). Before Governor Festus, when Paul spoke of Jesus rising from the dead, Festus blurted out, "Paul, you are beside yourself! Much learning is driving you mad!" (Acts 26:24).

Even in the centuries before Paul, many diverse beliefs about the soul and immortality began to take root among the Greeks. By 420 BC, just after Socrates fully refined the Greeks' belief that departed spirits went to Elysium or Tartarus, his student Plato (424–328 BC) took things in a new direction. In his *Timaeus*, Plato teaches that the human body and the entire physical world are a curse, and that when the spirit is free of this mortal flesh and has entered the spiritual world, it may finally begin to enjoy freedom.

The Greeks' disbelief in the resurrection parallels the views of many today. Even many Christians fail to understand the importance of the resurrection of our bodies. They look forward to dying and going to be with God and think that our spirits will then live forever in a spiritual realm. When reminded that our physical bodies will be transformed and reunited with our spirits, their question is, "Why?" Since they assume we can already enjoy Heaven fully as disembodied spirits,

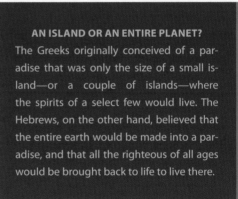

AN ISLAND OR AN ENTIRE PLANET?
The Greeks originally conceived of a paradise that was only the size of a small island—or a couple of islands—where the spirits of a select few would live. The Hebrews, on the other hand, believed that the entire earth would be made into a paradise, and that all the righteous of all ages would be brought back to life to live there.

what *need* is there to be encumbered with a physical body again?

But the Bible is clear: We won't be in a distant celestial realm forever. That's a temporary state. God's ultimate plan is to bring the heavenly city down to this planet so that we can enjoy both the presence of God *and* the physical earth. The Jews in Isaiah's day weren't yet aware that God's city would come to earth, but they believed that when the Messiah came, the resurrection of the dead would occur and the earth would be transformed into a paradise.

THE UNSAVED DEAD

The Jews believed that the righteous, while waiting for the resurrection, reposed in a pleasant afterlife. But it was bleaker for the wicked. If there were better parts of Sheol, there were also worse parts, and the deeper in Sheol one went, the worse it became. One king was told, "You shall be brought down to Sheol, to the lowest depths of the Pit" (Isaiah 14:15). In Moses' day, God declared, "A fire is kindled in My anger, and shall burn to the lowest hell" (Deuteronomy 32:22). Some of the departed were consigned to "the remotest parts of the pit" (Ezekiel 32:23 NASB). Even in ancient times, the Hebrews realized that the deep parts of the underworld were unpleasant places.

Around 700 BC, Isaiah wrote about the death of the king of Babylon, saying, "Hell from beneath is excited about you, to meet you at your coming; it stirs up the dead for you, all the chief ones of the earth; it has raised up from their thrones all the kings of the nations. They all shall speak and say to you: 'Have you also become as weak as we? Have you become like us? Your pomp is brought down to Sheol. . .the maggot is spread under you, and worms cover you'" (Isaiah 14:9–11). "Nevertheless you will be thrust down to Sheol, to the recesses of the pit. Those who see you will gaze at you, they will ponder over you, saying, 'Is this the man who made the earth tremble, who shook kingdoms?'" (Isaiah 14:15–16 NASB).

Over a century later, the prophet Ezekiel said of the Egyptians: "They will fall among those killed by the sword. . . . From within the realm of the dead [Sheol] the mighty leaders will say of Egypt and her allies, 'They have come down and they lie with the uncircumcised, with those killed by the sword'" (Ezekiel 32:20–21 NIV). These spirits most certainly survived death and had a conscious existence in the dark regions of the afterlife.

THE PIT AND TARTARUS

The Jewish historian Josephus (AD 37–100) writes, "They [the Pharisees] also believe that souls have an immortal vigor in them, and that *under the earth* there will be rewards or punishments, according as they have lived virtuously or viciously in this life; and the latter are to be detained in an everlasting prison, but that the former shall have power to revive and live again" (*Antiquities* 18.1.3, emphasis added). In chapter 1, we discussed the righteous who will "revive and live again." Now let's consider the "everlasting prison" to which the unrighteous were consigned.

The concept of the wicked being punished in the afterlife developed at the same time as the idea of the righteous being rewarded—and these themes are two sides of the same coin. Since we've already examined Greek views on Hades, let's see how this developed into a belief in Tartarus. Again, this concept appeared first among the Hebrews. Apart from describing people "going down to Sheol," the dark realm under the ground, the early scriptures also frequently describe dying as "going down to the Pit."

▶ Early scriptures describe Sheol as "going down to the pit," typically a long shaft leading deep into the earth. Here, an old industrial chimney shaft is photographed from the bottom, with blue sky and white clouds above the opening.

About 1000 BC, David prayed, "O LORD, You brought my soul up from the grave; You have kept me alive, that I should not go down to the pit" (Psalm 30:3). Solomon, about 950 BC, described robbers who said, "Let us swallow them alive like Sheol, and whole, like those who go down to the Pit" (Proverbs 1:12). "But You, O God, shall bring them [bloodthirsty and deceitful men] down to the pit of destruction" (Psalm 55:23). "Yet you shall be brought down to Sheol, to the lowest depths of the Pit" (Isaiah 14:15). "I will bring you down with those who descend into the Pit, to the people of old, and I will make you dwell in the lowest part of the earth, in places desolate from antiquity, with those who go down to the Pit" (Ezekiel 26:20).

From these passages, we see that the Pit is called "the pit of destruction," and that it is in Sheol, since the wicked are "brought down to Sheol, to the lowest depths of the Pit." In fact, the Pit seems to be the deepest part of Sheol, because it is "in the lowest part of the earth."

Homer, centuries after David and Solomon—and shortly after Isaiah—likewise described Tartarus as "the deepest pit under the earth" where the wicked dead went. In *The Iliad*, he has the god Jove say, "If I see anyone acting apart and helping either Trojans or Danaans. . .I will hurl him down into dark Tartarus far into the deepest pit under the earth, where the gates are iron and the floor bronze, as far beneath Hades as heaven is high above the earth." Homer later records Jove saying, "For aught I care, you may go to the lowest depths beneath earth and sea, where Iapetus and Saturn dwell in lone Tartarus with neither ray of light nor breath of wind to cheer them."

A SPIRITUAL PIT

The word *pit* comes from the Hebrew words *beer* and *bor*, which mean "a pit, a well." This was typically a long shaft leading deep into the earth. The Bible also describes a place of punishment called "the abyss" or "the bottomless pit."

Hesiod uses his poetic imagination to assert in *Theogony*, "For a brazen anvil falling down from heaven nine nights and days would reach the earth upon the tenth: and again, a brazen anvil falling from earth nine nights and days would reach Tartarus upon the tenth."

Earlier, I mentioned that the Greeks believed that the Garden of the Hesperides was located in Tartessos, a region in southern Spain—and that Elysium (the Greek equivalent of Heaven) was located a little farther west, beyond the Straits of Gibraltar. The Greek geographer and philosopher Strabo (64 BC–AD 24) makes an interesting—and likely accurate—observation about the origins of the name Tartarus: "Tartessos was known by hearsay as 'farthermost in the west,' where, as the poet [Homer]

> **THE FAR WEST**
> To the Greeks, Elysium/Paradise, the Garden of the Tree of Life, and Tartarus were all in the farthest west, in what was believed to be the edge of the physical world. In the Lord of the Rings trilogy, J. R. R. Tolkien draws from this when he places Aman, the Undying Lands, home of the Valar, in the Far West.

himself says, falls into Oceanus 'the sun's bright light drawing black night over earth, the grain-giver.' Now, that night is a thing of evil omen and associated with Hades, is obvious; also that Hades is associated with Tartaros. Accordingly, one might reasonably suppose that Homer, because he heard about Tartessos, named the farthermost of the nether-regions Tartaros after Tartessos, with a slight alteration of letters."

THE ABYSS—THE BOTTOMLESS PIT

To the Greeks, Tartarus was a great abyss, and was, in fact, called *Abussos* (Abyss), meaning "deep" or "bottomless." It later appears in the Greek New Testament (Revelation 9:11; 11:7; 17:8; 20:1, 3), where it is also translated "abyss" in the New International Version and the New American Standard Bible, but as "the bottomless pit" in the King James Version. The bottomless pit *is* the abyss. It is a real region, and it is distinct from the final place of punishment, the lake of fire. We know this because the devil is imprisoned in the Pit for a thousand years, then *later* cast into the lake of fire (Revelation 20:1–3, 7, 10).

The demons in the two men of Gadara cried out to Jesus, imploring Him not to send them to the bottomless pit before the appointed time. "And they begged Jesus repeatedly not to order them to go into the Abyss" (Luke 8:31 NIV). "And suddenly they cried out, saying, 'What have we to do with You, Jesus, You Son of God? Have You come here to torment us before the time?'" (Matthew 8:29). We see therefore that the abyss, Tartarus, was a place of punishment.

There is another fascinating correlation between Isaiah and Homer. Back in 700 BC, Isaiah described *kings* in the Pit, saying: "The realm of the dead below is all astir to meet you at your coming; it rouses the spirits of the departed to greet you—all those who were leaders in the world; it makes them rise from their thrones—all those who were kings over the nations. They will all respond, they will say to you, 'You also have become weak, as we are; you have become like us.'. . . But you are brought down to the realm of the dead, to the depths of the pit" (Isaiah 14:9–10, 15 NIV).

Not long after Isaiah, Homer wrote of kings in the pit of Tartarus. At this early time, the Greeks still believed that only the souls of wicked *kings* went there. Socrates (469–399 BC) noted that "he who has lived unjustly and impiously shall go to the house of vengeance and punishment, which is called Tartarus. . . . And Homer witnesses to the truth of this; for they are always kings and potentates whom he has described as suffering everlasting punishment in the world below: such were Tantalus and Sisyphus and Tityus. But no one ever described Thersites, or any private person who was a villain, as suffering everlasting punishment, or as incurable."

Isaiah had also said, "It shall come to pass in that day that the LORD will punish on high the host of exalted ones, and on the earth the kings of the earth. They will be gathered together, as prisoners are gathered in the pit, and will be shut up in the prison; after many days they will be punished" (Isaiah 24:21–22).

ANGELS AND TITANS IN TARTARUS

In *Theogony*, Hesiod states that Zeus defeated rebellious primordial gods named Titans, and cast them down into the deep pit of Tartarus: He "overshadowed the Titans. . .and bound them in bitter

A statue of an angel with one wing. The Greeks believed the Titans were sent to Tartarus and "bound in chains of darkness."

chains when they had conquered them by their strength for all their great spirit, as far beneath the earth to Tartarus. . . . The Titan gods are hidden under misty gloom, in a dank place where are the ends of the huge earth."

Compare the Titans being "bound. . .in bitter chains" in Tartarus to rebellious angels being bound in "chains of darkness" in Tartarus in the following verse: "God did not spare the angels who sinned, but cast them down to hell and delivered them into chains of darkness, to be reserved for judgment" (2 Peter 2:4). The expression "cast them down to hell" comes from the Greek word *tartaroo*, which means "send into Tartarus." This is the only place where a word referring to Tartarus is used in the New Testament, but its appearance is important. It was used because its imagery accurately describes the place where the rebellious angels were imprisoned. In fact, the New American Standard Bible translates the phrase "delivered them into chains of darkness" as "committed them to pits of darkness." The New International Version translators note that the same phrase could be rendered "gloomy pits."

Jude describes this same scene, saying, "The angels who did not keep their positions of authority but abandoned their proper dwelling—these he has kept in darkness, bound with everlasting chains for judgment on the great Day" (Jude 1:6 NIV). Tartarus is a gloomy prison where certain of the evil angels are presently being punished and tormented, but it is still not their final destination. Their destination is Gehenna (Matthew 25:41). Satan himself will be chained in the bottomless pit, the abyss, during the Millennium (Revelation 20:1–3).

SPIRITS IN PRISON

As was already mentioned, the Greeks not only believed that Tartarus was a prison for the Titans, but later considered it to be the deep abyss used as a dungeon of torment for wicked humans. Isaiah was the first to describe such imagery, and more than a century later, about 586 BC, Ezekiel wrote the following description of Hell: "The strong among the mighty shall speak to him out of the midst of hell with them that help him: they are gone down, they lie uncircumcised,

slain by the sword. Asshur is there and all her company: his graves are about him: all of them slain, fallen by the sword: whose graves are set in the sides of the pit, and her company is round about her grave: all of them slain, fallen by the sword, which caused terror in the land of the living" (Ezekiel 32:21–23 KJV).

This passage describes Asshur, referring to the notoriously cruel Assyrians, who didn't simply go into a gloomy Hades but were suffering in a deeper part of it. Ezekiel says that their "graves are set in the *sides* of the pit." Since the Pit is

▶ A photo of an old prison cell. The Greeks believed Tartarus was a prison for the Titans, as well as a dungeon to torment wicked people.

exceedingly deep, and the wicked angels are chained in prison at the very bottom, where do the most wicked humans go? In the deepest depths of Tartarus *with* the fallen angels? No. It appears that they're in prison "in the sides of the pit," extending some distance down.

These are quite likely the "spirits in prison" that Peter mentions: "Christ also suffered once for sins, the just for the unjust, that He might bring us to God, being put to death in the flesh but made alive by the Spirit, by whom also He went and preached to the spirits in prison, who formerly were disobedient, when once the Divine longsuffering waited in the days of Noah, while the ark was being prepared" (1 Peter 3:18–20). But whether Jesus preached a message of hope to these sprits in prison is another matter, which we will discuss later.

THE FIRES OF GEHENNA

A Jewish doctrine that differs markedly from early Greek myths is the belief in Gehenna, the everlasting fire. Jesus said, "It is better for you to enter the kingdom of God with one eye than to have two eyes and be thrown into hell [Gehenna], where 'the worms that eat them do not die, and the fire is not quenched'" (Mark 9:47–48 NIV). One day, Jesus will say to the wicked, "'Depart from Me, you cursed, into the everlasting fire prepared for the devil and his angels.' . . . And these will go away into everlasting punishment, but the righteous into eternal life" (Matthew 25:41, 46).

When Jesus described Gehenna, He was quoting Isaiah, who wrote about 680 BC: "They will go out and look on the dead bodies of those who rebelled against me; the worms that eat them will not die, the fire that burns them will not be quenched, and they will be loathsome to all mankind" (Isaiah 66:24 NIV). Isaiah was deeply grieved when King Ahaz burned infants in the fires in the Valley of Hinnom. Later, about 680 BC, he prophesied about the fiery punishment of the wicked. So ever since Isaiah's day, the Jews had been thinking of a fiery place of destruction for the wicked. In fact, the Jewish concept of a fiery hell has roots as far back as 1406 BC, when Moses

GEHENNA—A FIERY HELL

Jesus referred to Hell as *Gehenna*, called *ge-Hinnom* (the Valley of Hinnom) in Aramaic, a valley outside the south gate of Jerusalem. There, around 720 BC, idolatrous King Ahaz had cast infants into the flames while worshipping demonic idols (2 Chronicles 28:3). Later, King Josiah destroyed the idols (2 Kings 23:10) and godly Jews turned the valley into Jerusalem's garbage dump—filled with continuously burning trash and rotting refuse. The bodies of executed criminals were often burned there and worms (maggots) fed on the rotting corpses. Hence Jesus said that Hell was a place where "their worm does not die and the fire is not quenched" (Mark 9:44).

recorded God as saying, "For a fire is kindled in My anger, and shall burn to the lowest hell [*Sheol*]" (Deuteronomy 32:22).

The Jews didn't get this idea from the Greeks. The Greeks didn't envision a burning hell. There is no reference to it in the works of Homer or Hesiod, other than a brief mention in *The Iliad*, where Ulysses says, "I hate a man, even as I hate hell fire, who lets his poverty tempt him into lying." The Greek king Ixion was said to be tied to a flaming wheel in Tartarus, but his punishment was unique.

A SHIFT IN GREEK THEOLOGY

Pythagoras (570–495 BC), a Greek philosopher and mathematician of Samos, spoke about the souls of the dead being judged. But Greek views were slow to change. Until about 450 BC, most Greeks still believed that the majority of the dead went to Hades—not to Elysium to be rewarded or to Tartarus to be punished.

About 420 BC, however, Socrates (469–399 BC) said, "There existed a law respecting the destiny of man. . .that he who has lived all his life in justice and holiness shall go, when he is dead, to the Islands of the Blessed, and dwell there in perfect happiness out of the reach of evil; but that he who has lived unjustly and impiously shall go to the house of vengeance and punishment, which is called Tartarus" (quoted by Plato, in *Gorgias*, ca. 380 BC).

In *The Myth of Er*, Plato (424–348 BC) came out with a highly developed theology. In this purported vision, a man named Er

▶ The Jewish concept of Hell as an everlasting fiery place of torment goes back centuries to the time of Moses.

sees two openings in the earth and two in the sky, and judges tell departed souls which entrance to take: the good are directed into the sky, the bad are sent underground. At the same time, clean souls waft down from a celestial exit, exclaiming about beautiful sights and experiences. Others emerge from the earth, dirty and weary, weeping over their punishments. These souls are then allowed to choose their next reincarnation. Only the worst criminals cannot leave the underground.

DEMETER AND PERSEPHONE

The rise of Greek mystery cults between 800 and 480 BC also contributed to the belief that ordinary people could go to the Islands of the Blessed. The cult of Demeter and Persephone, based in Eleusis near Athens, and called the Eleusinian Mysteries, was the most influential.

Demeter had been worshipped as the goddess of harvest and fertility from antiquity, and a legend developed to explain the four months of drought in the Greek summer. The story was that the god Hades kidnapped Demeter's daughter, Persephone, and took her to the underworld. Demeter looked for her daughter for many months, neglecting her duties, so there was a drought. Zeus therefore ordered Hades to return Persephone to the upper world. However, Persephone had eaten four pomegranate seeds in the underworld, so was obliged to spend four months every year there—during which time Demeter again neglected her duties. Hence the annual summer drought.

From this fable, the belief apparently developed that if Persephone could escape Hades, so could ordinary people. Originally, only outstanding heroes and mortals related to the gods went to Elysium.

▶ A plaque by an artist named Ninion in the 4th century AD, depicting elements of the Eleusinian Mysteries and showing Persephone and Demeter; Persephone escaped Hades, which gave rise to the belief that if she could, so could ordinary people.

Later, those whom the gods chose were included. But as time went on, even ordinary people, if they went through a mystic initiation ceremony and lived good lives, could hope for a better afterlife in Elysium. People eventually joined this idea of a better afterlife with Homer's teaching about Elysium, and though certain philosophers had different ideas, this was the popular belief among common Greeks.

SWEET HOPE FOR ETERNITY

According to Isocrates (436–338 BC), the goddess Demeter's greatest gifts to mankind were agriculture and "the holy rite [i.e., the Eleusinian Mysteries] which inspires in those who partake of it sweeter hopes regarding both the end of life and all eternity" (Panegyricus 4.28). But as the early Christians told the Greeks, Jesus had declared, "I am the way, the truth, and the life. No one comes to the Father except through Me" (John 14:6).

THE ACCUMULATED WEIGHT OF REVELATIONS

By the time the Greeks conquered Jerusalem and the process of Hellenization began (ca. 322 BC), a great shift in Greek religious doctrine had occurred, and their concepts of Elysium and Tartarus were fully developed. It is from these circumstances that secular scholars have concluded that Greek thinking influenced the Jews—who, up until this time, it is claimed, had given almost *no* thought to the afterlife. But as I have explained, the reverse was true: the Jews already had received detailed revelations, had thought deeply upon them, had reached conclusions and developed doctrines, and had exported their views to the Greeks.

By Isaiah's day (700 BC), and certainly by Ezekiel's day (his last dated revelation was in 571 BC), the Hebrews had accumulated a tremendous wealth of revelation. Let's review it briefly. Scripture declares that people have immortal spirits, that these spirits survive the death of the body, and that they go to a ghostly region under

▶ Scripture describes Sheol as having separate chambers, gates, and doors. In the long, dark hallway behind this old metal gate are separate chambers.

the earth—called Sheol, the "land of darkness and the shadow of death" (Job 10:21). There they join those who have died before them. There are separate "chambers" there (Proverbs 7:27), meaning at least two distinct realms, and these regions have gates and doors (Job 17:16; 38:17).

Spirits there are "weak" (Isaiah 14:10), a mere shadow of their earthly selves, but they retain human appearance; dead kings still have thrones (Isaiah 14:9), and slain warriors go "down to hell with their weapons of war" (Ezekiel 32:27).

Spirits confined there are conscious of their surroundings and of new arrivals, and still have their reason and emotions (Isaiah 14:9). For the unrighteous dead, it is a land of utter darkness, disorder, and empty existence (Job 10:21–22), "the abode of silence" (Psalm 94:17 NASB), where they feel hopelessly "adrift among the dead" (Psalm 88:5). Some are relegated to "the lowest depths of the Pit" (Isaiah 14:15). For the righteous, however, it is a place of peace and light, from which they don't wish to be disturbed (1 Samuel 28:15).

In addition, the Bible clearly teaches that at the end of time, God will make a new heaven and a new earth, and will resurrect the dead of all ages. The righteous will be rewarded with eternal life on a transformed New Earth, and the wicked will suffer: "The worms that eat them will not die, the fire that burns them will not be quenched" (Isaiah 26:19; 65:17; 66:22–24 NIV).

WRITTEN RECORDS OF DOCTRINES

We can see how the Jewish scholars and scribes dedicated to copying, reading, thinking about, and discussing the scriptures were able to piece together an accurate picture of the afterlife. (In places where they came to the wrong conclusions, Jesus corrected them.) This doctrinal development began in David's day, proceeded from the exile in Babylon to the return to Judah, and continued through the Persian and Greek periods—all the way up to New Testament times. And these doctrines were widely taught among the Jewish population.

One question must be asked, however: If the Hebrews had been

▶ A portion of a photographic reproduction of Isaiah 53, found at Qumran; this scroll, known as the Great Isaiah Scroll, is the best preserved of the scrolls and is dated to around 200 BC.

developing their theology of Heaven and Hell since at least the days of Isaiah, why do we have no written record of these Jewish religious views until the third century BC, when apocryphal books, such as 1 Enoch, were written?

Well, other than the canonical scriptures, no Jewish religious writings of any kind, whether commentary or teaching, survive from 700–200 BC. Even books such as 1 Enoch (ca. 200 BC) aren't commentaries but were intended to be passed off as scripture. Not until about 100 BC do any commentaries on the scriptures or doctrines appear, and these are among the Dead Sea Scrolls written by the Essenes—and even their survival is exceptional and accidental.

Development of the Greek concept of Paradise is equally fragmentary: Although Homer described Elysium about 650 BC, it wasn't until hundreds of years later that Paradise, by that name, appeared again in Greek literature. Apollonius of Rhodes (300–250 BC) mentions it in *Argonautica,* making him the second writer since Homer to speak of Elysium. Other writers simply referred to "the Isles of the Blessed."

THE GREEK SEPTUAGINT

The Old Testament was written in Hebrew, with portions in Aramaic. But by 300 BC, most Jews scattered throughout the eastern Mediterranean spoke Greek instead of Hebrew. So the scriptures were translated into Greek between 285 and 132 BC in the city of Alexandria in Egypt. This translation was later referred to as the Septuagint. By the first century, most Jews had accepted the Septuagint as authoritative, and literary leaders such as Philo and Josephus considered it equal to the Hebrew text. Apparently, so did the writers of the New Testament, judging by the way they quoted it as authoritative in their epistles.

The Septuagint naturally used Greek expressions for Jewish words. Thus, *Sheol* was translated as *Hades*. Jesus says in Luke 16:22–23 (NIV), "The rich man also died and was buried. In Hades, where he was in torment, he looked up." Jesus didn't say, "In a place *similar* to Hades," but simply stated that the rich man was *in* Hades. Peter told a Jewish audience in Jerusalem that David "spoke concerning the resurrection of the Christ, that His soul was not left in Hades" (Acts 2:31).

In addition, the word *Tartarus* was used in the Septuagint translation in Job 40:20 and 41:21 and was familiar to the first-century Christians.

▶ A copy of the the Septuagint, an ancient Greek translation of the Old Testament, which naturally translated Hebrew words into Greek, such as *Hades* and *Tartarus*.

Thus, in the New Testament, when discussing the rebellious angels, Peter says that God "cast them down to hell," using a Greek word that means "to cast down to Tartarus" (2 Peter 2:4).

It might seem to the casual observer that the Jews borrowed their concepts from the Greeks, or that the New Testament endorses Greek views of the afterlife. But although they used the same terms, by this time the Jews already had their *own* fully developed doctrines about Hades, Tartarus, Paradise, and Heaven. It should be remembered that there were many divergent views on these subjects among the Greeks themselves.

Also, many Greek expressions had passed into common usage divorced from their original meaning. For example, of the many hundreds of times that the New Testament writers refer to Heaven, they use the Greek word *ouranos*, which

> **THE SEPTUAGINT**
> The Greek translation of the Hebrew scriptures was called the Septuagint, from the Latin word *septuaginta* (meaning "seventy"), based on the tradition that seventy Jewish scholars had worked on it.

originally referred to the mythical Greek god Uranus. Yet by the first century, it commonly referred to the sky and the heavens above, so that Jesus could say without any confusion, "Repent, for the kingdom of heaven [*ouranos*] is at hand" (Matthew 4:17).

Also, Hades originally referred to the Greek god Hades, and his domain was called "the house of Hades." But by New Testament times, *Hades*, too, had become a place name so that Jesus could say to John in AD 96, "I am He who lives, and was dead, and behold, I am alive forevermore. Amen. And I have the keys of Hades and of Death" (Revelation 1:18).

THE APOCRYPHAL BOOK OF 1 ENOCH

During the last two centuries before Christ, Jewish writers produced a number of apocryphal books about Heaven and Hell. The book of 1 Enoch, claiming to be written by the biblical Enoch, is the best-known. I quote it here, not because it's scripture, but because it reflects Jewish theology of the afterlife in the centuries just before Christ. Though most of the so-called visions of Enoch and other spurious books are merely the product of human imagination, the fact remains that they reflect contemporary doctrinal development—a process that God Himself had guided.

In R. H. Charles's 1917 translation of 1 Enoch 22:2, the writer describes seeing "four hollow places, deep and wide" and separate from one another. He claims that an angel told him, "These hollow places have been created for this very purpose, that the spirits of the souls of the dead should assemble therein. . .till the great judgment (comes) upon them. . . . Here their spirits shall be set apart in this great pain till the great day of judgment" (1 Enoch 22:3–4, 11).

Note that 1 Enoch states that the spirits of the unrighteous experience torment in Hades *before* the final day of judgment. This parallels what Jesus taught about the rich man suffering in Hades even before being cast into Gehenna, the final lake of fire. As for "the spirits

of the righteous," 1 Enoch says they were in a hollow place, "in which there is the bright spring of water" (1 Enoch 22:9). Again, this parallels Jesus' account of the beggar Lazarus being in a blessed place with plenty of water.

Jesus, however, gives a more logical view of Paradise than does the writer of 1 Enoch, who relies on natural reasoning. A normal Jew living in 200 BC couldn't understand how two dimensions could coexist, so when the writer describes Hades and Abraham's Bosom, he refers to separate "hollow places, deep and wide and very smooth" (1 Enoch 22:2). To his understanding, for spirits to live under the earth, they had to be in giant caverns. Jesus, on the other hand, describes both Hades and Abraham's Bosom as separate realms with "a great gulf" (Luke 16:26 NKJV) or "chasm" (Luke 16:26 NASB) between them—*not* two deep caverns with solid rock between them.

First Enoch also claims that God placed an archangel named Uriel "in charge of the world and of Tartarus" (1 Enoch 20:2). Again,

Jesus described both Hades and Abraham's Bosom as separate realms with a "great gulf" or chasm between them; Refrigerator Canyon in Zion National Park, Utah, helps make sense of this Jewish understanding.

though its statement about Uriel is a flight of fancy, this passage is important to our study because it uses "Tartarus" to describe the deepest region of Hades—something the New Testament also does in 2 Peter 2:4. As for the angels bound in Tartarus, 1 Enoch says, "In those days they shall be led off to the abyss of fire: and to the torment and the prison in which they shall be confined for ever" (1 Enoch 10:13–14).

THE AUTHOR OF 1 ENOCH
The book of 1 Enoch is *not* inspired scripture; it was written by an anonymous Greek-speaking Jew about 200 BC, not by the biblical Enoch, as it claims.

The question will be asked, however, "If 1 Enoch isn't scripture, why does Jude quote from it in his epistle?" Jude 1:14–15 says, "Now Enoch, the seventh from Adam, prophesied about these men also, saying, 'Behold, the Lord comes with ten thousands of His saints, to execute judgment on all, to convict all who are ungodly among them of all their ungodly deeds which they have committed in an ungodly way, and of all the harsh things which ungodly sinners have spoken against Him.'" This quote comes from 1 Enoch 1:9.

Why did Jude quote a prophecy from this book as if it were inspired? Well, just because this book wasn't accepted into the canon doesn't mean that it *entirely* lacks truth. Also, the fact that Jude quoted a sentence from it doesn't mean he considered the entire book inspired. He was quoting a well-known statement that illustrated his point.

The apostle Paul often quoted Greek authors for the same reason. For example, Paul writes, "One of them, a prophet of their own, said, 'Cretans are always liars, evil beasts, lazy gluttons.' This testimony is true" (Titus 1:12–13). Paul is quoting *Cretica* by Epimenides (500s BC), a Cretan poet said to have made several true predictions. Does this mean Paul endorsed everything Epimenides said? By no means. Two lines later in *Cretica*, Epimenides says of the pagan god Zeus, "Thou livest and abidest forever."

In Acts 17:28, Paul again quotes Epimenides, as well as citing the Cilician poet Aratus (315–240 BC). In 1 Corinthians 15:33, he quotes the play *Thais* by the Greek playwright Menander (342–291

BC). *Thais* is a comedy about a prostitute—so Paul wouldn't have considered it inspired by God. (He didn't even need to have watched the play. The quote he repeated was a common proverb among Greeks of his day.)

OTHER JEWISH APOCRYPHAL WRITINGS

There were other apocryphal books written in this era as well. The book of Judith was written about 120 BC and builds on Isaiah 66:24—"the worms that eat them will not die, the fire that burns them will not be quenched"—stating, "Woe to the nations that rise up against my people! The Lord Almighty will take vengeance on them in the day of judgment; fire and worms he will give to their flesh; they shall weep in pain forever" (Judith 16:17 RSV).

The book of 4 Maccabees was written about 90 BC and states a belief that the righteous went to Abraham's Bosom when they died: "Let us not fear him who thinks he is killing us, for great is the struggle of the soul and the danger of eternal torment lying before those who transgress the commandment of God. . . . For if we so die, Abraham and Isaac and Jacob will welcome us, and all the fathers will praise us" (4 Maccabees 13:14–15, 17 RSV).

Written during the century before Christ, the apocryphal Apocalypse of Zephaniah contains a highly developed belief in punishments and rewards in the afterlife, saying, "You have escaped from the Abyss and Hades, now you will cross over the crossing place. . .to all the righteous ones, namely Abraham, Isaac, Jacob, Enoch, Elijah, and David" (Apocalypse of Zephaniah 9:2).

This book also describes the fires of Hell. "Again I turned back and walked, and I saw a great sea. . . . I discovered that it was entirely a sea of flame like a slime which casts forth much flame and whose waves burn sulfur and bitumen" (Apocalypse of Zephaniah 6:1–2). This imagery was accurate; in the book of Revelation, John describes "the fiery lake of burning sulfur" (Revelation 19:20 NIV).

Again, I quote them here not because they're scripture—they are *not*—but because they give us a look at Jewish theology of the afterlife in the centuries just before Christ.

▶ Burning sulfur steams in a geothermal area of New Zealand. A lake of burning sulfur is the image the Bible uses to describe what the fires of Hell are like.

THE JEWS INFLUENCING ZOROASTRIANISM

Finally, a word about Zoroastrianism. Zoroaster was the founder of the Zoroastrian religion of Persia and is thought by many scholars to have lived between 628 BC and 551 BC—though others maintain that he lived several centuries earlier. By the 500s BC, however, Zoroastrianism had become the state religion of the Persians.

A number of scholars believe that Zoroastrianism had an influence on Judaism. It's commonly believed that before the Babylonian Captivity (605–539 BC), the Jews had no concept of the devil, no belief in the resurrection, and no doctrine of final judgment. Scholars say that the Jews borrowed these doctrines from the Zoroastrians while living in the Persian Empire.

The Zoroastrians believed that the earth would be renovated in the end times and that there would be some kind of resurrection of the dead; but according to scholar Franz König, they didn't hold the doctrine of the resurrection before the 300s BC. By this late date, the Jews had already been released from captivity for two centuries (in 539 BC). And because the Jewish scriptures as early as 700 BC taught a clear doctrine of the resurrection, it's obvious that if any borrowing of ideas happened, the Zoroastrians were the ones borrowing from the Jews.

As for the Jewish belief in Satan, the evil spirit who accursed God's people and caused diseases and disasters, the book of Job plainly talked about him as early as 1600 BC. Zoroaster didn't believe in the scriptural concept of the devil, but taught a dualism: there was a good god, Ahura Mazda, who was the source of all good, and an evil god, Ahriman, who was the source of all evil. But the Jewish scriptures teach that the one true God is all-powerful and created all things—including the devil. The first two chapters of the book of Job make it clear that the devil has to get permission from God before acting.

Also, the name of the supreme "good" Persian god is Ahura Mazda, but some scholars point out the similarity between the Zoroastrian word *Ahura* and the Vedic word *Asura* (meaning "demon"). Whatever the relation between these two words, we know that Zoroaster reformed an earlier polytheistic religion and exalted one of its many gods, Ahura Mazda (the deity of wisdom), to the position of supreme being and creator, while demoting other gods to secondary roles. The Bible, on the other hand, from the very beginning, declares the Lord God to be the one true God and Creator.

The writers of the Bible were inspired by the Holy Spirit of God, not by the philosophers and priests of the pagan religions around them. "For prophecy never came by the will of man, but holy men of God spoke as they were moved by the Holy Spirit" (2 Peter 1:21).

Jesus, who created all things in the heavens and earth, ascended to Heaven after His death and resurrection; His ascension was depicted by Plockhorst in the mid-1800s in this painting that can be found at Grace Church in Chiangmai, Thailand.

3 | JESUS AND THE KINGDOM OF HEAVEN

JESUS' TEACHINGS ON HEAVEN

Jesus has an absolutely unique perspective on Heaven. His views on the subject are authoritative. That's because He *created* Heaven. The Gospel of John states, "In the beginning was the Word, and the Word was with God, and the Word was God. He was in the beginning with God. All things were made through Him, and without Him nothing was made that was made" (John 1:1–3). Paul adds, "For by Him all things were created, *both in the heavens* and on earth, visible and invisible, whether thrones or dominions or rulers or authorities—*all things* have been created through Him and for Him" (Colossians 1:16 NASB, emphasis added).

After His resurrection, Jesus ascended to Heaven and sat down on God's throne with Him (Revelation 3:21; Mark 16:19). But even before

> **THE ONLY BEGOTTEN GOD**
>
> In the New King James Version, the translators' note to John 1:18 tells us that an alternate Greek text renders the phrase "the only begotten Son" as "the only begotten God." Indeed, the NIV translates the verse as follows: "No one has ever seen God, but the one and only Son, who is himself God and is in closest relationship with the Father, has made him known."

His incarnation, Jesus was enthroned with His Father and knew Heaven better than anyone else. John describes him as "the only begotten Son, who is in the bosom of the Father" (John 1:18).

Jesus not only knows the Father intimately and made Him known to mankind, but also knows Heaven intimately and described it to us. He said that He "came down from heaven" (John 3:13; see also John 6:38.) If anyone, therefore, could accurately explain what Heaven is like, Jesus could. "He who comes from heaven is above all. And what He has seen and heard, that He testifies" (John 3:31–32). Jesus Christ is the ultimate authority on Heaven.

THE KINGDOM OF HEAVEN

Jesus talked frequently about Heaven, referring to it most often as "the kingdom of Heaven" (Matthew 3:2) and "the kingdom of God" (Matthew 6:33). This makes it clear that Heaven is not simply a beautiful otherworldly realm, but a kingdom belonging to and ruled by God, the great King. Many modern people envision a Heaven to which all people—good, mediocre, and bad—go. In their version of Heaven, both Jesus and the Father are conspicuously absent.

But Heaven is *God's* kingdom, which is why Jesus taught us to pray, "May your Kingdom come soon. May your will be done on earth, as it is in heaven" (Matthew 6:10 NLT). God's will is obeyed completely in Heaven, but we need to pray that His kingdom comes and that His will is done on *earth* as well. This obedience starts with us. Jesus said, "Not everyone who says to Me, 'Lord, Lord,' shall enter the kingdom of heaven, but he who does the will of My Father in heaven" (Matthew 7:21). Heaven isn't simply a happy place where everyone goes after they die; going to Heaven means entering into the eternal presence of the God whom we love and obey.

> **GOD'S KINGDOM IS FOR US**
> Jesus said, "I confer on you a kingdom, just as my Father conferred one on me" (Luke 22:29 NIV). God and His Son don't want the kingdom of Heaven all for themselves; they want to *share* it with us.

Jesus also referred to Heaven as "My Father's kingdom" (Matthew 26:29). Because He is the Son of God and the Messiah, He also said, "My Father has granted Me a kingdom" (Luke 22:29 NASB). He later referred to Heaven as "My kingdom" (John 18:36). Paul, in fact, calls it "the kingdom of Christ and God" (Ephesians 5:5).

However, if we love and trust God, He will lavish the riches of His kingdom on us. When talking about the righteous, Jesus called Heaven "the kingdom of their Father" (Matthew 13:43), and He promised that God would tell them, "Come, you who are blessed by my Father; take your inheritance, the kingdom *prepared for you* since the creation of the world" (Matthew 25:34 NIV, emphasis added). Heaven belongs to God, but ever since the creation of the world and mankind, our Father's kingdom is being prepared as an inheritance for *us*, His children.

God takes particular delight in preparing Heaven to give us pleasure and joy. This task began at the creation of the world and has continued for thousands of years. Just before Jesus returned to Heaven, He said, "I go to prepare a place for you. . .that where I am, there you may be also" (John 14:2–3).

Jesus also said, "Blessed are the poor in spirit, for *theirs* is the kingdom of heaven" (Matthew 5:3, emphasis added). In a very special way, the kingdom of Heaven belongs to *us*. Though we're spiritually poor, God has prepared astounding riches for us.

HEAVEN PAST, PRESENT, AND FUTURE

It's important to understand what we *mean* when we talk about Heaven. For most people, Heaven is a place of beauty and light and happiness, in some spiritual dimension, completely separate from and unrelated to this physical earth. But this picture is only partially true.

As we've seen, when the Old Testament saints died, they went to a realm known as Abraham's Bosom. We could consider this the "past Heaven," because the righteous who went there enjoyed the bliss of Paradise but didn't have access to the presence of God in His eternal city. That limitation is now past.

When the New Testament describes Heaven *now*, the "present Heaven," it refers principally to the New Jerusalem, where God dwells. As the book of Hebrews says, we "have come to. . .the city of the living God, the heavenly Jerusalem, to an innumerable company of angels, to the general assembly and church of the firstborn who are registered in heaven, to God the Judge of all" (Hebrews 12:22–23). This present Heaven is centered in the heavenly city.

Also, in a very real sense, *part* of this present Heaven exists in our

▶ Jesus assured his listeners that the righteous would live on a restored Eden-like earth. Jan Breughel the Elder painting *Landscape with Animals* (1613) brings to life his version of what Paradise looks like.

hearts now. Although we live on this fallen planet, we're already citizens of Heaven. As Jesus declared, the kingdom is not simply something that is to come, but it exists right now, because "the kingdom of God is within you" (Luke 17:21).

However, the *ultimate* kingdom of God, the "future Heaven," is yet to be established. It will come into being when the New Jerusalem emerges from the spiritual dimension and settles on this physical planet (Revelation 21:1–3). Though the eternal city will continue to be the capital of Heaven, God's kingdom will include the renewed planet Earth, which will have been transformed into a global Garden of Eden.

THE FATE OF THE RIGHTEOUS AND THE WICKED

The Jews in the first century didn't envision eternal life in a heavenly realm someplace beyond the earth. Certainly they understood that the spirits of the dead were presently in Abraham's Bosom in an unseen state, and they knew that God was somewhere in the heavens, but they were convinced that after the resurrection of the dead, the righteous would live on a restored Eden-like earth, where the wicked would be no more. "The righteous shall inherit the land, and dwell in it forever" (Psalm 37:29). The Messiah, the Son of David, would rule over them for unending days in a reign of perfect peace, justice, and joy.

The unrighteous, if they were even raised from the dead, would rise in the "resurrection of condemnation," only to be destroyed. Isaiah writes: "'As the new heavens and the new earth that I make will endure before me,' declares the LORD, 'so will your name and descendants endure. . . . And they will go out and look on the dead bodies of those who rebelled against me; the worms that eat them will not die, the fire that burns them will not be quenched, and they will be loathsome to all mankind'" (Isaiah 66:22, 24 NIV).

Based on this passage, the Jews had various ideas about the fate of the wicked. Some claimed that the wicked would be utterly burned and reduced to ashes. After all, God had promised, "You will tread down the wicked, for they will be ashes under the soles of your feet" (Malachi 4:3 NASB). Others believed that the unrighteous—or at least some of them—would suffer eternally in a lake of burning sulfur. Still others believed that the wicked would suffer for a season but be released when they'd been sufficiently punished. We'll discuss all these views in detail later.

Meanwhile, what would the righteous do in Paradise on earth? They fully expected to be with "Abraham, Isaac and Jacob and all the prophets in the kingdom of God" (Luke 13:28 NIV). But Jesus repeatedly disconcerted His listeners by pointing out that Jews wouldn't be the only ones to enjoy this. He said, "I say to you that many will come from the east and the west, and will take their places at the feast with Abraham, Isaac, and Jacob in the kingdom of heaven" (Matthew 8:11 NIV).

THE CONTEXT OF JESUS' TEACHINGS

It's worth noting that when Jesus talked about Heaven and Hell, He didn't have to explain to the Jews that the righteous would sit down at a banquet table with Abraham, Isaac, and Jacob (Matthew 8:11). This was a widely accepted belief, and His listeners were familiar with the concept. When He mentioned it, they understood what He was talking about. The same applied when He discussed the wicked suffering in Hades (Luke 16:19–26), or the existence of the

> **JOSEPHUS AND THE RESURRECTION**
>
> Josephus writes, "They [the Pharisees] also believe that souls have an immortal vigor in them, and that under the earth there will be rewards or punishments, according as they have lived virtuously or viciously in this life; and the latter are to be detained in an everlasting prison, but that the former shall have power to revive and live again" (*Antiquities* 18.1.3).

fires of Gehenna (Mark 9:47–48), or the fact that the devil and his angels would be punished in everlasting fire (Matthew 25:41). Jesus wasn't introducing concepts that his audience had never heard before; but he gave fresh insight to already familiar subjects.

By Jesus' day, most Jews believed there would be a resurrection and

Jesus made it clear in scripture that He was returning soon; His second coming is depicted in a magnificent stained glass window at St. Matthew's Lutheran Church in Charleston, South Carolina.

SECOND COMING OF CHRIST

a final judgment of both the righteous and the wicked. As Martha said about Lazarus, "I know that he will rise again in the resurrection at the last day" (John 11:24). These were mainstream beliefs—at least among the Pharisees, whose teachings were embraced by the majority of Jews.

We see from the quote by Josephus (see sidebar on p. 105) that all the Pharisees didn't necessarily believe that the wicked would rise again; only the righteous. But Jesus taught that there would be *two* resurrections and that *all* people would come forth, "those who have done good, to the resurrection of life, and those who have done evil, to the resurrection of condemnation" (John 5:29).

EMPHASIZING THE SPIRITUAL DIMENSION

Jesus also surprised many listeners by emphasizing the spiritual side of the kingdom of God. Though the Jews expected a physical, material kingdom in the land of Israel, and Jesus definitely affirmed this belief, He also spoke repeatedly about the spiritual heavens and the spiritual realm of Hell. And after His resurrection, instead of staying on the earth, He "ascended far above all the heavens" and "was received up into heaven, and sat down at the right hand of God" (Ephesians 4:10; Mark 16:19). This was an unexpected turn of events.

Jesus had warned His enemies: "I am going away, and. . .where I go you cannot come" (John 8:21). To His disciples, He spoke of "going away" and then inviting them to join Him, and also of returning to be with them—but these concepts baffled them (John 13:33; 14:2–6, 19–23, 28; 16:5–6, 16–18). Wasn't the kingdom of God supposed to be on the earth in Israel, and once the Messiah came, wasn't He supposed to rule forever? "The people answered Him, 'We have heard from the law that the Christ remains forever'" (John 12:34).

Jesus taught that eventually He would return (Matthew 24:29–31) and set up His kingdom on the earth. When He reigned in the ancient city of Jerusalem over all the nations of the earth (Revelation 20), this would finally fulfill Jewish expectations. They would have eternal life, yes, but would dwell in the land of Israel in a natural earth that would be made over into a beautiful paradise.

They weren't anticipating what would happen *next*. Yet if they had taken the following promises literally, they would have. Isaiah writes, "For behold, I create new heavens and a new earth" (Isaiah 65:17 NASB). "'I am coming, and I will live among you,' declares the LORD" (Zechariah 2:10 NIV). "My dwelling place also will be with them; and I will be their God, and they will be My people" (Ezekiel 37:27 NASB). Sure enough, as Revelation 21 brings out, the entire earth will be remade as the Garden of Eden, and the heavenly city—the home of God—will descend to earth. There will be a greater Paradise on earth than the Jews had ever imagined.

However, often when Jesus spoke of the kingdom of God, He seemed to be focusing on a *spiritual* hereafter. For example, when asked by Pilate, "Are You the King of the Jews?" Jesus answered, "My kingdom is not of this world" (John 18:33, 36). At that time it wasn't. . .*yet*. It wasn't an either/or situation, but that's how it appeared to many people, and this was a stumbling block for many Jews.

For the Greeks, a purely spiritual kingdom was no problem. That's what they expected. Ever since the days of Plato—who declared physical matter evil and the spiritual realm good—they had looked for a permanent escape from this present world. When they became Christians, a number of Greeks had difficulty with the teaching that their physical bodies would rise again and live on the earth. Paul had to directly address this issue. He asked, "If it is preached that Christ has been raised from the dead, how can some of you say that there is no resurrection of the dead?" (1 Corinthians 15:12 NIV).

To this day, many Christians believe that "going to Heaven" in a spiritual dimension is the end of the story. They fail to understand the importance of the resurrection of our physical bodies and of an unending life in the natural world.

EATING AND DRINKING IN THE KINGDOM

When we consider the activities most often described as happening in the kingdom of Heaven, we're in for a surprise. The Jews put great emphasis on eating and drinking in the kingdom of God, and Jesus talked about this as well. It may seem unspiritual to many Christians, but feasting in Heaven is prominent in the scriptures because it epitomizes the best, the happiest, and the most joyful times—the exact opposite of lack and suffering and misery. And in the kingdom of God, these happy times will last forever.

Jesus said, "I tell you this, that many Gentiles will come from all over the world—from east and west—and sit down with Abraham, Isaac, and Jacob at the feast in the Kingdom of Heaven" (Matthew 8:11 NLT). This is most likely not describing a gigantic banqueting hall filled with millions of people who can't even see Abraham from some seat ten miles away. It probably refers to the patriarchs holding *continual* feasts, day after day, with new groups of believers.

Jesus taught that when hosting a banquet, we should invite the poor, the lame, and the destitute. "'Then at the resurrection of the righteous, God will reward you for inviting those who could not repay you.' Hearing this, a man sitting at the table with Jesus exclaimed, 'What a blessing it will be to attend a banquet in the Kingdom of God!'" (Luke 14:14–15 NLT). Jesus responded by informing him that many

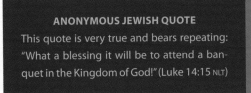

ANONYMOUS JEWISH QUOTE
This quote is very true and bears repeating: "What a blessing it will be to attend a banquet in the Kingdom of God!" (Luke 14:15 NLT)

people who are invited to God's great banquet are so preoccupied with the things of this world that they can't be bothered to accept the invitation.

At the Last Supper, after drinking from "the cup of blessing" (1 Corinthians 10:16 KJV), Jesus told His twelve disciples, "I will not drink of this fruit of the vine from now on until that day when I drink it new with you in My Father's kingdom" (Matthew 26:29 NASB). Notice the words "with you." Apparently, while many believers will be privileged to sit down to feast with Abraham, Isaac, and Jacob, only a select few will have the privilege of dining regularly with the Son of God. To the Twelve, Jesus said, "And I bestow upon you a kingdom. . .that you may eat and drink at My table in My kingdom, and sit on thrones judging the twelve tribes of Israel" (Luke 22:29–30).

Of course, there *will* be times when Jesus will feast personally with every single believer. After all, He promised, "I stand at the door and knock. If anyone hears my voice and opens the door, I will come in and eat with that person, and they with me" (Revelation 3:20 NIV).

Though Jesus and the Jews put considerable emphasis on feasting in God's kingdom, some people believe this must be purely symbolic,

because Paul tells us that "the kingdom of God is not eating and drinking, but righteousness and peace and joy in the Holy Spirit" (Romans 14:17). But this verse must be understood in context: Paul isn't denying that we will feast in the kingdom of God. In this passage, he's talking about dietary scruples *in this life*, and that we're not to eat nonkosher food if it offends a brother or sister (see Romans 14:14–23).

When we have our new bodies, we may not *need* to eat, but Jesus ate food in His glorified body after His resurrection. He ate food

Jesus shares His last meal on earth with His disciples, pictured here in Leonardo da Vinci's (1452–1519) painting *The Last Supper*.

the very day He rose from the dead (Luke 24:40–43), and His disciples repeatedly "ate and drank with him after he rose from the dead" (Acts 10:41 NIV).

THE KINGDOM OF HEAVEN WITHIN

Jesus frequently referred to the physical establishment of God's kingdom on earth as a future event, but He also emphasized its spiritual dimension by stating that it was happening *right now*. "When He was asked by the Pharisees when the kingdom of God would come, He answered them and said, 'The kingdom of God does not come with observation; nor will they say, "See here!" or "See there!" For indeed, the kingdom of God is within you'" (Luke 17:20–21).

People were entering God's kingdom at that very time—without dying and going to Heaven. Jesus said, "The law and the prophets were until John. Since that time the kingdom of God has been preached, and everyone is pressing into it" (Luke 16:16). This thought is presented slightly differently elsewhere: "From the days of John the Baptist until now the kingdom of heaven suffers violence, and the violent take it by force" (Matthew 11:12).

Again, many Jews were dismayed to hear this. They were looking forward to an *exclusively* material kingdom that would be a considerable improvement on what they were presently experiencing. Love and joy and unselfishness in this *present* life were all well and fine, but they surely hoped for a glorious material kingdom.

Paul also emphasized the present reality of the kingdom, saying that God has enabled us "to share in the inheritance of his holy people in the kingdom of light. For he has rescued us from the dominion of darkness and brought us into the kingdom of the Son he loves"

> **SEIZING GOD'S KINGDOM**
> In the New American Standard Bible, the translators' notes to Matthew 11:12 point out that this passage could also read: "The kingdom of heaven is forcibly entered, and violent men seize it for themselves." They were earnest and insistent. Jesus had said, "*Strive* to enter through the narrow gate" (Luke 13:24, emphasis added), and people were doing just that.

(Colossians 1:12–13 NIV). God has *already* brought us into His Son's kingdom. This "dominion of darkness" refers not only to eternal death in Hell, but also to the devil's kingdom of darkness in this present age. Likewise, the kingdom of light, the kingdom of God's Son, refers not only to Heaven and the world to come, but also to our life in Christ in this present era.

God has already "raised us up together, and made us sit together in the heavenly places in Christ Jesus" (Ephesians 2:6). It may not *seem* this way much of the time, but it's a reality. Of course, we must still humbly submit ourselves and our petitions to God, not get the idea that we sit enthroned as glorified lords, free to command miracles, overflowing prosperity, and perfect health.

SURETY OF GOING TO HEAVEN

What's the most important thing we need to know about Heaven? More than anything else, we need to know if we are personally *going* there.

So how do we enter God's kingdom? Jesus said, "I tell you the truth, unless you turn from your sins and become like little children, you will never get into the Kingdom of Heaven" (Matthew 18:3 NLT). He added that "no one can see the kingdom of God unless they are born again" (John 3:3 NIV). We're born again when the Spirit of Christ enters our being and fills us with the life of God. "God has sent the Spirit of his Son into our hearts" (Galatians 4:6 NLT), and "the Spirit gives life" (John 6:63 NIV).

Paul tells us that "he who is joined to the Lord is one spirit with Him" (1 Corinthians 6:17), and when we're united with God's Spirit, we have the life of God inside us—eternal life. "Therefore, if anyone

COMING ALIVE IN GOD

Being saved is more than simply holding a particular belief or giving mental assent to the existence of God and the fact that Jesus died to save us. Being saved is when our faith and sincere heart cry opens us up to the Holy Spirit, and He comes in with His mighty power and "plugs us in" to God.

A stained glass window of Jesus with little children; Jesus told His disciples that to enter the kingdom of Heaven they needed to turn from sin and become like little children.

is in Christ, he is a new creation" (2 Corinthians 5:17).

We absolutely *cannot* save ourselves. Our own efforts to live righteously aren't enough to earn us a place in Heaven. "For it is by grace you have been saved, through faith—and this is not from yourselves, it is the gift of God" (Ephesians 2:8 NIV). Grace is an unearned gift, something you can only gratefully receive. Receiving this gracious gift is what saves us.

Many sincere believers, however, are worried by Jesus' statement that one day many people will profess to know Him and will list all the good things they've done in His name—yet Jesus will tell them, "I never knew you. Away from me, you evildoers!" (Matthew 7:23 NIV). They worry that if even those who have done wonderful miracles in Jesus' name think they're saved, but find out to their shock that they aren't, then what hope do *they*—ordinary Christians who have done no mighty works or miracles in Jesus' name—have of being assured of their salvation?

The key to understanding Jesus' statement is that those people who claimed to be serving Jesus were hypocrites. They may have outwardly appeared good, but they were actually doing evil and were aware of it. They were never actually "joined to the Lord." They knew all *about* Jesus, but they never knew *Him*. Paul tells us, "They profess to know God, but by their deeds they deny Him" (Titus 1:16 NASB). They don't obey Him. "For this you know with certainty, that no immoral or impure person or covetous man, who is an idolater, has an inheritance in the kingdom of Christ and God" (Ephesians 5:5 NASB; see also 1 Corinthians 6:9–10; Galatians 5:19–21).

But we who love God, believe in His Son, trust Jesus to save us, and obey Him in love can be assured that we're saved. We're not saved by our good works, but if we truly have the Spirit of Christ dwelling in us, good works will naturally follow. We may stumble and fall, but if our faith and love and repentance are sincere, we won't live our lives in disobedience to God. And we can be sure that God loves us and will make good His promise to save us.

THE FINAL JUDGMENT

Jesus taught that there would be a judgment in the last day—something the Jews of His day surely believed. But though His listeners were of the opinion that God the Father would judge them, Jesus taught that "the Father judges no one, but has entrusted all judgment to the Son, that all may honor the Son just as they honor the Father. . . . Very truly I tell you, a time is coming and has now come when the dead will hear the voice of the Son of God and those who hear will live. . . . And he has given him authority to judge because he is the Son of Man" (John 5:22–23, 25, 27 NIV).

Elsewhere Jesus explains, "But when the Son of Man comes in His glory, and all the angels with Him, then He will sit on His glorious throne. All the nations will be gathered before Him; and He will separate them from one another, as the shepherd separates the sheep from the goats; and He will put the sheep on His right, and the goats on the left" (Matthew 25:31–33 NASB).

Jesus clarifies that He will not personally pass judgment on people, however: "If anyone hears My sayings and does not keep them, I do not judge him; for I did not come to judge the world, but to save the world. He who rejects Me and does not receive My sayings, has one who judges him; the word I spoke is what will judge him at the last day" (John 12:47–48 NASB).

> **FAITH AND GOOD WORKS**
>
> Good deeds can't save you, but once God redeems you, you'll desire to love and obey Him, and love others and do good to them. True faith results in acts of love and obedience. "The only thing that counts is faith expressing itself through love" (Galatians 5:6 NIV). Jesus said, "If you love Me, you will keep My commandments" (John 14:15 NASB).

Jesus' teachings are the perfect law of liberty, so James urges us to be merciful. "So speak and so do as those who will be judged by the law of liberty. For judgment is without mercy to the one who has shown no mercy. Mercy triumphs over judgment" (James 2:12–13).

Jesus explains that if we are to enter the kingdom of Heaven, we must be "born again" (John 3:3 KJV) as children of light. And

▶ The Last Judgment mosaic at Saint Mark's Basilica in Venice depicts a scene Jesus describes in Matthew 25 where the Son of Man comes in glory, with His angels, and sits on the throne where He will separate the sheep from the goats.

besides our faith that we are saved, there are outward evidences as well—namely, we will *live* like God's children. As Paul said, "Walk as children of light" (Ephesians 5:8). After all, many in the day of judgment shall call Him, "Lord, Lord" (Matthew 7:22), and proclaim how many great things they've done in His name, but He will ask, "But why do you call Me 'Lord, Lord,' and not do the things which I say?" (Luke 6:46). We may insist that we love God, but Jesus said, "If you love me, obey my commandments" (John 14:15 NLT).

"Then the King will say to those on His right hand, 'Come, you blessed of My Father, inherit the kingdom prepared for you from the foundation of the world: for I was hungry and you gave Me food; I was thirsty and you gave Me drink; I was a stranger and you took Me in; I was naked and you clothed Me; I was sick and you visited Me; I was in prison and you came to Me'" (Matthew 25:34–36). When the righteous ask when they did these things for Him, Jesus will answer, "Assuredly, I say to you, inasmuch as you did it to one of the least of these My brethren, you did it to Me" (Matthew 25:40).

"Then He will also say to those on the left hand, 'Depart from Me, you cursed, into the everlasting fire prepared for the devil and his angels: for I was hungry and you gave Me no food; I was thirsty and you gave Me no drink; I was a stranger and you did not take Me in, naked and you did not clothe Me, sick and in prison and you did not visit Me'" (Matthew 25:41–43). When they ask when they saw Him in need and failed to minister to Him, Jesus will answer, "'Assuredly, I say to you, inasmuch as you did not do it to one of the least of these, you did not do it to Me.' And these will go away into everlasting punishment, but the righteous into eternal life" (Matthew 25:45–46).

THE JOY SET BEFORE HIM

The Bible tells us, "For the joy set before him he [Jesus] endured the cross, scorning its shame, and sat down at the right hand of the throne of God" (Hebrews 12:2 NIV). Jesus had to endure the excruciating physical pain of crucifixion *and* the shame of being rejected and publicly humiliated. How did He do this? He focused on "the joy set before him." The fact that the hope of this joy sustained Christ Himself in His darkest hour tells us in unequivocal terms that Heaven is a place overflowing with tremendous joy, just waiting for us.

Jesus knew that He would have joy for several reasons: For one thing, He would once again be united with His Father. He would once again take up all the fullness of His deity that He had set aside to become human and would be highly exalted (Philippians 2:5–11). He would once again have the magnificent glory that His Father had given Him (John 17:5, 24). And He would be satisfied that His immense sacrifice had been worth it, because it had brought millions of people into the eternal presence of God (Isaiah 53:11–12).

Heaven will be a place of unsurpassed joy for us as well—and God intends for this hope to help us overcome all the trials and tribulations of this life. Jesus said, "You now have sorrow; but I will see you

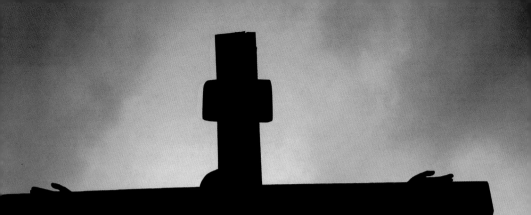

▶ Scripture says Jesus endured the cross, and the pain and rejection that went with it, for the joy set before Him, indicating Heaven will be a place of immense joy.

again and your heart will rejoice, and your joy no one will take from you" (John 16:22). "Be very glad—for these trials make you partners with Christ in his suffering, so that you will have the wonderful joy of seeing his glory when it is revealed to all the world" (1 Peter 4:13 NLT).

We will have the joy not only of seeing His glory revealed, but also of knowing that we have given *God* joy, for we will hear Him say, "Well done, good and faithful servant. . . . Enter into the joy of your lord" (Matthew 25:23). "In Your presence is fullness of joy" (Psalm 16:11 NASB). We shall also have great joy when God rewards us greatly for serving Him. And we will certainly experience great joy in being reunited with our departed loved ones. Heaven will be a place of tremendous joy for everyone who is there.

JESUS GOES TO HADES

As we've already seen, after Jesus died on the cross, He went to Paradise (Abraham's Bosom) with the penitent thief. This is what Paul refers to when he writes, "Now this, 'He ascended'—what does it mean but that He also first descended into the lower parts of the earth?" (Ephesians 4:9). Most Christian scholars agree with this interpretation, because, after all, Abraham's Bosom was where the righteous were waiting.

However, differences in opinion have arisen regarding Peter's sermon on Pentecost. After first quoting Psalm 16:10, where David says, "For You will not leave my soul in Sheol [Hades], nor will You allow Your Holy One to see corruption," Peter explains that David "spoke concerning the resurrection of the Christ, that His soul was not left in Hades, nor did His flesh see corruption" (Acts 2:27, 31–32).

Because Abraham's Bosom is technically *part* of Hades, but is separate from the dark part, many scholars contend that when the Bible says that Jesus descended to Hades, He went *only* to Abraham's Bosom. They say that the following scripture should be understood in that context: "For this reason the gospel was preached also to those who are dead, that they might be judged according to men in the flesh, but live according to God in the spirit" (1 Peter 4:6).

This makes sense: the departed righteous, even though they had lived under the Law of Moses, loved God and had faith in Him. "Now faith. . .is what the ancients were commended for" (Hebrews 11:1–2 NIV). They had hoped for the Messiah and gladly believed in Jesus when they heard

> **THE APOSTLES' CREED**
>
> The basic statement of Christian faith, the Apostles' Creed, declares: "I believe in Jesus Christ, God's only Son, our Lord, who. . .was crucified, died, and was buried; he descended into Hell [Hades]. On the third day he rose again."[3]

Him preaching. "He who is of God hears the words of God" (John 8:47 NASB). And as we saw earlier, seven months before Jesus' crucifixion, Moses and Elijah came from Paradise to talk with Jesus. When they returned there, they would've told everyone that the Messiah would soon come to them. So, yes, it's certain that "the gospel was preached to those who [were] dead" in Abraham's Bosom.

However, other scholars point to the following passage, which says that "He went and preached to the *spirits in prison*, who formerly were *disobedient*"—and say it means that Jesus then *also* preached the Gospel to the unrighteous in the dark regions of Hades: "For Christ also suffered once for sins, the just for the unjust, that He might bring us to God, being put to death in the flesh but made alive by the Spirit, by whom also He went and preached to the spirits in prison, who formerly were disobedient, when once the Divine long-suffering waited in the days of Noah, while the ark was being prepared" (1 Peter 3:18–20).

This passage has two main interpretations: First, it could mean that Jesus went and preached the Gospel, offering the hope of salvation to the spirits of people who had died long ago. They "formerly were disobedient," but apparently their suffering in Hades had caused them deep remorse and they were now ready to believe the truth. If that's the case, then the following verse could be referring to it: "Because of the blood of your covenant, I will set your prisoners free from the waterless pit" (Zechariah 9:11).

There are two difficulties with this interpretation, however: "People are destined to die once, and after that to face judgment" (Hebrews 9:27 NIV). There doesn't appear to be a second chance to receive salvation for those who reject God in this life. Also, the word *spirits* is normally used of human beings in the Bible only when it's qualified (e.g., "the spirits of just men made perfect" [Hebrews 12:23 KJV]). Otherwise it refers to nonhuman spirits.

The other main interpretation is that these "disobedient spirits" were fallen angels who are elsewhere said to be imprisoned in Tartarus—the abyss (2 Peter 2:4; Jude 1:6). The theory here is that during the days of Noah, these angels were the "sons of God" who married mortal women and had giant offspring (Genesis 6:1–4). They've been in prison ever since. The Gospel that Jesus would have preached to them would have simply been a declaration of victory over the power of the enemy, a word of condemnation (2 Corinthians 2:16). The main problem with this interpretation is that it's only conjecture that fallen angels could have had intercourse with humans.

Furthermore, the Bible states that Jesus not only went to Paradise between His death and resurrection, but *also* descended into the abyss—also known as the bottomless pit or Tartarus—where the fallen angels and the worst sinners were imprisoned. Paul writes in Romans 10:6–7: "Do not say in your heart, 'Who will ascend into heaven?' (that is, to bring Christ down from above) or, 'Who will descend into the abyss?' (that is, to bring Christ up from the dead)." This visit was surely to declare His victory over the forces of evil. Jesus didn't offer *them* hope of salvation.

The one place we know that Jesus *didn't* go was Gehenna, the lake of fire. He didn't need to suffer there for our sins, contrary to what some people believe. This error arose because the King James Version translates both *Hades* and *Gehenna* as "hell." Thus, when Acts 2:31 (referring to Christ being in Hades) says, "He. . .spake of the resurrection of Christ, that his soul was not left in hell," many people mistakenly assume that Christ's soul was in Gehenna for a time. Because *we* deserve to go to Hell, and Jesus took our punishment for us, they reason that He must have suffered torments in the lake of fire between His death and His resurrection. This is simply *not* what happened.

Jesus suffered on the cross for our sins and didn't need to suffer any more after He died. He said just *before* He died, "It is finished" (John 19:30 NIV). By hanging on the cross and shedding His blood for our sins, Jesus paid the full price for our salvation. The Greek word translated here as "finished" was commonly written on debt notices after they were paid in full. So Jesus didn't need to suffer torment in Hell in place of *our* suffering there. "For it pleased the Father. . .to reconcile all things to Himself, by Him. . .having made peace through the blood of His cross" (Colossians 1:19–20). Christ's blood on the cross, not His supposed torments in Gehenna, is what saves us.

THE HARROWING OF HELL

The Bible says about the Old Testament saints: "These were all commended for their faith, yet none of them received what had been promised, since God had planned something better for us so that only together with us would they be made perfect" (Hebrews 11:39–40 NIV). They had to wait in Abraham's Bosom for thousands of years until the arrival of Jesus, unable to enter the heavenly city until we too could go directly to Heaven when we die.

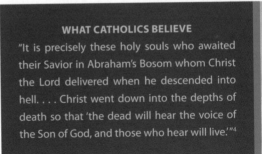

WHAT CATHOLICS BELIEVE

"It is precisely these holy souls who awaited their Savior in Abraham's Bosom whom Christ the Lord delivered when he descended into hell. . . . Christ went down into the depths of death so that 'the dead will hear the voice of the Son of God, and those who hear will live.'"[4]

It is commonly believed that when Jesus rose from the dead, He took the spirits of the Old Testament saints to Heaven with Him. Many people believe that evidence for this appears in the following scripture: "The tombs were opened, and many bodies of the saints who had fallen asleep [died] were raised; and coming out of the tombs after His resurrection they entered the holy city and appeared to many" (Matthew 27:52–53 NASB). Unfortunately, this *isn't* evidence. The Old Testament saints weren't physically resurrected at this time. Their bodies remained in the ground and only their spirits entered Heaven. They will only rise from the dead when *all* people rise in the final day.

This verse refers only to certain righteous Jews who had *recently* died and who then came back to life. If this was the resurrection of all the righteous of millennia past, why did only some of them rise? The text says that "*many* [not all] bodies of the saints. . .were raised." And why did those who *did* rise from the dead wander around and enter Jerusalem when they should have been entering Heaven with Jesus and the rest of the Old Testament saints?

The Catholic catechism states that the dead Christ went down to the realm of the dead to preach to the just who had gone before Him. Even though most evangelical Christians don't accept everything in this catechism, most would agree that Christ's preaching availed only the righteous Old Testament saints, *not* the general multitudes of the lost in Hades.

This event is called "the harrowing of Hell." To *harrow* means to "despoil," and the concept is of Christ triumphing over Hell (Hades) and releasing its captives. It's believed that He then led these redeemed spirits in a great victory procession from Abraham's Bosom into the heavenly city. The prophet Amos had declared, "The LORD Almighty . . .builds his lofty palace in the heavens" (Amos 9:5–6 NIV), and now that everything was finally ready, the righteous men and women of ages past were able to enter God's eternal palace.

When Moses and Elijah appeared with Jesus on the Mount of Transfiguration, "they spoke about his departure, which he was about to bring to fulfillment at Jerusalem" (Luke 9:31 NIV). The Greek word for departure is *exodos* ("going out"), from which we get the English word *exodus*. Moses and Elijah didn't necessarily talk *only* about Jesus' decease, His departure from this life. When Moses led the exodus from Egypt, he brought more than two million Hebrews to the Promised Land. Jesus led an exodus of millions of souls from Abraham's Bosom into the New Jerusalem.

GOING UP TO HEAVEN

After His resurrection, instead of staying on the earth, Jesus "was received up into heaven, and sat down at the right hand of God" (Mark 16:19). For the present, both Jesus and the heavenly city in which He dwells remain in the celestial dimension. As Peter explains, "Heaven must receive him until the time comes for God to restore everything, as he promised long ago through his holy prophets" (Acts 3:21 NIV).

Peter was chiefly referring to the prophet Isaiah, through whom God had promised, "For behold, I create new heavens and a new earth" (Isaiah 65:17 NASB). God's original creation will be restored to

▶ Andrea di Bonaiuto's (1343–1377) painting *Descent of Christ to Limbo*. Catholic catechism teaches that when Christ died, He went down to the realm of the dead to preach to the just who had gone before Him.

its pristine state before the Fall, and the entire planet will become like the Garden of Eden. Only then, when God has "restored everything," will the heavenly city come down and God and His Son will dwell on the earth with mankind (Revelation 22:1–3).

Until that day, Christians go up to join God in Heaven when they die. Consider what happens to the two end-time witnesses who are martyred in Jerusalem: "And they heard a loud voice from heaven saying to them, 'Come up here.' And they ascended to heaven in a cloud" (Revelation 11:12).

THE SEVEN HEAVENS

You will often hear the expression "the seventh heaven." This is because Jewish mystics of the Kabala, as recorded in the Talmud, list seven separate heavens, together with the angels who supposedly rule each one. Medieval Jewish scholars elaborated greatly on this theme. There is, however, no scriptural evidence in the Old Testament for such divisions of the heavens. They are purely an invention of highly imaginative Jewish scholars.

Some people point out, however, that Paul said he was "caught up to the third heaven. . .caught up into Paradise" (2 Corinthians 12:2, 4). According to the Talmud, the third heaven, Shehaqim, was considered the abode of the Garden of Eden, and was indeed called Paradise. Also, Hebrews 4:14 states that "we have a great High Priest who has passed through the heavens, Jesus the Son of God." And Paul adds, in Ephesians: "He. . .is the very one who ascended higher than all the heavens, in order to fill the whole universe" (Ephesians 4:10 NIV). The fact that these verses use the word *heavens* is not evidence that there are seven distinct heavens. After all, the Old Testament

Benvenuto Tisi da Garofalo's (1481–1559) *Ascension of Christ*, showing Jesus going up to Heaven. We too will go up to Heaven to join Jesus when we die.

▶ Dante and Beatrice from Dante's *Divine Comedy* gaze upon the highest sphere of Heaven, as rendered by artist Gustave Doré (1832–1883).

uses the phrase "the heavens" (plural) to describe the sky.

Many people think that Catholics believe in "seven heavens," but this has never been an official or even unofficial doctrine of the Roman Catholic Church. Also, it's commonly thought that Dante speaks of seven heavens in his *Divine Comedy*, but this isn't the case. Dante instead mentions "nine concentric spheres of heaven," the sun, moon, five inner planets, and two spheres beyond them.

In the final analysis, however, there is some truth to

THE SEVEN HEAVENS

According to the Talmud, the seven heavens are Vilon (also called Arafel), Raqi'a, Shehaqim, Ma'on, Makhon, Zebul, and finally, Araboth, the highest heaven, where God's throne is.

the belief that Heaven consists of different levels, each one higher and more glorious than the other. In the King James Version, we're told that God "buildeth his stories in the heaven" (Amos 9:6), and it's entirely plausible that the heavenly city, being 1,400 miles high, consists of a multitude of levels, culminating in the highest level where God's throne is. This, however, would entail far more than seven levels.

SPIRITS AND GHOSTS

Ever since Jesus opened the way into the presence of God by dying on the cross and rising from the dead, the spirits of the saved go directly to Heaven when their bodies die. Paul writes, "We are confident. . .to be absent from the body and to be present with the Lord" (2 Corinthians 5:8). Thus, he also writes, "I long to go and be with Christ" (Philippians 1:23 NLT).

Meanwhile, the unsaved go to Hades when they die, where they're confined until Judgment Day. According to popular folk theology, however, many spirits of the departed go neither to Heaven nor to Hades, but hang around the physical world as disembodied spirits. It's commonly believed that troubled spirits "who aren't ready to move on" remain, often at their former habitation—resulting in "haunted houses."

It's also believed that the spirits of the good—and according to folk theology, *most* departed loved ones are good—often remain close at hand to watch over their families. Thus, when a father dies, and sometime later one of his children is spared in an accident, people will smile and say, "He's still here. He's watching over them." If you wonder why they believe that the departed do the jobs of angels, it's because they mistakenly believe that humans *become* angels when they die. (See "Of Angels and Men" in chapter 4.)

In Jesus' day, many Jews believed that a person's spirit remained near the body for three days after physical death. After a person dies, his or her body becomes stiff through a process called rigor mortis, but the corpse doesn't begin to decompose until approximately

▶ The Jews believed a person's spirit stayed near their body for three days after they died, before leaving for its eternal destination. This is why Lazarus's resurrection was so miraculous to them, depicted here by painter Leon Bonnat (1833–1922).

forty-eight hours after death. The Jews believed that after a body began to rot and all hope of returning to life was gone, the spirit then went to its eternal destination. This is why the resurrection of Lazarus, after he'd been dead for *four* days, was seen as such a miracle (John 11:39).

So the Jews believed that disembodied spirits could remain in their familiar haunts and even appear to people—but only for a very limited time. This is why, when the disciples were in a boat on the storm-tossed Sea of Galilee and saw Jesus walking on the waves, they cried out, "It is a ghost!" (Matthew 14:26). The Greek word translated "ghost" is *phantasma*, from which we get our word *phantom*. The disciples thought they were seeing someone who had just died.

This is also why, after Jesus rose from the dead and materialized among His disciples, "they were terrified and frightened, and supposed they had seen a spirit. And He said to them, 'Why are you troubled? And why do doubts arise in your hearts? Behold My hands and My feet, that it is I Myself. Handle Me and see, for a spirit does not have flesh and bones as you see I have'" (Luke 24:37–39). The word translated "spirit" comes from the Greek word *pneuma*.

Jesus didn't deny the existence of disembodied spirits. Instead, He proved to His disciples that He *wasn't* one, but that He was physically alive. On the other hand, He wasn't confirming modern superstitious beliefs that the spirits of the departed can hang around for years, even decades. Shortly after death—often immediately following it—the spirits of the unsaved go to Hades, where they're confined.

So-called haunted houses are usually a result of demonic activity, not of troubled human spirits. This is especially the case if a murder or another crime was committed in a place. The demons that inspired and empowered that evil can sometimes remain in the location and cause continued paranormal activity and disturbances.

When loved ones have died, it's important to release them and to acknowledge that they're gone—not attempt to hang on to them. This is why the practice of setting a plate at the table for a departed loved one, though done in sincere love, isn't a good idea. It's especially not advisable to invite departed loved ones back to visit you, or to attempt to communicate with them. Though it's technically possible to "summon" the departed, not only is this forbidden by scripture, but it can also open the door to demons and allow them to manifest their presence.

BOOKS ABOUT VISITS TO HEAVEN

In recent years, several books describing personal visits to Heaven have become bestsellers. For example, *Heaven Is for Real* by Todd Burpo (2010) describes a visit by his four-year-old son, Colton, to Heaven, and *Proof of Heaven* by Eben Alexander, MD (2012), describes the after-death experiences of a formerly skeptical neurosurgeon. These books, though very different from one another, have generated tremendous interest in the hereafter.

Of course, quite a number of other books have been written by people who claim to have visited Heaven, including *Nine Days in Heaven* by Dennis and Nolene Prince (2006), *Revealing Heaven* by Kat Kerr (2007), *A Glimpse of Eternity* by Ian McCormack (2008), *My Time in Heaven* by Richard Sigmund (2010), *Flight to Heaven* by Capt. Dale Black (2010), *The Boy Who Came Back from Heaven* by Kevin and Alex Malarkey (2010), *My Journey to Heaven* by Marvin J. Besteman (2012), and *Waking Up in Heaven* by Crystal McVea (2013).

David E. Taylor, author of *My Trip to Heaven*, claims that Jesus promised to appear personally to everyone

▶ Many have written books about their after-death journeys to Heaven or Hell. This painting, titled *Ascent of the Blessed,* is Hieronymus Bosch's (1450–1516) interpretation of spirits being escorted to the doorway of Heaven.

who reads Taylor's book. In addition, he assures his readers that they can all expect to be taken by the Lord on a personal tour of Heaven.

Mary K. Baxter wrote a book called *A Divine Revelation of Hell* (1997), in which she claims to have toured Hell for forty consecutive days. She states that it's in the form of an enormous human body—with many tortured souls, for example, in the "left leg of hell"—even though Jesus stated that Hell wasn't designed for mankind (Matthew 25:41). Baxter also claims she was taken to Heaven, and she wrote another book titled *A Divine Revelation of Heaven* (1998). Another book that describes a marathon visit to Paradise is *40 Days in Heaven* (1909) by Seneca Sodi.

Apart from these books, there are numerous online videos and articles in which people from all over the world, from America to Chile to Ukraine to Ethiopia to Nigeria to Rwanda to Burma, describe their visits to Heaven or Hell. Though some may seem almost beyond belief, and a few seem to reflect the person's own doctrines, others are highly documented and very credible.

Some people don't claim to have visited Heaven itself. Mary Neal, in her book, *To Heaven and Back: A Doctor's Extraordinary Account of Her Death, Heaven, Angels, and Life Again*, says that she was stopped before she could actually enter the door of Heaven.

A PUBLISHING PHENOMENON

Mark Galli, editor of *Christianity Today*, writes, "Every few years, such books have been a regular publishing phenomenon. But the recent spate of afterlife books is new in two respects: they feature visits to heaven, and in increasing numbers, they are written by orthodox Christians."[5]

WHAT DO WE MAKE OF ALL THIS?

Though we may find these personal accounts of visits to Heaven fascinating or exhilarating, many of them fail to line up with scripture. Many people are thrilled, however, because such accounts at least declare the reality of the world to come. Others are more cautious, wondering if these books describe Heaven accurately. I confess that I'm skeptical in this regard, especially when an author claims to have visited Paradise day after day.

▶ This oil-on-canvas painting by Francisco Ricci (1614–1685) of the Annunciation shows the angel Gabriel with Mary; some books about after-death travels to Heaven and Hell have inaccurately depicted such things as angels.

Choo Thomas, in her book, *Heaven Is So Real* (2006), describes her frequent trips to Heaven and her many personal visits with Jesus, including a time He cooked fish for her on a heavenly barbecue. She claims that Jesus told her she was an end-time prophetess and that He'd make her rich and give her a huge house and a red luxury car. She repeatedly insists that tithing is so important that those who fail to tithe go to Hell. She claims that to reject her message is to reject the words of Jesus.

For its part, *Proof of Heaven*, while describing breathtaking trips on the wings of enormous, beautiful butterflies, and emphasizing the vivid reality of the afterlife, describes God's presence as a deep "darkness" pervaded by an "Om" chant. When the author meets God, God tells him, "There is nothing you can do wrong."[6] So much for God hating sin. The best discussion of this book I have read is Donald S. Whitney's online review.[7] If you have questions about Alexander's book, you will want to read Whitney's thoughtful analysis.

Though I'm convinced that some of these accounts of visiting Heaven are genuine, we must exercise caution. Not every story is true. The Bible tells us, "Beloved, do not believe every spirit, but test the spirits, whether they are of God" (1 John 4:1). Don't let it be said that "you happily put up with whatever anyone tells you, even if they preach a different Jesus than the one we preach, or a different kind of Spirit than the one you received, or a different kind of gospel than the one you believed" (2 Corinthians 11:4 NLT; see also 2 Corinthians 11:13–15).

Even *Heaven Is for Real*, though written from a mainstream Christian perspective and undoubtedly representing a real experience, describes departed humans with *wings*, which is nowhere stated or even implied in scripture. It also states that the angel Gabriel sits on a throne at the left hand of God—whereas scripture states, "I am Gabriel, who *stands* in the presence of God" (Luke 1:19, emphasis added). He stands before God's throne like all the other angels. He does not rule at God's left hand. These inaccuracies have led some to conclude that while it's fine to read such books for inspiration, they shouldn't be consulted as a final authority on doctrine.

Nevertheless, I'm convinced that several claimed visits to Heaven are genuine and that God intends for them to encourage us. A good example of this is *Flight to Heaven* by Capt. Dale Black. It has all the earmarks of a genuine experience and left me wishing the description of his experience wasn't so brief. The same goes for Crystal McVea's moving book, *Waking Up in Heaven*, whose deeply resonating message is that God loves you more than you can possibly imagine.

REGULAR RUNS TO HEAVEN

Some people claim that it's as easy as catching a bus downtown to visit God's eternal city. Indeed, they ride there frequently in heavenly contraptions and teach that *all* Christians can enjoy the privilege of visiting Heaven...*often*.

But other books, such as *My Time in Heaven* by Richard Sigmund, give so *many* details that it becomes information overload. Mixed with the believable and almost-believable descriptions are some incredible elements. Sigmund describes fountains and containers in Heaven filled with the *actual* blood of Christ and mentions giant statues of Jesus that can move. But with Christ personally there in all His glory, who needs automated statues of Him?

Some of these books seem like attempts to make up for the Bible's supposed lack of information. However, when the all-knowing God gave the apostle John a glimpse of Heaven and told him, "What you see, write in a book" (Revelation 1:11), surely He was aware that this was the perfect opportunity to let John see as much of Heaven as we needed to know. Yet God decided that there were certain things we didn't need to know (2 Corinthians 12:4; Revelation 10:3–4).While books about visits to Heaven can serve as the icing on the cake, they should not be the cake itself. The Bible provides that.

We need not depend on such experiences to "fill in the blanks," because the Bible—particularly Isaiah and Revelation—provides a rich source of information about Heaven, containing many more details about our heavenly home than many people suspect.

THE EARLY CHRISTIANS' VIEW OF HEAVEN

As we noted in chapter 2, the Jews had very definite ideas about what eternal life in the kingdom of God would be like: They envisioned it as a more blessed extension of life on earth. And they definitely didn't think of the kingdom of Heaven as being in some distant, spiritual realm. They expected to be living in physical bodies on the physical earth. Jews who became Christians after Christ's resurrection continued in these beliefs. The difference was that they had now *found* the Messiah and were waiting for Him to return to set up this kingdom.

On the other hand, the Greeks and Romans—who soon made up the majority of the church—lacked this knowledge of Old Testament scriptures. They were steeped in the Greco-Roman concept of a paradise called Elysium in the spiritual realm. And though Paul and other Jewish Christians taught them about Heaven on earth, this teaching isn't apparent in the New Testament epistles. The only place it's touched on is in 1 Corinthians 15, where Paul reproves the Greeks for not believing in a bodily resurrection.

In his epistles, Paul repeatedly mentions that Jesus rewards faithful believers, but the *nature* of these rewards isn't often specified. The kingdom of Heaven is briefly described in the three synoptic Gospels—Matthew, Mark, and Luke—but because the Gospel of John wasn't published until AD 85 or 90, even some basic concepts, such as "mansions" in Heaven (John 14:2), weren't widely known until then. In addition, the book of Revelation, which we take for granted today, wasn't written until AD 96. About all that was recorded in the meantime was a brief mention in the first epistle to the Thessalonians, in which Paul says of Heaven, "Then we will be with the Lord forever" (1 Thessalonians 4:17 NLT).

The early Christians went for about sixty years with little written scriptural knowledge of Heaven. But certainly they were hungry to know, and Jewish evangelists and apostles traveled around preaching and teaching, passing on Christ's sayings handed down by word of mouth. So the church would have received accurate teaching in this way. But there were also some inaccurate teachings. Some Christians promoted incredible statements that Jesus never said. The following fragment, taken from *The Oracles of the Lord* by Papias (AD 70–155), purports to be Christ's teaching on the kingdom of Heaven: "The days will come in which vines shall grow, having each ten thousand branches, and in each branch ten thousand twigs, and in each true twig ten thousand shoots, and in every one of the shoots ten thousand clusters, and on every one of the clusters ten thousand grapes, and every grape when pressed will give twenty-five *metretes* [one thousand liters] of wine. . . . In like manner, that a grain of wheat would produce ten thousand ears, and that every ear would have ten thousand grains, and every grain would yield ten pounds of clear, pure, fine flour; and that apples, and seeds, and grass would produce in similar proportions."

The Christian historian Eusebius (AD 260–340) wrote about Papias in *The History of the Church*, "The same person, moreover, has set down other things as coming to him from unwritten tradition, amongst these some strange parables and instructions of the Savior, and some other things of a more fabulous nature."[8]

Fabulous indeed! Then, as now, it was important to discern between genuine and fabricated descriptions of Heaven.

4 : THE INHABITANTS OF HEAVEN

GOD IS LIGHT

Throughout the Bible, we're given glimpses of Heaven— of angels, cherubim, seraphim, and departed believers. Although these glimpses are wonderful, the most beautiful visions are of God in all His glory.

Heaven is bathed in indescribably beautiful light. The apostle John writes, "God is Light, and in Him there is no darkness at all" (1 John 1:5 NASB). The Psalms say of the Lord: "You are radiant with light," and "The LORD wraps himself in light as with a garment" (Psalm

▶ No one can imagine the brilliance of the light of God's glory that scripture says floods the heavenly Jerusalem; we have mere shadows of this glory, as seen in this beautiful photograph of sunlight on a gray cloud.

76:4; 104:2 NIV). When Ezekiel saw God, he remarked that "brilliant light surrounded him" (Ezekiel 1:27 NIV).

Jesus is the Son of God and shares His Father's glory. He is "the brightness of His glory and the express image of His person" (Hebrews 1:3). That's why Jesus declared, "I am the Light of the world" (John 8:12 NASB). The disciples had a glimpse of "the brightness of His glory" when Jesus was transfigured on a mountain: "His face shone like the sun, and His clothes became as white as the light" (Matthew 17:2). Again, when John saw Jesus in a vision on the island of Patmos, "His face was like the sun shining in all its brilliance" (Revelation 1:16 NIV).

Paul writes of "God, the blessed and only Ruler, the King of kings and Lord of lords, who alone is immortal and who lives in unapproachable light, whom no one has seen or can see" (1 Timothy 6:15–16 NIV). When Paul says that God lives in "unapproachable light" and that no man *has* seen him or *can* see him, he means that our frail human bodies, while in this physical realm, cannot withstand the sight of God in His full glory. As God warned Moses, "You cannot see My face, for no man can see Me and live!" (Exodus 33:20 NASB).

The Israelites knew this. That's why Manoah said to his wife after they'd seen the angel of the Lord, "We shall surely die, because we have seen God!" (Judges 13:22). They were astounded and relieved that they lived. "When Gideon saw. . .the angel of the LORD, he said, 'Alas, O Lord GOD! For now I have seen the angel of the LORD face to face.' The LORD said to him, 'Peace to you, do not fear; you shall not die'" (Judges 6:22–23 NASB).

They had obviously seen only a fraction of God's holiness and glory—as much as God knew they could bear. One day, in Heaven, when we have our eternal spiritual bodies, we'll be able to bear much more. Then we shall see Jesus in His full glory: "But we know that when Christ appears. . .we shall see him as he is" (1 John 3:2 NIV).

The light and glory of God absolutely fill every corner of the heavenly Jerusalem, even now. "The city had no need of the sun or of the moon to shine in it, for the glory of God illuminated it. The Lamb is its light" (Revelation 21:23–24). "There shall be no night there: They need no lamp nor light of the sun, for the Lord God gives them light" (Revelation 22:5). And one day we will live in that city whose every facet, every stone, every blade of grass, is permeated by God's presence.

GOD IS THE HEART OF HEAVEN

Remember, God is the very center of Paradise, the One on whom all the heavenly hosts are focused. He is the One whom all the angels and saints worship. When the Bible describes the throne room of God, we glimpse the very heart of Heaven.

Throughout the Bible, God appeared to men who were "in the Spirit" and thus able to bear looking upon Him. As they described the glory of God, they also described a few details of His throne. The first time God appeared in His glory was on Mount Sinai: "Then Moses, Aaron,

Nadab, Abihu, and the seventy elders of Israel climbed up the mountain. There they saw the God of Israel. Under his feet there seemed to be a surface of brilliant blue lapis lazuli, as clear as the sky itself" (Exodus 24:9–10 NLT).

Many centuries later, God appeared to Isaiah: "In the year that King Uzziah died, I saw the Lord, high and exalted, seated on a throne;

▶ The glory of the Lord in Heaven is described as fire and brightness like a rainbow; Hans Memling (1474–1479) depicted his idea of what God's enthronement in Heaven looks like.

Paradise Lost by Gustave Doré (1832–1833), an illustration showing Jesus sitting at the right hand of the throne of the Father, the place of honor.

and the train of his robe filled the temple" (Isaiah 6:1 NIV).

About one hundred years after this, God appeared to Ezekiel: "Then I looked, and behold, a whirlwind was coming out of the north, a great cloud with raging fire engulfing itself; and brightness was all around it and radiating out of its midst like the color of amber, out of the midst of the fire. Also from within it came the likeness of four living creatures. . . .

"And above the firmament over their heads was the likeness of a throne, in appearance like a sapphire stone; on the likeness of the throne was a likeness with the appearance of a man high above it. Also from the appearance of His waist and upward I saw, as it were, the color of amber with the appearance of fire all around within it; and from the appearance of His waist and downward I saw, as it were, the appearance of fire with brightness all around. Like the appearance of a rainbow in a cloud on a rainy day, so was the appearance of the brightness all around it. This was the appearance of the likeness of the glory of the LORD" (Ezekiel 1:4–5, 26–28).

A few decades later, Daniel had a vision of God: "I beheld till. . .the Ancient of days did sit, whose garment was white as snow, and the hair of his head like the pure wool. . . . Thousand thousands ministered unto him, and ten thousand times ten thousand stood before him" (Daniel 7:9–10 KJV).

JESUS ENTHRONED IN HEAVEN

As Daniel's vision continued, he saw something astonishing: "I saw in the night visions, and, behold, one like the Son of man came with the clouds of heaven, and came to the Ancient of days, and they brought him near before him. And there was given him dominion, and glory, and a kingdom, that all people, nations, and languages, should serve him: his dominion is an everlasting dominion, which shall not pass away, and his kingdom that which shall not be destroyed" (Daniel 7:13–14 KJV). This was none other than Jesus Christ, the Son of God. Jesus used this same expression to describe Himself, saying, "They shall see the Son of man coming in the clouds of heaven with power and great glory" (Matthew 24:30 KJV).

The New Testament tells us that after Jesus was resurrected, He ascended to His Father's throne. "So then after the Lord had spoken unto them, he was received up into heaven, and sat on the right hand of God" (Mark 16:19 KJV). "This is the same mighty power that raised Christ from the dead and seated him in the place of honor at God's right hand in the heavenly realms" (Ephesians 1:19–20 NLT). Jesus "sat down at the right hand of the throne of the Majesty in heaven" (Hebrews 8:1 NIV).

Jesus said that the right hand of the throne of God is *part* of God's throne: "I also overcame and sat down with My Father on His throne" (Revelation 3:21). Jesus Christ is worthy to sit on God's throne with Him because He *is* God. Christians down through the ages have worshipped not only God the Father, but also God the Son.

While Jesus was still on earth, He longed for His followers to be with Him in Heaven, and for them to see His splendor and magnificence. He prayed: "Father, I want those you have given me to be with me where I am, and to see my glory, the glory you have given me because you loved me before the creation of the world" (John 17:24 NIV). The greatest joy that we'll experience in Heaven will be to see the Father and the Son in all of their glorious beauty.

JOHN'S VISIONS OF JESUS

In AD 96, the apostle John was caught up to Heaven and saw the throne of God: "At once I was in the Spirit, and there before me was a throne in heaven with someone sitting on it. And the one who sat there had the appearance of jasper and ruby. A rainbow that shone like an emerald encircled the throne. . . . From the throne came flashes of lightning, rumblings and peals of thunder" (Revelation

▶ The apostle John's vision of the throne of Jesus depicted by German Renaissance painter Lucas Cranach (1472–1553) in his illustration *The Apocalypse*.

4:2–3, 5 NIV). And there, in the midst of the throne of God in heaven, stood Jesus, the Lamb of God. Then the four fearsome beasts, and the twenty-four elders, who had been praising God, fell down and worshipped Jesus. And all the millions upon millions of angels gathered around God's throne also worshipped the Son of God (Revelation 5:8–14).

Jesus appeared to John on the island of Patmos, and this is John's amazing description of Him: "I saw one like a son of man, clothed in a robe reaching to the feet, and girded across His chest with a golden sash. His head and His hair were white like white wool, like snow; and His eyes were like a flame of fire. His feet were like burnished bronze, when it has been made to glow in a furnace, and His voice was like the sound of many waters. . . . His face was like the sun shining in its strength" (Revelation 1:13–16 NASB).

THE SEVEN SPIRITS OF GOD

Now let's have a look at those who surround the throne of God. One of the most mysterious, otherworldly visions John saw was of "seven lamps of fire burning before the throne, which are the seven Spirits of God" (Revelation 4:5 NASB). How can this be? After all, scripture plainly states, "There is one body, and *one Spirit*" (Ephesians 4:4 KJV, emphasis added).

In the scriptures, however, seven is the number of perfection and completeness, and it's significant that the Bible refers to Jesus as "He who has the seven Spirits of God" (Revelation 3:1). "The seven Spirits" literally means "the sevenfold Spirit"—in other words, *one* Spirit with seven facets—and it's fascinating to see the relationship

▶ Matthias Gerung's (1500–1570) painting of John's vision of Heaven, showing his rendition of the seven Spirits of God, which are represented by the seven lamps of fire burning behind the throne.

between Jesus and this sevenfold Spirit in the next passage.

"And I saw. . .a Lamb standing, as if slain, having seven horns and seven eyes, which are the seven Spirits of God, sent out into all the earth" (Revelation 5:6 NASB). In this vision, Jesus is pictured with seven eyes, which are declared to be the seven Spirits of God. This imagery is drawn from the vision of Zechariah, who saw "a lamp-stand of solid gold with a bowl on top of it, and on the stand seven lamps" (Zechariah 4:2). He was told that these seven blazing lamps were "the eyes of the LORD, which scan to and fro throughout the whole earth" (Zechariah 4:10).

This demonstrates the intimate relationship that Jesus has with the Spirit of God. Now we begin to understand how Jesus can send the Holy Spirit into the hearts of all believers throughout the entire earth (John 15:26), and why "the Spirit of God" is also called "the Spirit of Christ" (Romans 8:9).

CHERUBIM—CELESTIAL CREATURES

There are astonishing creatures associated with God's throne. Isaiah declared, "O LORD of Heaven's Armies, God of Israel, you are enthroned between the mighty cherubim!" (Isaiah 37:16 NLT). These mighty, spiritual beings closely surround God and serve Him as gatekeepers and honor guards.

God "is enthroned above the cherubim" (Isaiah 37:16 NASB), who bear God's throne. David declared, "O God, enthroned above the cherubim, display your radiant glory" (Psalm 80:1 NLT). The cherubim bear God when He travels through the heavens: "He rode upon a cherub, and flew; He flew upon the wings of the wind" (Psalm 18:10).

In the apostle John's vision of Heaven in AD 96, he saw four cherubim. "And in the midst of the throne, and around the throne, were four living creatures full of eyes in front and in back. The first living creature was like a lion, the second living creature like a calf, the third living creature had a face like a man, and the fourth living creature was like a flying eagle. The four living creatures, each having six wings, were full of eyes around and within" (Revelation 4:6–8).

Exactly 689 years earlier, in 593 BC, the prophet Ezekiel had also seen these incredible celestial creatures. He writes: "As I looked, behold. . .a great cloud with fire flashing forth continually and a bright light around it, and in its midst something like glowing metal in the midst of the fire. Within it there were figures resembling four living beings. And this was their appearance: they had human form. Each of them had four faces and four wings. Their legs were straight and their feet were like a calf's hoof, and they gleamed like burnished bronze. Under their wings on their four sides were human hands. As for the faces and wings of the four of them, their wings touched one another; their faces did not turn when they moved, each went straight forward. As for the form of their faces, each had the face of a

► Cosmas Damian Asam's (1686–1739) work displayed at the St. Martin Basilica in Germany portrays cherubim, God's personal servants who bear Him as He travels through the heavens.

man; all four had the face of a lion on the right and the face of a bull on the left, and all four had the face of an eagle. Such were their faces. Their wings were spread out above; each had two touching another being, and two covering their bodies. . . . And the living beings ran to and fro like bolts of lightning" (Ezekiel 1:4–11, 14 NASB).

Later, Ezekiel gives additional details about these beings: "One of the cherubim reached out his hand to the fire that was among them. He took up some of it. . . . Under the wings of the cherubim could be seen what looked like human hands. . . . Their entire bodies, including their backs, their hands and their wings, were completely full of eyes" (Ezekiel 10:7–8, 12 NIV).

Note that John describes the cherubim as four distinct creatures: the first like a lion, the second like a calf, the third like a man, and the

fourth like an eagle. And they each had *six* wings. Ezekiel describes *each* cherubim as having all four faces, and having *four* wings. Either there are different types of cherubim, or, more likely, these unusual creatures are capable of altering their appearance—just as Jesus did when "He appeared in another form" (Mark 16:12).

Whatever the cherubim's real nature, it is commonly believed that they're described in *symbolic* terms. For example, their bodies covered with eyes represent their all-seeing nature, and their three bestial faces symbolize their great strength, power, and majesty. Others assert that the four different faces symbolize the four Gospels, with Matthew represented by the lion, Mark by the bull, Luke by the man, and John by the flying eagle. However, though parallels can certainly be drawn, the cherubim are *actual creatures* in the spiritual realm, not mere symbols.

The cherubim seem to be closely identified with bulls. Note in the following verse how the word *cherub* is used instead of *bull*: "Each of the cherubim had four faces: One face was that of a cherub, the second the face of a human being, the third the face of a lion, and the fourth the face of an eagle" (Ezekiel 10:14 NIV). Possibly, therefore, the cherubim have the *bodies* of bulls, although

> **CHERUBIM AND ANCIENT GODS**
> Some scholars think that God deliberately created the cherubim with the appearances of the main gods the pagans worshipped—lions, bulls, and eagles—to show that God truly is the "God of gods" (Psalm 136:2). This, however, implies that God first saw people worshipping animal idols and then created the cherubim—whereas cherubim have existed since before the creation of the physical world. After all, Satan is a fallen cherub (Ezekiel 28:14, 16).

Ezekiel says "they had human form" (Ezekiel 1:5 NASB). Again, however, these astonishing creatures seem to be able to alter their appearance.

Others point out that the Assyrians and ancient Mesopotamians worshipped creatures called *lamassu*, usually depicted with the bodies of bulls (sometimes with lions' bodies), having eagle's wings and human heads—incorporating some of the imagery of the cherubim, albeit in different form. The Assyrians considered them protective spirits, and not only built giant replicas of them at their city gates to guard their cities, but also buried engravings of them on clay tablets under their doorways to protect their houses.

> **THE WORD *CHERUBIM***
>
> The word *cherubim* is the Hebrew masculine plural form of *cherub*, which is borrowed from the Assyrian word *kirubu*, which in turn derives from *karâbu*, "to be near." Hence, it means near ones, personal servants, bodyguards.

But if the cherubim were merely copies of the *lamassu*, they would have borne a similar name, especially considering that their name is borrowed from another Assyrian word, *kirubu*. Plus, the Israelites were easily led astray into folk superstition and syncretism, yet there's no written or archaeological record of their worshipping the cherubim *or* burying tablets with cherubim inscribed on them under their thresholds. It's far more likely that the Assyrians and other ancient pagans had dim glimpses of the cherubim and copied them.

These beings, which closely surround the throne of God, are more than just God's bestial entourage; they are sentient, holy beings, dedicated to continually worship God. "And they do not rest day or night, saying: 'Holy, holy, holy, Lord God Almighty, who was and is and is to come!'" (Revelation 4:8).

DEPICTING THE CHERUBIM

Ezekiel wasn't the first person to see the incredible cherubim. After Adam and Eve were sent out of Paradise, "the LORD God stationed mighty cherubim to the east of the Garden of Eden" (Genesis 3:24 NLT).

Moses saw the cherubim as well. The earthly sanctuary that he gave instructions to build was "a copy and shadow of what is in heaven. This is why Moses was warned when he was about to build the tabernacle: 'See to it that you make everything according to the pattern shown you on the mountain'" (Hebrews 8:5 NIV). Thus Moses gave

▶ Franz Stuck's (1863–1928 beautiful oil-on-canvas painting of a cherub, *The Guardian of Paradise*). No one knows for sure what these cherubim, who guarded the entrance to the Garden of Eden, actually looked like.

exact specifications for "the cherubim of glory overshadowing the mercy seat" (Hebrews 9:5). He had artisans create golden cherubim to cover the ark of the covenant (Exodus 25:18–20).

God had warned, "You shall not make for yourself an idol, or any likeness of what is in heaven above" (Exodus 20:4 NASB). But the prohibition against making graven images didn't apply in this case, perhaps because the people weren't making these images as objects to worship. In addition, God instructed them to decorate the curtains of the Tabernacle (the worship tent). "Then Bezalel decorated the curtains with. . .skillfully embroidered cherubim" (Exodus 36:8 NLT).

Some 480 years later, when Solomon built the Temple, he filled it with replicas and carvings of cherubim: "He made two cherubim of wild olive wood, each 15 feet tall, and placed them in the inner sanctuary. The wingspan of each of the cherubim was 15 feet, each wing being 7½ feet long. . . . Their outspread wings reached from wall to wall, while their inner wings touched at the center of the room. He overlaid the two cherubim with gold" (1 Kings 6:23–24, 27–28 NLT).

"[Solomon] decorated all the walls of the inner sanctuary and the main room with carvings of cherubim, palm trees, and open flowers. . . . These double doors were decorated with carvings of cherubim. . . . Carvings of cherubim, lions, and palm trees decorated the panels and corner supports wherever there was room" (1 Kings 6:29, 32; 7:36 NLT). The fact that cherubim were depicted throughout the Temple *wherever there was room* meant that they were very important, and God went to great lengths to emphasize them.

> **THE MYSTERIOUS CHERUBIM**
> Despite their being so frequently depicted in scripture, no portrayals of cherubim have survived to the present. Jewish scholars admit that no one knows for sure exactly what these creatures look like.

SERAPHIM: "THE BURNING ONES"

There are other mighty, mysterious spiritual beings in Heaven called seraphim. This name comes from the Hebrew word *seraph*, which means "to burn," so *seraphim* most probably means "the burning ones." The following passage is the only reference to them in scripture:

"I saw the Lord sitting on a throne, lofty and exalted, with the train of His robe filling the temple. Seraphim stood above Him, each having six wings: with two he covered his face, and with two he covered his feet, and with two he flew. And one called out to another and said, 'Holy, Holy, Holy, is the LORD of hosts, the whole earth is full of His glory.' And the foundations of the thresholds trembled at the voice of him who called out, while the temple was filling with smoke . . . . Then one of the seraphim flew to me with a burning coal in his hand, which he had taken from the altar with tongs. He touched my mouth with it and said, "Behold, this has touched your lips; and your iniquity is taken away and your sin is forgiven" (Isaiah 6:1–4, 6–7 NASB).

The word *saraph* is also translated twice in the Bible as "fiery flying serpent" (Isaiah 14:29; 30:6) and three times as "fiery serpents" (Numbers 21:6, 8; Deuteronomy 8:15). The latter instances refer to venomous snakes that bit the Israelites in the desert—called "fiery" because their bites stung like fire. However, there's no indication that the seraphim had a snakelike appearance. They are simply holy, fiery beings with human form. Like the cherubim, these are not angels, but a distinct kind of heavenly being.

The seraphim seem particularly focused on God's holiness and His worship. And they have tremendous spiritual power. When one of them cried out, "'Holy, Holy, Holy, is the LORD of hosts," the physical foundations of the Temple doors trembled. The seraph also handled a white-hot coal that purified Isaiah from sin, indicating that they are deeply dedicated to maintaining purity.

ANGELS: GOD'S MESSENGERS

The angels—and all other celestial beings—were brought into existence by God and His Son, Jesus Christ, before the creation of the physical universe. "For by Him all things were created, both in the heavens and on earth, visible and invisible, whether thrones or dominions or rulers or authorities—all things have been created

A mosaic of seraphim displayed in the dome of the Hagia Sophia, Istanbul, Turkey. Seraphim focus on God's holiness and worship, and have great spiritual power.

through Him and for Him" (Colossians 1:16 NASB). How did He do it? "He issued his command, and they came into being" (Psalm 148:5 NLT). We know this happened sometime before Creation, because God says, "When I laid the foundations of the earth. . .the morning stars sang together and all the angels shouted for joy" (Job 38:4, 7 NLT).

The most important angelic messenger was the mighty angel Gabriel, who constantly stands in the very presence of God (Luke 1:19). In the Old Testament, he took a revelation to the prophet Daniel and helped him understand heavenly visions (Daniel 8:16–17; 9:21–22), and in the New Testament, he bore messages to Zacharias and to Mary (Luke 1:11–19, 26–33).

Of course, *all* angels see God, even if not as intimately as Gabriel does. Jesus said the angels guarding little children "always see the face of My Father who is in heaven" (Matthew 18:10). Many lower-ranking angels carry messages of comfort and encouragement to God's people, such as the angel who appeared to Paul during a great storm (Acts 27:23–24).

How many angels are there? The apostle John writes, "I looked and heard the voice of many angels, numbering thousands upon thousands, and ten thousand times ten thousand" (Revelation 5:11 NIV).

MALAK MEANS "MESSENGER"

The Hebrew word for "angel" is *malak* and means "messenger." Though angels have many different duties, one of their primary functions is to serve as God's messengers. From their first appearance in Genesis, we see them repeatedly bearing messages from God to people.

That's one hundred million angels! The prophet Daniel saw the same number attending to God and standing before Him (Daniel 7:10). Of course, they likely didn't see every angel in existence, simply those who were crowded around God's throne. After all, there are more than seven billion people in the world today, and lots of angels are required to attend to them all. That's why Hebrews 12:22 says there is "an innumerable company of angels."

▶ Archangels Michael and Gabriel, God's messengers. According to scripture, there are untold numbers of angels who serve God and bring messages from Him to His people.

WHAT ANGELS LOOK LIKE

People typically imagine angels with white robes, blond hair, and big white wings—more like oversized feather-dusters than powerful spiritual beings. Yet the Bible calls them "mighty angels" (2 Thessalonians 1:7) and states that "angels. . .are greater in power and might" than mere mortals (2 Peter 2:11). They also "excel in strength" (Psalm 103:20).

At the same time, angels normally have "the appearance of a man" when we see them (Daniel 8:15). That's why they're often able to walk among us undetected (Hebrews 13:2). Nevertheless, their great glory still shines through at times and there's often something "very awesome" about them (Judges 13:6).

Some angels are especially awesome. As Daniel observed, "I

▶ Angels are described in the Bible as having the appearance of a man, and their clothes are often "gleaming like lightning." Peter Paul Rubens (1612–1615) reveals his understanding of what angels look like in his painting *The Holy Women at the Sepulchre*.

looked up and there before me was a man dressed in linen, with a belt of fine gold from Uphaz around his waist. His body was like topaz, his face like lightning, his eyes like flaming torches, his arms and legs like the gleam of burnished bronze, and his voice like the sound of a multitude" (Daniel 10:5–6 NIV). The King James Version says that the angel had "eyes as lamps of fire." However, this was a chief angel, so he was more powerful and glorious than a regular angel.

Another powerful angel appeared when Jesus rose from the dead: "An angel of the Lord descended from heaven and came and rolled away the stone and sat upon it. And his appearance was like lightning, and his clothing as white as snow. The guards shook for fear of him and became like dead men" (Matthew 28:2–4 NASB). Another angel at the tomb is described as wearing "clothes that gleamed like lightning" (Luke 24:4 NIV).

John also had a vision of a magnificent angel in Heaven: "I saw still another mighty angel coming down from heaven, clothed with a cloud. And a rainbow was on his head, his face was like the sun, and his feet like pillars of fire" (Revelation 10:1). "I saw another angel coming down from heaven, having great authority, and the earth was illuminated with his glory" (Revelation 18:1). You can understand why John, in the presence of such a magnificent being, mistakenly bowed to worship him (Revelation 22:8–9). The angel, however, commanded him to worship God.

OF ANGELS AND MEN

The belief that we somehow sprout wings in heaven is based on a misunderstanding. Many people believe that when humans die they become angels. According to television shows and movies, new arrivals in Heaven have to "earn their wings" to become angels. Not so. Angels are distinct beings created by God before He brought the galaxies into being. Human beings were created last. After the resurrection, humans will have glorious bodies and powers *like* angels, but we won't *become* angels. It's a case of apples and oranges. In Revelation 7, John first describes an innumerable multitude of saved

▶ Carl Heinrich Bloch (1834–1890) painted his understanding of an angel in his work *An Angel Comforting Jesus Before His Arrest in the Garden of Gethsemane*. Angels are unique creatures, different and separate from humans.

humans in Heaven (verse 9), then describes a separate multitude of angels (verse 11).

Part of the mistaken belief that people become angels stems from concern over loved ones. Parents who have watched over their children for years—even when their children are grown adults—often think that they'll continue looking out for them after going to Heaven. But guarding our loved ones is the job of angels, not departed saints.

We aren't angels, nor will we ever become angels. God has sent His angels to serve human beings. "Are not all angels ministering spirits sent to serve those who will inherit salvation?" (Hebrews 1:14 NIV). Angels are already immortal and don't inherit the salvation Christ gives us. They don't understand how God saves us, though they wish they did (1 Peter 1:12). Nevertheless, "there is rejoicing in the presence of the angels of God over one sinner who repents" (Luke 15:10 NIV).

ANGELIC GUARDS AND ESCORTS

One of the most comforting promises in the Bible says, "The angel of the LORD encamps around those who fear Him, and rescues them" (Psalm 34:7 NASB). If we revere the Lord, His mighty battle angels take up positions around us.

Angels not only protect us in our homes, they also accompany and safeguard us all the time. "If you make the LORD your refuge, if you make the Most High your shelter, no evil will conquer you. . . . For he will order his angels to protect you wherever you go" (Psalm 91:9–11 NLT). God also promised the Israelites, "I am sending an angel ahead of you to guard you along the way and to

GUARDIAN ANGELS

Many people believe that two guardian angels are permanently assigned to believers, because in speaking of those who look after "little ones" on earth, Jesus refers to *"their"* angels (Matthew 18:10). And when the servant girl Rhoda told other Christians that she had seen Peter (who had been freed from prison), they insisted, "It is *his* angel" (Acts 12:15, emphasis added). So there's likely truth to the belief that we have the same angels guarding us throughout our lives.

▶ The Bible is clear that angels guard souls who have died and escort them to heaven, as depicted in Adolphe William Bouguereau's (1825–1905) painting *A Soul Brought to Heaven*.

bring you to the place I have prepared" (Exodus 23:20 NIV).

When it comes our time to die and go to Heaven, God will also send angels to guard us and bring us safely to the wonderful place He has prepared. We won't have to attempt that journey alone. In the story of Lazarus and the rich man, Jesus said that "the poor man died and was carried by the angels to be with Abraham" (Luke 16:22 NLT). Jesus also said that in the coming Rapture, God "will send His angels . . .and they will gather together His elect" (Matthew 24:31).

So, yes, angels will escort us to Heaven when we die. Many people who have been allowed to briefly visit Heaven have told of angels taking them there. They have also described seeing multitudes of other angels.

ARCHANGELS, PRINCES, AND COMMANDERS

One thing we'll discover when we get to Heaven is that it's a very organized place. It's not like a giant anthill with millions of angels running around all on their own, with no overseer or ruler (Proverbs 6:6–8). All of the one hundred million angels mentioned by John are organized into ranks and dominions.

▶ Guido Reni's (1575–1642) oil-on-canvas painting of the archangel Michael. Michael is God's chief angel, whose primary job is to protect God's people.

Earlier we learned that Jesus created all things, "both in the heavens and on earth, visible and invisible, whether thrones or dominions or rulers or authorities" (Colossians 1:16 NASB). We see, therefore, that there are rulers in the heavenly realm and that they sit on thrones of authority. Paul refers to them in Ephesians as "the rulers and the authorities in the heavenly places" (Ephesians 3:10 NASB). These angelic rulers have dominion over other angels.

MICHAEL AND OTHER ARCHANGELS

In the New Testament, Michael is called "Michael the archangel" (Jude 1:9). *Arch* is a Greek word meaning "chief," so *archangel* simply means "chief angel." Therefore, all of the other chief princes are *also* technically archangels.

Daniel 12:1 refers to the archangel Michael as "the great prince." And Daniel also says that Michael is "*one of* the chief princes" (Daniel 10:13, emphasis added). This indicates that there are many other lower-ranking angelic princes, plus a number of *chief* angelic princes, such as Gabriel. However, Michael appears to be the most prominent of all the rulers.

God told Daniel that Michael is "the great prince who protects your people" (Daniel 12:1 NIV), so we know that Michael's specific assignment is to guard the people of God. When Joshua was getting ready to besiege Jericho, he met a mighty angel who announced that he was "Commander of the army of the LORD" (Joshua 5:14). Very likely, this commander was Michael, because when there was war in Heaven, we read that "Michael and *his* angels fought against the dragon. . .and his angels" (Revelation 12:7 KJV, emphasis added). Just as Michael is the prince of the angels, Satan (Beelzebub) is the "prince of the devils" (Matthew 9:34 KJV).

God's angelic army also has a vast chariot corps. One time, when the prophet Elisha and his servant were in the city of Dothan, the Arameans sent an army there. When Elisha's servant awoke in the morning, he saw a huge army around the city and went to warn Elisha. The prophet told him, "Don't be afraid. Those who are with us are more than those who are with them." Then the Lord opened the servant's eyes, and he "saw the hills full of horses and chariots of fire all around Elisha" (2 Kings 6:15–17 NIV).

When the prophet Elijah went up to Heaven, "a chariot of fire and horses of fire" came for him (2 Kings 2:11 NASB). How many horses and chariots does God have? "The chariots of God are twenty thousand, even thousands of thousands" (Psalm 68:17). God's army also has cavalry units (Revelation 19:11–14) and scouts on horseback (Zechariah 1:8–10). The angels of God aren't wispy wimps floating around on clouds; they're a highly organized and powerful fighting force.

ANGELS PRAISING GOD

In the Psalms, the angels are commanded, "Bless the LORD, you His angels" (Psalm 103:20), and "Praise Him, all His angels; praise Him, all His hosts!" (Psalm 148:2). Repeatedly, this is what we see the angels doing, both in Heaven and on earth. When John visited the throne room of God, he said, "I heard the voice of many angels around the throne. . .saying with a loud voice: 'Worthy is the Lamb who was slain to receive power and riches and wisdom, and strength and honor and glory and blessing!'" (Revelation 5:11–12).

And again, "All the angels were standing around the throne and around the elders and the four living creatures. They fell down on

▶ Many angels are constantly in God's presence; Giovanni Di Paolo (1403–1482), an Italian artist, painted this image in his rendering of a host of angels beneath the Holy Trinity.

their faces before the throne and worshiped God, saying: 'Amen! Praise and glory and wisdom and thanks and honor and power and strength be to our God for ever and ever. Amen!'" (Revelation 7:11–12 NIV). Angels have a terrific, joyful time praising God. A note by the translators of the New American Standard Bible tells us that the phrase "myriads of angels" in Hebrews 12:22 could also be rendered "angels in festive gathering."

Angelic choirs praise God on earth as well. After an angel announced Jesus' birth to the shepherds near Bethlehem, "suddenly there was with the angel a multitude of the heavenly host praising God and saying, 'Glory to God in the highest, and on earth peace among men with whom he is pleased!'" (Luke 2:13–14 RSV). God also commands His angels to worship Jesus, His Son: "When He again brings the firstborn into the world, He says: 'Let all the angels of God worship Him'" (Hebrews 1:6).

ANGELS REPORTING TO GOD

God's angels report to Him on a regular basis: "Now there was a day when the sons of God came to present themselves before the LORD. . . . Again there was a day when the sons of God came to present themselves" (Job 1:6; 2:1 NASB). God's angels are constantly appearing before Him—apparently at set times—reporting to Him, making requests, as well as being sent forth on assignments. As a mighty angel told Zacharias, "I am Gabriel! I stand in the very presence of God. It was he who sent me to bring you this good news!" (Luke 1:19 NLT).

Gabriel is not the only angel who constantly stands in the presence of God. Revelation 8:2 says, "I saw the seven angels who stand

> **GOD JUDGES THE *ELOHIM***
> Isaiah refers to the heavenly city as "the mount of the congregation" (Isaiah 14:13). And Psalm 82:1 states that "God stands in the congregation of the mighty; He judges among the gods." The Hebrew word translated as "gods" is *elohim*, which in this case means "mighty ones." Picture God surrounded by hosts of exalted angels and mighty celestial beings, judging them and rendering decisions as they appear before Him.

▶ Angels who watch over children have constant access to God's throne; Pietro da Cortona's (1596–1669) painting *The Guardian Angel* gives us a picture of what he believed guardian angels look like.

before God, and to them were given seven trumpets." We often pay close attention to the fact that they're given trumpets of judgment and yet overlook the fact that they are referred to as "*the* seven angels who stand before God" (emphasis added). We aren't given more details on the rank or authority of these seven amazing angels, other than that they initiate great judgments on the earth.

The angels who watch over children also have continual access to God's throne. Jesus told His disciples, "See that you do not despise one of these little ones; for I tell you that in heaven their angels always behold the face of my Father who is in heaven" (Matthew 18:10 RSV).

Another thought: police officers have the authority to bear arms and to *use* them, but they must write a report justifying their actions every time they fire their weapons. Are angels similar? Could this be why they "present themselves before the LORD" (Job 1:6 NIV)—to account for their actions? Remember, although God's angels' intentions are good, they don't *always* make the wisest decisions, which is why God sometimes "charges His angels with error" (Job 4:18).

ALL ABOUT ANGELS

Angels aren't human, yet they often take human form and can even enjoy mortal food. Consider when Lot prepared food for his angelic visitors: "Now the two angels. . .entered his house; and he prepared a feast for them, and baked unleavened bread, and they ate" (Genesis 19:1, 3 NASB). Earlier that day, those same two angels had eaten a meal that Abraham had prepared (Genesis 18:6–8). Angels also eat their own food in Heaven—the same food that God used to sustain the nation of Israel in the wilderness after the Exodus: "He rained down manna upon them to eat and gave them food from heaven. Man did eat the bread of angels" (Psalm 78:24–25 NASB).

Some angels can bake bread. And the bread is so nutritious and supernatural that eating one loaf of it, and drinking one jug of miraculous water, gave Elijah the strength to make a forty-day trek across the desert (1 Kings 19:1–8).

Where do angels live in Heaven? Do they have lodgings there, or are they always serving God, always on the go, and basically homeless? The Bible doesn't give a definitive answer, though it does indicate that the angels have dwellings in the heavenly city. After all, they lived with God in the New Jerusalem for thousands of years before the first people went there. If they didn't have lodgings there, the entire vast city would have stood unused. A hint of the angels'

▶ An old painting by an unknown artist in the 18th century shows an angel protecting a child; it is unknown where angels dwell in Heaven, although there are hints of heavenly places of lodging.

▶ Fra Angelico's *The Last Judgment* (1425–1430) shows the twenty-four elders surrounding God's throne.

dwellings might be found in Job 4:18–19: "If He charges His angels with error, how much more those [mortal men] who dwell in houses of clay?" Angels are contrasted to mortals, who live in temporal "houses of clay." So where do angels live if not "eternal dwellings"? (Luke 16:9 NIV). But the fact is, we simply don't know.

Some people go into great detail about the supposed hierarchies and categories and names of angels, but most of this is nothing but human imagination and speculation, and the Bible cautions us: "Do not let anyone who delights in. . .the worship of angels disqualify you. Such a person also goes into great detail about what they have seen; they are puffed up with idle notions by their unspiritual mind" (Colossians 2:18 NIV).

THE TWENTY-FOUR ELDERS

Another fascinating detail about Heaven is that there are *two dozen* thrones surrounding the throne of God. "Surrounding the throne were twenty-four other thrones, and seated on them were twenty-four elders. They were dressed in white and had crowns of gold on their heads. . . . Whenever the living creatures give glory, honor and thanks to him who sits on the throne. . .the twenty-four elders fall down before him who sits on the throne and worship him who lives for ever and ever. They lay their crowns before the throne and say:

'You are worthy, our Lord and God, to receive glory and honor and power'" (Revelation 4:4, 9–11 NIV).

Elsewhere, John writes that "the twenty-four elders fell down before the Lamb, each one holding a harp and golden bowls full of incense, which are the prayers of the saints" (Revelation 5:8 NASB). The twenty-four elders repeatedly prostrate themselves before the throne of God and worship Him (Revelation 11:16; 19:4).

Who are these elders? One guess is that they're angels, since the Bible declares that angelic princes have thrones in Heaven. But if so, it's odd that they're referred to as "elders"—a term almost exclusively reserved in the Bible for human beings. In fact, this is likely what they are. A number of Bible commentators propose that these elders consist of the twelve greatest saints of the Old Testament, together with the twelve apostles of the New Testament. After all, Jesus promised His apostles that when "the Son of Man sits on the throne of His glory, you. . .will also sit on twelve thrones, judging the twelve tribes of Israel" (Matthew 19:28).

THE SPIRITS OF THE DEPARTED

The Bible says that we "have come to Mount Zion and to the city of the living God, the heavenly Jerusalem, to an innumerable company of angels, to the general assembly and church of the firstborn who are registered in heaven, to God the Judge of all, to the spirits of just men made perfect" (Hebrews 12:22–23). There is not only "an innumerable company of angels" in the heavens, but even now "we are surrounded by such a great cloud of witnesses" (Hebrews 12:1 NIV). These witnesses are departed Christians who are now watching us from Heaven and cheering us on.

There are great multitudes of the saved in Heaven. "After these things I looked, and behold, a great multitude which no one could count, from every nation and all tribes and peoples and tongues, standing before the throne and before the Lamb, clothed in white robes. . . . They have washed their robes and made them white in the blood of the Lamb. For this reason, they are before the throne of

God; and they serve Him day and night in His temple; and He who sits on the throne will spread His tabernacle over them. They will hunger no longer, nor thirst anymore. . . for the Lamb in the center of the throne will be their shepherd, and will guide them to springs of the water of life; and God will wipe every tear from their eyes" (Revelation 7:9, 14–17 NASB).

We have a wonderful hope, which is why Paul says we should give "joyful thanks to the Father, who has qualified you to share in the inheritance of his holy people in the kingdom of light" (Colossians 1:12 NIV).

▶ Those who are saved will one day stand before the throne of God and will serve Him day and night with joy; this image is titled *Paradise*, from *De Civitate Dei* by the French School.

REUNITED WITH LOVED ONES

Since time immemorial, men and women have hoped for life after death in a place where they will be joyously reunited with departed loved ones. If your family members were believers, and you are as well, then this desire will most certainly come true. Not only will you see them again, but you'll be able to enjoy their company forever.

Many people believe that when they arrive in Heaven, the first people to greet them will be their loved ones who are already there. The Bible doesn't say this, but neither does it say that such is *not* the case. We know that angels are very well informed about what happens here on earth: they know when we're born again (Luke 15:10), they know when our bodies die, and they bring us to Heaven. It would be a small thing for the angels to inform our departed loved ones so that they can greet us as we enter Heaven. This isn't clearly stated in scripture, but it's very possible.

However, many people who claim they have visited Heaven *don't* say that they met a departed loved one. Rather, they speak of having an audience with the Son of God. It may well be that the first person we meet in Heaven will be Jesus. This seems to be what's indicated by Stephen, who, just before he is martyred, exclaims, "I see heaven open and the Son of Man standing at the right hand of God" (Acts 7:56 NIV). Normally, Jesus is *seated* at the right hand of God (Luke 22:69; Colossians 3:1; Hebrews 8:1). But He apparently rose from His throne to greet Stephen when he died.

Though we often long to see our departed parents or other loved ones who've passed away, for many of us, the greatest joy will be to see a beloved husband or wife who has gone to Heaven. And the question is, "Will we still be married in Heaven?" Despite what certain religions teach, the answer is *no*. In Luke 20:27–33, some religious leaders tell Jesus about a woman who'd been married seven times, taking one husband after another after each had died. They then ask Jesus whose wife she will be in the kingdom of God, since she had been the wife of all seven men. Jesus replies, "The people of this age marry and are given in marriage. But those who are considered worthy of taking part in the age to come and in the resurrection from the dead will neither marry nor be given in marriage, and they can no longer die; for they are like the angels. They are God's children, since they are children of the resurrection" (Luke 20:34–36 NIV).

We'll undoubtedly feel a tender love for those who were our marriage partners on earth, feel a special bond with them, and enjoy spending a great deal of time in their company, but we will no longer be involved in a physical marriage union. Instead, the Bible tells us, we'll all be spiritually married to Jesus. (For more on this, see "The Marriage Supper of the Lamb" in chapter 7.)

HOW MANY PEOPLE IN HEAVEN?

Some people think that only a small fraction of Earth's population will ever enter Heaven and that the overwhelming majority are destined for Hell, because Jesus said, "Enter by the narrow gate; for wide is the gate and broad is the way that leads to destruction, and there are many who go in by it. Because narrow is the gate and

▶ While being stoned, Stephen saw Jesus standing at the right hand of God, shown in this painting called *The Stoning of St. Stephen*, by Annibale Carracci (1560–1609).

difficult is the way which leads to life, and there are few who find it" (Matthew 7:13–14). Depending on whom you talk to, 51 percent to 99.99 percent of people who have ever lived won't inherit eternal life.

This can cause us great grief. We wonder why God created so many billions of people, knowing that the majority would go to Hell instead of enjoying Heaven. However, John tells us, "I looked, and behold, *a great multitude which no one could count*, from every nation and all tribes and peoples and tongues, standing before the throne and before the Lamb" (Revelation 7:9 NASB, emphasis added).

We know that the New Jerusalem and the New Earth are both

immense, with room for many billions of people; but even though God isn't willing that *any* should perish (Matthew 18:14) and has arranged accommodations for more than those who will accept His invitation, not all will accept it. In one parable, Jesus records the King (God) telling His servant to go out into the city and bring in whomever he could find. "And the servant said, 'Master, it is done as you commanded, and *still there is room.*' Then the master said to the servant, 'Go out into the highways and hedges, and compel them to come in, *that my house may be filled*'" (Luke 14:22–23, emphasis added).

Jesus said there are many mansions in His Father's house; and because it is God's will that His house be *filled*, He will see to it that it *is* filled.

CHILDREN IN HEAVEN

Many people who have been taken to visit Heaven report seeing myriad small children there. This is entirely in keeping with what Jesus has told us. He said, "Let the little children come to me, and do not hinder them, for the kingdom of heaven belongs to such as these" (Matthew 19:14 NIV). Several people, when in Heaven, were told that the children either died young or were aborted. We know that "it is not the will of your Father which is in heaven, that one of these little ones should perish" (Matthew 18:14 KJV), so they apparently go to Heaven.

But even if these visions of visiting Heaven are true, the question arises, "Where do all these children come from?" The answer may be found in a related question: "Do children who die before they're old enough to understand the Gospel and receive it go to Heaven or Hell?" There are two main views. The first is that there are *no* exceptions—that even small infants who didn't have faith in Jesus will suffer eternal torments in Hell. This view is understandably abhorrent to Christians.

The second view is that God doesn't hold children responsible for sins until they reach "the age of accountability," the age at which a child knows the difference between good and evil. Proponents of this view believe that a child who dies *before* reaching that age—regardless of what religion his or her parents were—is received into Heaven. So which view is accurate?

Those who hold the first view point out that "*all* have sinned" and that "the wages of sin is death" (Romans 3:23; 6:23, emphasis added). They also point out that David confesses, "Behold, I was brought forth in iniquity, and in sin my mother conceived me" (Psalm 51:5 NASB). In other words, he was *born* a sinner.

Those who hold the second view don't dispute that everyone is born in sin. What they affirm, however, is that scripture *also* teaches that God doesn't hold children accountable until they're old enough to know the difference between good and evil. In Deuteronomy 1:39, God speaks of "your lit-tle ones and your chil-dren. . .who today have no knowledge of good and evil" and speaks of a time "before the child shall know to refuse the evil, and choose the good" (Isaiah 7:16 KJV). And God asks Jonah, "Should I not pity Nineveh, that great city, in which are more than one hundred and twenty thousand persons who cannot discern between

▶ A picture of children joyfully flying a kite; though there are differing views, it appears there will be vast numbers of children in Heaven.

their right hand and their left?" (Jonah 4:11). He was talking about the young children.

Though the scriptures are not conclusive in this matter, it appears that very young children are spared and that much of the present population of Heaven is children.

WHERE DO SPIRITS COME FROM?

Some people believe that when children are aborted, they return to God, who originally sent them. These people imagine that all human spirits preexist with God before coming to earth, and that we are sent from Heaven into our human bodies. However, if all spirits originate in Heaven, this would mean that *all* human spirits are saved. Many people would happily agree with this conclusion, and Jewish mystics state that unborn human souls wait in Araboth, the seventh Heaven, to be born. But this *isn't* the picture scripture gives.

Some people see an alternative in this statement from Jesus to His enemies: "You are from below, I am from above; you are of this world, I am not of this world" (John 8:23 NASB). Since Jesus was referring to Heaven when He said, "I am from above," the argument goes, then he must have been referring to Hell when He said, "You are from below." The natural conclusion, then, is that people are predestined before birth, either to salvation or to damnation, depending on whether their spirit originated in Heaven or Hell. This idea comes from a careless reading of the scriptures. Jesus was plainly referring to *this physical world* when He said, "You are from below. . . you are of this world."

Where then do human spirits come from? The prophet Zechariah said that the Lord "stretches out the heavens, lays the foundation of the earth, and forms the spirit of man within him" (Zechariah 12:1). God forms a new eternal human spirit within the fertilized egg at the moment of conception. The scriptures simply don't support the view that humans are eternally preexistent.

MAGNIFICENT HEAVENLY HORSES

Besides cherubim, angels, and people in Heaven, there are also animals. The apostle John tell us there are vast herds of horses there (Revelation 19:11, 14). The horses in this portion of John's vision were all pure white, but heaven's horses come in many colors, including the common sorrel.

The white horses in Revelation aren't ordinary horses, however;

▶ The book of Revelation describes white horses in Heaven that fly through the air and are often spoken of in connection with fire.

they are actually able to fly through the air. In fact, the horses that pull God's fiery chariots are called "horses of fire" (2 Kings 2:11 NASB; see also 2 Kings 6:17). Does this mean that at times they literally burn with divine fire? Possibly. The burning bush was alight with the fire of God. "Though the bush was engulfed in flames, it didn't burn up" (Exodus 3:2 NLT).

On the other hand, remember that the gems that make up the heavenly city are called "stones of fire" (Ezekiel 28:16 NASB). This isn't because they're literally burning, but because they glow with an intense light, like white-hot coals. So the "horses of fire" could look "like burnished bronze, when it has been made to glow in a furnace" (Revelation 1:15 NASB). Either way, these celestial steeds will be truly awe-inspiring.

SORREL CELESTIAL STALLIONS

The Bible tells us that some of the horses of Heaven are sorrel colored. *Sorrel* means "chestnut colored" or "a copper-red shade of chestnut."

God even sends angels forth on horseback to patrol the earth. "I saw by night, and behold, a man riding on a red horse, and it stood among the myrtle trees in the hollow; and behind him were horses: red, sorrel, and white. Then I said, 'My lord, what are these?' . . . And the man who stood among the myrtle trees answered and said, 'These are the ones whom the LORD has sent to walk to and fro throughout the earth'" (Zechariah 1:8–10).

5 : SPIRITUAL PLACES AND THINGS

THE REALITY OF SPIRITUAL MATTER

Some Christians think that the Bible's description of Heaven is completely symbolic, so there's no telling whether it exists in any kind of real, tangible way. Every physical object mentioned, every number quoted, and every measurement given is said to simply represent perfection, completeness, purity, joy, or some other intangible value or emotion.

As proof that we can't actually know what Heaven is like, they quote 1 Corinthians 2:9, which says, "Eye has not seen, nor ear heard, nor have entered into the heart of man the things which God has prepared for those who love Him." However, Paul says in the very next verse, "But God has revealed them to us through His Spirit" (1 Corinthians 2:10). Paul wrote this letter to the Corinthians in AD 55, and when the book of Revelation came out forty-one years later, in AD 96, the nature of Heaven was much more fully revealed.

Many people argue that the book of Revelation, which describes Heaven in great detail, shouldn't be taken literally, that it's all symbols and metaphors for some incomprehensible higher spiritual reality. If that's true, Revelation ultimately describes nothing whatsoever. Others believe, however, that, apart from cases of obvious symbolism (e.g., Revelation 5:6; 14:14–16), John's descriptions of Heaven are intended to be taken at face value, and that even his symbolic portrayals represent a concrete reality.

Jesus admonishes us to store up treasures in heaven; the question is, how *real* is this treasure? Is it merely a figurative way of saying we'll have happiness there, or will this treasure be more tangible? After the resurrection, when we receive our glorified bodies, they'll be made of supernatural elements but will nevertheless be solid and material. So we'll be able to enjoy tangible possessions. We won't simply drift in a cloud bank feeling joyful. God has promised us mansions to dwell in and streets of gold to walk on. It just remains to be seen precisely what form these mansions and streets of gold will take.

> **TANGIBLE SPIRITUAL MATERIALS**
> Even if the Bible's descriptions of Paradise are metaphors for something else, they nevertheless describe *tangible* spiritual realities. Whatever picture we have in our minds, the reality we'll one day encounter will be even better. And it will be solid and real.

Randy Alcorn, in his excellent book titled *Heaven*, contends that Heaven is an actual, physical place, as physical and as real as this present world we live in.[9] He's absolutely right. However, in popular usage, "physical" and "spiritual" are polar opposites, with physical objects seen as solid and *real*, and spiritual objects seen as intangible and unreal. So instead of referring to spiritual things as *physical*, perhaps it would be best to refer to them as *material*, and to refer to *heavenly* materials as opposed to *earthly* materials.

THE HEAVENLY JERUSALEM

As mentioned earlier, the city where God dwells is presently in the heavenly dimension and is therefore called "Jerusalem which is above" (Galatians 4:26 KJV). This heavenly place is God's residence, His capital, the center of the universe. It's made out of amazing materials that are *more than* physical. In other words, while they have all the properties that physical earthly objects have, they also have *extra* dimensions and properties to them. These have not only the capability of making them invisible to our eyes but also intangible to our other senses.

One day, the New Jerusalem will come down out of the heavenly dimension and exist on the earth. However, whether the New Jerusalem is in the spiritual dimension (as it is presently) or on the earth (as it one day will be), it will always be the abode of God. The Bible says that Heaven is "His holy habitation" (Zechariah 2:13). It's therefore appropriate that we devote this chapter to looking at God's eternal city.

THE STAIRS OF HEAVEN

In chapter 1, we learned that Jacob "saw a stairway resting on the earth, with its top reaching to heaven, and the angels of God were ascending and descending on it. There above it stood the LORD" (Genesis 28:12–13 NIV).

Also, Jesus said to Nathanael, "Very truly I tell you, you will see

▶ A pen, ink, and watercolor titled *Jacob's Dream* by William Blake (1757–1827), showing heavenly stairs ascending to and descending from the doorway of Heaven.

HEAVEN

'heaven open, and the angels of God ascending and descending on'
the Son of Man" (John 1:51 NIV). The New International Version
puts part of Jesus' statement in quotes because He's referring to the
passage in Genesis. Apparently, two thousand years after Jacob, these
heavenly stairs still existed and were still used by angels.

The earthly Temple in Jerusalem also had stairs; pilgrims ascended
stone steps to reach the Temple courts from the south. Archaeologists
uncovered the largest of these sets of steps, 215 feet wide, in 1968.
These are but a copy of the heavenly stairway.

THE DOOR OF HEAVEN

The apostle John writes, "After these things I looked, and behold, a
door standing open in heaven" (Revelation 4:1). He heard a voice calling him to come up, and immediately he was transported through the
door into Heaven itself. This doorway does *not* appear to be synonymous with one of the twelve "gates of pearl" that Revelation describes,
but it is a portal from the physical dimension through to the spiritual
realm. And though a number of people who claim to have visited
Heaven report following a pathway leading to the gates of the heavenly
city, in John's case, this door led directly to the throne room of God.

THE WALL AROUND THE CITY

All ancient cities had thick, protective walls around them to keep out
enemies, and the heavenly Jerusalem also has "a great, high wall" to
keep out anyone who doesn't belong there (Revelation 21:12 NIV).
Since the base of the city is a square, 1,400 miles (12,000 stadia) long
by 1,400 miles wide, this wall runs for a total of 5,200 miles around
the city. It is also 216 feet thick (Revelation 21:16–17).

The wall is made of a glorified type of jasper (Revelation 21:18).
On earth, jasper is a precious stone that's usually red in color, though
sometimes it's yellow, brown, or green—or even blue. This wall also
has "twelve foundation stones, and on them [are] written the names
of the twelve apostles of the Lamb" (Revelation 21:14 NLT).

The wall is "inlaid with twelve precious stones: the first [is] jasper, the second sapphire, the third agate, the fourth emerald, the fifth onyx, the sixth carnelian, the seventh chrysolite, the eighth beryl, the ninth topaz, the tenth chrysoprase, the eleventh jacinth, the twelfth amethyst" (Revelation 21:19–20 NLT). Some of these precious stones are very hard substances, but they aren't just natural gemstones. If they were, eventually—after untold millennia—even a soft wind would wear them away. But they too consist of eternal elements.

THE GATES OF THE CITY

The New Jerusalem has "twelve gates, and twelve angels at the gates, and names written on them, which are the names of the twelve tribes of the children of Israel: three gates on the east, three gates on the north, three gates on the south, and three gates on the west. . . . The twelve gates were twelve pearls: each individual gate was of one pearl" (Revelation 21:12–13, 21). Since the wall around the city is 5,200 miles long, if the gates are spaced at equal distances, and this is probably the case, then there are 466 miles between each gate.

The gates of ancient cities were shut at sundown and barred, but not so with these. "On no day will its gates ever be shut, for there will be no night there. The glory and honor of the nations will be brought

▶ *Reconstruction of the Temple of Herod* by James Tissot (1886–1894), showing the gates of the earthly Temple. The gates of the heavenly temple will never be shut; angels will guard the city to make sure nothing impure enters it.

into it. Nothing impure will ever enter it, nor will anyone who does what is shameful or deceitful, but only those whose names are written in the Lamb's book of life" (Revelation 21:25–27 NIV).

But if the gates are never shut, doesn't that mean that anyone is free to enter? No. That's why the angels stand guard at the gates, to make sure that no impure person enters the city. "And the nations of those who are saved shall walk in its light" (Revelation 21:24). "Blessed are those who wash their robes, that they. . .may go through the gates into the city" (Revelation 22:14 NIV). This means that they're saved and "have washed their robes and made them white in the blood of the Lamb" (Revelation 7:14 NASB).

Will the gates actually be gigantic spheres of layered calcium carbonate like earthly pearls? Very likely they'll be orbs of luminous, *eternal* material resembling pearls. They haven't, after all, been fashioned like common pearls inside an oyster, nor are they even made of natural, physical substances.

THE THRONE OF GOD

Now let's have a look *inside* the heavenly city, beginning with the throne of God. As we discussed in chapter 1, God's throne is at the very summit of the New Jerusalem, the crystal-gold mountain of the Lord's house. We're given many details about God's throne room. The most magnificent thing there is the throne of God. Isaiah writes, "I saw the Lord, high and exalted, seated on a throne" (Isaiah 6:1 NIV). Ezekiel also saw God's throne and writes, "I saw the likeness of a throne of lapis lazuli" (Ezekiel 10:1 NIV; see also Ezekiel 1:26).

However, compare this to what John saw several centuries later: "Then I saw a great white throne and him who was seated on it" (Revelation 20:11 NIV). Is God's throne pure white, or is it deep blue with gold flecks? The answer is probably *both*. Ezekiel saw God's throne

A THRONE OF LAPIS LAZULI

Lapis lazuli is a deep-blue precious stone prized for its intense color. It's streaked and spotted with gold-colored flecks. God's throne therefore is astonishingly colorful and beautiful.

during normal times, and John saw it when God was judging the world. Daniel also saw God's throne of judgment, which he describes as "a fiery flame" (Daniel 7:9). When God judges the world, physical matter will flee from the brilliance of His majesty (Revelation 20:11), and His throne will blaze with white light.

God's throne is high and lofty and incredibly beautiful, and it's apparently not a single seat, but a complex structure. The Bible tells us that Jesus "sat down at the right hand of the throne of the Majesty in heaven" (Hebrews 8:1 NIV). Jesus states that the right hand of the throne of God is *part* of God's throne. He says, "I also overcame and sat down with My Father on His throne" (Revelation 3:21). And Jesus told His disciples that He "will sit on His glorious throne" (Matthew 25:31 NASB), also called "the throne of His glory" (Matthew 19:28).

King Solomon's throne was a pale copy of God's celestial throne.

▶ Andreas Brugger (1737–1812) painted *Solomon at His Throne*, described in the Bible as beautiful ivory overlaid with pure gold—and yet no comparison to God's heavenly and lofty throne.

"The king made a great throne of ivory, and overlaid it with pure gold. The throne had six steps, and the top of the throne was round at the back; there were armrests on either side of the place of the seat, and two lions stood beside the armrests. Twelve lions stood there, one on each side of the six steps; nothing like this had been made for any other kingdom" (1 Kings 10:18–20).

In Daniel's vision, God's throne glows with so much light that it appears fiery: "The Ancient of days did sit. . . . His throne was like the fiery flame, and his wheels as burning fire" (Daniel 7:9 KJV). Ezekiel also mentions these wheels, saying, "I saw a wheel on the ground beside each [cherubim] with its four faces. This was the appearance and structure of the wheels: They sparkled like topaz, and all four looked alike. Each appeared to be made like a wheel intersecting a wheel. . . . Their rims were high and awesome, and all four rims were full of eyes all around" (Ezekiel 1:15–16, 18 NIV).

These wheels are associated with the four cherubim: "The spirit of the living beings was in the wheels" (Ezekiel 1:21 NASB). Whatever their purpose, they're referred to as *wheels*, causing some to suggest that, because the cherubim are throne-bearers, and because Ezekiel saw God's throne appear in Babylonia, these wheels somehow transport God's throne throughout the universe. But as we see in Daniel's vision, these wheels are also present when His throne is stationary in Heaven.

THE SEA OF GLASS

John writes, "Also in front of the throne there was what looked like a sea of glass, clear as crystal" (Revelation 4:6 NIV). He later describes it further, saying, "I saw something like a sea of glass mingled with fire, and [the saved] standing on the sea of glass" (Revelation 15:2).

Try to imagine the beauty of this pavement. It's like "glass, clear as crystal. . .mingled with fire." This surface reminded John of glass, because he could gaze down into its crystalline depths as if it were a pure sea, and fiery light was mingled with it, moving through it in brilliant waves and sparks and swirls. However, when Moses saw

God, "under his feet was something like a pavement made of lapis lazuli, as bright blue as the sky" (Exodus 24:10 NIV). Either Moses saw God's throne in a different location, or, quite possibly, the pavement of the throne room can change appearance and color.

The word *sea* is drawn from the imagery of the gigantic bronze basin in front of the Temple in Jerusalem. It was filled with water and called "the Sea of cast bronze" (1 Kings 7:23–25). In addition, perhaps the enormous crystal pavement with fire surging and sweeping through it—making it seem as if it were in motion—reminded John of the wave-tossed Sea of Galilee of his youth. Whatever the reason for its name, we can be certain that, being before God's throne, it is one of the most beautiful areas of Heaven.

THE ALTAR OF INCENSE AND PRAYER

There was an altar in the Temple at Jerusalem dedicated to burning incense to God. John the Baptist's father, Zacharias, was offering

▶ Lucas Cranach's (1472–1553) illustration titled *The Martyrs beneath the Altar*. Under this altar in Heaven, where incense is burned before God's presence, are souls slain for their testimony to the Word of God.

incense there when he saw the angel Gabriel (Luke 1:8–11). There is a similar altar in Heaven. King David prayed, "May my prayer be set before you like incense" (Psalm 141:2 NIV), and an angel told the centurion Cornelius, "Your prayers. . .have come up as a memorial offering before God" (Acts 10:4 NIV). This same imagery appears in Revelation: "Then another angel, having a golden censer, came and stood at the altar. He was given much incense, that he should offer it with the prayers of all the saints upon the golden altar which was before the throne. And the smoke of the incense, with the prayers of the saints, ascended before God from the angel's hand" (Revelation 8:3–4). Note that the golden altar is in front of the throne. In the earthly Temple, the altar of incense was in front of the Holy of Holies, where God manifested His presence between the golden cherubim. In Heaven, the golden altar is *also* before the presence of God, who is enthroned between the cherubim.

The above passage says that incense mixed with prayers ascended up to God. However, in another place, the incense is described as prayer itself: John tells us that "each one [of the twenty-four elders] had a harp and they were holding golden bowls full of incense, which are the prayers of God's people" (Revelation 5:8 NIV). The relationship between incense and prayer is obviously very close.

This altar is where the saints make petitions to God. John writes, "I saw under the altar the souls of those who had been slain for the word of God and for the testimony which they held. And they cried with a loud voice, saying, 'How long, O Lord, holy and true, until You judge and avenge our blood on those who dwell on the earth?'" (Revelation 6:9–10). The writer of Hebrews tells us, "Let us therefore come boldly unto the throne of grace, that we may obtain mercy, and find grace to help in time of need" (Hebrews 4:16 KJV). When we come before God's throne in spirit, it's very likely that we stand at this heavenly altar (where incense and prayers are offered).

THE TEMPLE OF GOD

John remarks about the city, "I saw no temple in it, for the Lord God the Almighty and the Lamb are its temple" (Revelation 21:22 NASB). Nevertheless, the book of Revelation refers frequently to "the temple which is in heaven" (Revelation 14:17), indicating some kind of structure around the throne room. How do we reconcile these statements? One explanation is that God is spread like a tabernacle over everyone—because the presence of God the Father and His Son fills the entire city.

However, the presence of God is *centered* in His throne room; thus His sanctuary is rightly said to be there. This is borne out by the following passage: "[The ones who come out of the great tribulation] are before the throne of God; and they serve Him day and night in His temple; and He who sits on the throne will spread His tabernacle over them" (Revelation 7:15 NASB).

God's throne room is not open to outer space, as some people assume. There is a massive vaulted ceiling *above* it, making the throne room an enclosed sanctuary. This verse describes that ceiling: "Spread out above. . .was what looked something like a vault, sparkling like crystal, and awesome" (Ezekiel 1:22 NIV). As proof that God's throne is in this celestial temple, John says that "a loud voice came out of the temple of heaven, from the throne" (Revelation 16:17).

The Bible says, "We have a High Priest who. . .ministers in the heavenly Tabernacle, the true place of worship that was built by the Lord and not by human hands" (Hebrews 8:1–2 NLT). The Bible describes this as the "greater and more perfect" Temple, saying, "When Christ appeared as a high priest of the good things that have come, then through the greater and more perfect tent [tabernacle]. . .he entered once for all into the Holy Place" (Hebrews 9:11–12 RSV).

We've seen that there's an altar of incense before the throne, and in the earthly Temple, this altar was in the Holy Place inside the Temple, in front of the Most Holy Place. The following verses indicate the proximity of their heavenly counterparts: "Then another angel came out of the temple which is in heaven. . . . And another angel came out from the altar" (Revelation 14:17–18).

God dwells in this heavenly temple, and on occasion His glory fills it with intense power: "After these things I looked, and behold, the temple of the tabernacle of the testimony in heaven was opened. . . . The temple was filled with smoke from the glory of God and from His power, and no one was able to enter the temple" (Revelation 15:5, 8).

> **THE HEAVENLY ARK**
>
> Just as the earthly ark of the covenant was contained in the Temple at Jerusalem, so the celestial ark (of which the earthly ark was a copy) is housed in Heaven's Temple: "Then, in heaven, the Temple of God was opened and the Ark of his covenant could be seen inside the Temple" (Revelation 11:19 NLT).

NEARNESS TO GOD IN HEAVEN

Revelation 15:8 brings out an important point. We see God exuding such intense glory that it prevents anyone from coming near Him. The same thing happened when the earthly Temple was dedicated: "When Solomon finished praying. . .the glory of the LORD filled the temple. The priests could not enter the temple of the Lord because the glory of the LORD filled it" (2 Chronicles 7:1–2 NIV).

Jesus said, "Blessed are the pure in heart, for they will see God" (Matthew 5:8 NIV). The writer of Hebrews says, "Follow peace with all men, and holiness, without which no man will see the Lord" (Hebrews 12:14 KJV). Some Christians earnestly desire to draw close to God, but many are satisfied with a more distant relationship. Like Peter, they "followed him afar off" (Matthew 26:58 KJV).

Could it be that the closer we are to God on earth, the closer we'll be able to approach Him in Heaven? While the love and acceptance that emanate from His presence are inviting, God is also holy, and the closer we are to Him, the more we become aware of His holiness. For the pure in heart, being intimately close to God will be a wonderful experience; however, it may be overwhelming for those who weren't near to God in this life. They won't be able to *bear* being too close,

▶ This piece by Carl Heinrich Bloch (1834–1890) was painted using oil on copper, and it depicts the nearness of Jesus to little children. For the pure in heart, it is wonderful—not overwhelming—to be near God.

unless God deliberately conceals most of His glory.

Many Christians believe that the more they live for God now, the more glorious their mansion will be. But, very likely, part of their eternal reward includes the *location* of their heavenly dwelling place—whether high in the city near the throne of God, or on a lower level. Those farthest from the throne will still be in the city, but may only be as close to God as they desired to be in this life.

ENJOYING GOD FOREVER

Our nearness to God ties in with another thought: many people fear they'll be bored to tears, eternally gathered around God's throne praising Him for ever and ever, but that's not what the Bible indicates. God is transcendently beautiful and glorious, and seeing Him face-to-face will make adoring Him spontaneous. Worshipping God will likely give us rapturous pleasure, far surpassing the pleasures of sex or the most transcendent joy we experience here on earth. We'll probably have a hard time tearing our eyes away from Him. Jesus is one with God, His Father, and is "the brightness of his glory, and the express image of his person" (Hebrews 1:3 KJV). Therefore we will have great joy seeing Jesus face-to-face, in all His beauty.

Few people on earth have had such an encounter with God, or experienced the magnificence of His presence, but in Heaven we'll all have that privilege. David writes, "One thing have I desired of the LORD, that will I seek after; that I may dwell in the house of the LORD all the days of my life, to behold the beauty of the LORD, and to enquire in his temple" (Psalm 27:4 KJV).

We'll derive enormous pleasure from praising God in His heavenly kingdom and will greatly enjoy being in His presence. David declares, "In Your presence is fullness of joy; in Your right hand there are pleasures forever" (Psalm 16:11 NASB). This bears repeating: "In Your presence is *fullness of joy.*" Of course, we'll also experience pleasure and joy even during those times when we're not before God's throne. Although His glory is most intense there, His Spirit is everywhere in creation (Psalm 139:7–12), and we'll experience Him with us everywhere. Jesus promised, "I am with you always" (Matthew 28:20 KJV).

In fact, God and the Spirit of His Son dwell within our very hearts,

▶ In Heaven we will experience God's presence everywhere, filling us with unspeakable joy; God's right hand will guide us forever. Michelangelo's (1475–1569) *Creation of Adam* illustrates man in the presence of God.

and will do so forever. So no matter *where* we are in the universe, we'll experience God's joy. "If I take the wings of the morning, and dwell in the uttermost parts of the sea, even there Your hand shall lead me, and Your right hand shall hold me" (Psalm 139:9–10). We could be in a distant galaxy, and still God's right hand will be holding us. His right hand will lead us, and in His "right hand there are pleasures forever."

There will be untold millions or billions of people in Heaven, and though the sea of glass is a very large area able to accommodate immense crowds, it's only so big. So the honor of *constantly* being before God might be reserved for the twenty-four elders and other Christians privileged to be "before the throne of God and serve him day and night" (Revelation 7:15 NIV).

THE RIVER OF LIFE

John writes, "He showed me a pure river of water of life, clear as crystal, proceeding from the throne of God and of the Lamb" (Revelation 22:1). Because the throne of God is in the heights

BEFORE GOD'S THRONE
Something to consider: not only will we *not* spend our entire time in Heaven before God's throne, but we may not actually be invited to do so as much as we might like.

of the heavenly city, it's quite likely that this river not only flows through that level, but also cascades down in glorious waterfalls into all the levels below, coursing throughout the entire city.

A fascinating thing about this river is that Daniel describes it quite differently, saying: "His throne was a fiery flame. . .a fiery stream

▶ Jesus offered the Samaritan woman water that would quench her thirst forever, beautifully portrayed in this painting, *Christ and the Samaritan Woman*, by Ange Angels are described in the Bible as having the appearance of a man, and their clothes are often "gleaming like lightning." Peter Paul Rubens (1612–1615) reveals

issued and came forth from before Him" (Daniel 7:9–10). How do we reconcile these images? John saw a crystal-clear stream proceeding from God's throne, while Daniel saw a fiery stream issuing forth.

They likely saw the same stream at different times. Daniel's vision took place when "the books were opened" (Daniel 7:10) and God was judging the world—at which time the throne of God itself was ablaze like a "fiery flame." John saw the stream *after* the judgment (Revelation 20:11–15; 21:1), when things had calmed down and the saints were enjoying God's blessing. This river therefore seems to be the "water of life" for the saved, but a "fiery stream" to the condemned.

There are also fountains of the water of life throughout the city. John says that "the Lamb. . .will shepherd them and lead them to living fountains of waters." Note that he speaks of *fountains*, plural. Very likely there are numerous magnificent, cascading fountains in gardens throughout the city, probably all fed by the river of the water of life that flows from God's throne. And Jesus promises, "I will give of the fountain of the water of life freely to him who thirsts" (Revelation 7:17; 21:6).

David seems to describe one of these fountains with vivid imagery, saying, "For with You is the fountain of life; in Your light we see light" (Psalm 36:9 NASB). This may indicate that the water in the fountains is glowing with light.

In another place, Jesus says that His spiritual water will give us eternal life: "But those who drink the water I give will never be thirsty again. It becomes a fresh, bubbling spring within them, giving them eternal life" (John 4:14 NLT).

OUR HEAVENLY MANSIONS

One of the most well-known promises Jesus made regarding Heaven is about the dwellings we'll have in the next world. He promised: "In My Father's house are many mansions; if it were not so, I would have told you. I go to prepare a place for you. And if I go and prepare a place for you, I will come again and receive you to Myself; that where I am, there you may be also" (John 14:2–3).

Not surprisingly, this promise has inspired believers for the last two thousand years—not just those who were used to fine things in this life and looking for something even *better* in the next life, but particularly the poor, the oppressed, the destitute. Many believers have envisioned these "mansions" as sprawling marble palaces, complete with spiral staircases made of gold, paradisiacal gardens, fountains, Olympic-sized swimming pools, and even angels for servants.

The New International Version translates Jesus' statement as "My Father's house has many rooms" (John 14:2). When He refers to His

Father's "house," Jesus means the *entire, gigantic city.* However, that doesn't necessarily mean that the New Jerusalem consists of endless apartments joined by a warren of hallways.

The city of God is 1,400 miles high, consisting of myriad levels, from the base all the way up to the lofty summit. In the King James Version, we're told that God "buildeth his stories in the heaven" (Amos 9:6). The New International Version specifies that the Lord "builds his lofty palace in the heavens." Both represent the same idea, as a *lofty* palace would consist of many different stories or levels. If each level has a "ceiling" a quarter of a mile high, the city would have 5,600 individual levels, leaving ample space for our dwelling places to be stand-alone mansions surrounded by walkways, fountains, and enormous trees in open-air settings. If each level had a ceiling only 500 feet high, the city would have nearly 15,000 different levels—room for many billions of people.

A desire for a heavenly mansion may seem materialistic, but if we believe that God will provide such a place for us in the next life, we're less inclined to strive to provide a mansion for ourselves in the here and now. We're more likely to hold physical possessions with a loose hand. We're more likely to value service to our fellow man over pursuit of personal riches. We're more likely to give generously as Jesus commanded.

WHAT MANSIONS MEANS

The Greek word *moné*, translated "mansions" or "rooms," comes from the root word *méno*, which means "to remain, abide." So *moné* means "an abiding dwelling place." The emphasis is on the permanent nature of these dwellings, lodgings, or abodes, whatever form they may take.

Jesus said, "Where your treasure is, there will your heart be also" (Matthew 6:21 KJV). Whatever these mansions—or chambers within God's city-sized mansion—are like, they're a part of our treasure in Heaven, and they're worth desiring. We're to set our hearts on them, because the greatest palaces on earth are nothing compared to what we'll enjoy in Heaven.

Some people insist that we should desire only *God*, not any rewards He may give us in Heaven. They cite Psalm 73:25, which says, "Whom have I in heaven but You? And there is none upon earth that I desire besides You." But it was said of even the greatest saints of the Bible that "they desire a better country, that is, a heavenly one" (Hebrews 11:16 NASB). They desired not only God, but the heavenly country He created for them. If we give God first place in our lives, it's not a conflict to *also* desire the rewards that He delights to give us (Matthew 6:33). "Here we have no lasting city, but we seek the city which is to come" (Hebrews 13:14 RSV). There we "will be welcomed into eternal dwellings" (Luke 16:9 NIV).

▶ No matter what form our "mansions" in Heaven may take, we can rest assured that God is preparing our forever home where we will abide in Him. Whatever is in store, we can't help but imagine it will be even more beautiful than this lakeside village in Austria.

A garden of trees at sunset; heavenly Jerusalem will include breathtakingly beautiful trees and gardens.

THE TREES OF LIFE

Of all the trees in Heaven, the most wondrous are the trees of life: "Then the angel showed me a river with the water of life, clear as crystal, flowing from the throne of God and of the Lamb. It flowed down the center of the main street. On each side of the river grew a tree of life, bearing twelve crops of fruit, with a fresh crop each month. The leaves were used for medicine to heal the nations" (Revelation 22:1–2 NLT).

Jesus promises, "To him who overcomes I will give to eat from the tree of life, which is in the midst of the Paradise of God" (Revelation 2:7). How do we become overcomers? The Bible says, "Who is he who overcomes the world, but he who believes that Jesus is the Son of God?" (1 John 5:5). He later states, "Blessed are those who do [God's] commandments, that they may have the right to the tree of life" (Revelation 22:14). What are God's commandments? "This is His commandment: that we should believe on the name of His Son Jesus Christ and love one another" (1 John 3:23).

When it says that "the leaves were used for medicine to heal the nations" (Revelation 22:2 NLT), some people believe this refers to nations of the unsaved. But the most likely interpretation is that the leaves of the tree of life will be used as medicine to heal brokenhearted and deeply wounded Christians

> **THE GARDENS OF IRMO**
>
> In *The Silmarillion*, J. R. R. Tolkien writes that the transcendently beautiful Gardens of Irmo were in Valinor, the Blessed Realm; there, Estë the gentle, "healer of hurts and of weariness," assuaged all griefs and gave rest to the weary.[10] This is truly a picture of Heaven.

from all nations of the earth. The Bible tells us that "the Lamb. . .will shepherd them and lead them to living fountains of waters. And God will wipe away every tear from their eyes" (Revelation 7:17).

John tells us that "the tree of life. . .is in the midst of the Paradise of God" (Revelation 2:7). As we've already noted, the word *paradise* comes from an ancient Persian word meaning "an enclosed garden." Apart from the two trees of life flanking the river of life, there will be a profusion of breathtakingly beautiful trees and gardens in the heavenly Jerusalem.

STREETS OF GOLD

The Bible declares: "The street of the city was pure gold, like transparent glass" (Revelation 21:21). Are the streets of the New Jerusalem actually made of transparent gold? It definitely appears that the answer is "yes." In fact, all of Heaven is just as glorious. Not just the streets, but the *entire city* is made of translucent gold: "The city was pure gold, as clear as glass" (Revelation 21:18 NLT).

Because God Himself dwells in this city, it stands to reason that it would be so wonderful and fantastic, and made of such transcendent materials, that it would make earthly gold and jewels seem like cheap imitations. Why *wouldn't* the streets of God's capital be made of gold—and not only gold, but supernatural, transparent gold? If God can change our mortal, physical bodies into glorious bodies that never die and that glow with light, what can He do with mere gold?

We're told that the river of life "flowed down the center of the main street" (Revelation 22:2 NLT), and that's only the *main* street. There are streets everywhere in the city. Remember, it's 1,400 miles high, which very likely means there are untold thousands of levels in the city, each story containing hundreds of thousands of square miles of mansions, parks, fountains, streams, waterfalls, and ponds. Streets and avenues and boulevards and walkways of gold are woven throughout.

TREASURES IN HEAVEN

Once we realize that Heaven is our true home, the place where we'll live for eternal ages, we see things in proper perspective. There's no point in wasting years striving to get ahead and focus on gaining wealth on this earth, because we'll soon have to leave it all behind. Real life is more than the accumulation of material things. Jesus warns, "Watch out! Be on your guard against all kinds of greed; life does not consist in an abundance of possessions" (Luke 12:15 NIV). "For we brought nothing into this world, and it is certain we can carry nothing out" (1 Timothy 6:7 KJV).

Because we're on earth only a short time, and we'll be in Heaven forever, our priorities should be on heavenly things. This is why Jesus tells us to store up treasures in Heaven, not on earth. "Lay not up for yourselves treasures upon earth, where moth and rust doth corrupt, and where thieves break through and steal: But lay up for yourselves treasures in heaven, where neither moth nor rust doth corrupt, and where thieves do not break through nor steal: For where your treasure is, there will your heart be also" (Matthew 6:19–21 KJV).

> **WISE INVESTMENT PLANS**
> If we have the foresight to save money in the bank for our retirement years in this life, we're considered wise. How much wiser is it to have the forethought to store up treasure in Heaven for the *next* life, a world where we'll spend all eternity!

There are many ways to send treasure ahead to Heaven, and some of the surest ways are to be generous with our love, our time, our possessions, and our money. As Jesus advised one overly materialistic young man, "If you want to be perfect, go, sell what you have and give to the poor, and you will have treasure in heaven; and come, follow Me" (Matthew 19:21). The young man's heart was so ensnared by riches that Jesus advised a radical solution. He may not ask you to give away every earthly thing you own, but the principle of giving still applies if you want treasure in Paradise.

IMAGINING THE BEAUTY OF HEAVEN

The Bible gives us many details about Heaven and promises us great rewards there. God has also given us keen imaginations to picture the reality of the New Jerusalem, so it's perfectly acceptable to try to imagine how wonderful life there will be. In fact, the Bible says, "Since you have been raised to new life with Christ, set your sights on the realities of heaven" (Colossians 3:1 NLT). Heaven will have so much beauty and variety that there's probably no typical dwelling or neighborhood there. Nevertheless, let's ponder what one might look like.

Say you've been invited to feast with an Arab Christian who was martyred for her faith in Christ. You leave your own mansion, step onto a sparkling diamond dais, which envelops you with light as it effortlessly lifts you up one hundred levels. You emerge in the center of a park ringed by twelve large trees with pale blue leaves and glowing amber fruit. A multilevel fountain sends a white plume of water high into the air. Goldfish dart through the water in the fountain's copper-colored basin.

You stroll down a winding pathway of transparent gold, bordered by impossibly beautiful flowers. To your left, a grove of slender saplings shivers, even though there's no breeze, and the rustling silver leaves seem to sing, "Holy is the Lord!" A pride of seven lions lies

▶ The beauty of Heaven can only be imagined by comparing it with material things on earth, such as this picture of the stunning and colorful Dong Pee Sua Waterfall in the Kanchanaburi Province, Thailand.

sprawled across the path ahead, with no inclination to move, so you step over them, stopping to stroke under the chin of a regal lioness.

As you come around the flank of an enormous white pagoda, the sound of happy music and children's laughter rapidly approaches. A moment later, a bright swirl of butterflies—sparkling like shards of blue topaz—encircles you, their wings radiating music. Three deliriously happy children are in pursuit, trying to catch the elusive butterflies. Then they sweep past and the sound fades.

You pass a dizzying array of buildings, from palaces resembling magnificent French châteaus to a sprawling Greek villa, whose gem-encrusted walls glisten with waves of radiance. Then you're in front of a three-level palatial estate, built of gleaming white ivory and semitransparent gold edged with silver. Upon closer inspection, you see that the simple architecture is outlined and bordered with thousands of intricate, elegant curves. Graceful Arabic script is inscribed on the walls, and somehow you know it declares the glory of God and of the Lamb.

The immense, deep-brown gate swings open as you approach, and melodic music welcomes you. There is a short walk through the front garden to the mansion itself, where you mount a flight of snow-white steps to find the front door nestled between elegant pillars. The door also opens of its own accord, and this time soft, melodic bells echo, heralding your arrival. What you see as you step inside takes your breath away. You pause in the hall as the exquisite richness of your friend's eternal reward fills your senses.

Then she emerges from the kitchen, her face glowing with joy. She's dressed in radiant white and purple robes in a mixture of biblical and Arabic style. "You're just in time!" she exclaims. "The feast is almost ready!" The aroma of delicious food wafts into the hallway. After an embrace, she suddenly exclaims, "Oh! There's a special guest here! Why don't you go into the back garden and meet him while I finish?"

You walk into the enclosed estate behind the mansion, not sure which saint of God you should expect to find, and are overcome by the sheer beauty of your friend's personal paradise. You gasp as a wave of holiness and peace, mingled with the fragrance of a hundred exotic blooms, washes over you. You've heard that your friend prayed a lot on earth, and somehow that spiritual intimacy with God was translated to her garden here.

In a corner of the walled estate, beneath a tree with rose-colored foliage, stands a fierce young man arrayed in a glistening robe, with a great golden scabbard slung over his back. He's running an ivory brush through the mane of a magnificent stallion. The horse's body glows like burnished bronze shimmering in the heat of a furnace, and its eyes are coals of fire. The man glances your way and smiles—and without a word being said, you know that he is your friend's guardian angel.

Suddenly, there's a shriek of joy from inside the house. You hear your friend exclaim, "Father Abraham! What a surprise! You never told me you were coming!"

The angel chuckles. "Heaven is full of surprises."

Does this sound too good to be real? While it's admittedly only an imaginative peek into Paradise, it actually falls *far short* of the beauty and wonder of our eternal homes. "Eye has not seen, nor ear heard, nor have entered into the heart of man the things which God has prepared for those who love Him" (1 Corinthians 2:9).

THE BOOK OF LIFE

One of the most important objects in Heaven is the Book of Life. Paul talked about his "fellow workers, whose names are in the Book of Life" (Philippians 4:3), and Jesus promised, "The one who is victorious will. . .be dressed in white. I will never blot out the name of that person from the book of life, but will acknowledge that name before my Father and his angels" (Revelation 3:5 NIV).

Many people believe that the following passages refer to the same Book of Life. After the children of Israel had sinned, Moses interceded for them, saying, "Yet now, if You will forgive their sin—but if not, I pray, blot me out of Your book which You have written." But the Lord answered, "Whoever has sinned against Me, I will blot him out of My book" (Exodus 32:32–33). David also prayed against the wicked, "Let them be blotted out of the book of the living, and not be written with the righteous" (Psalm 69:28).

> **THE BOOK OF LIFE**
>
> The moment you accept Jesus as your Savior, you become spiritually alive. Although you're still on earth, your name is now written in the Book of Life. Your paperwork is already processed. You're already a citizen of Heaven. When you die, you will automatically be granted entry.

However, it's just as likely that this book refers to people's *physical* lives, and that being blotted out of this book means having one's life terminated. Remember, there are numerous books in Heaven—even a book describing every person's physical body and its development in the womb (Psalm 139:13–16). There are books recording all our sorrows and tears. David said to God, "You keep track of all my sorrows. You have collected all my tears in your bottle. You have recorded each one in your book" (Psalm 56:8 NLT).

The following verses, however, definitely refer to the Book of Life: "Nothing evil will be allowed to enter, nor anyone who practices shameful idolatry and dishonesty—but only those whose names are written in the Lamb's Book of Life" (Revelation 21:27 NLT). "And I saw the dead, the great and the small, standing before the throne, and books were opened; and another book was opened, which is the book of life. . . . And if anyone's name was not found written in the book of life, he was thrown into the lake of fire" (Revelation 20:12, 15 NASB; see also Daniel 12:1–2).

The Bible says that we "have come to Mount Zion and to the city of the living God, the heavenly Jerusalem, to an innumerable company of angels, to the general assembly and church of the firstborn who are registered in heaven" (Hebrews 12:22–23). What does it mean that the spirits of just men and women are "registered in heaven" in "the heavenly Jerusalem"? Well, Jesus said to "rejoice because your names are written in heaven" (Luke 10:20).

RECORDS OF DEEDS AND WORDS

There are also other books in Heaven. Daniel writes, "I watched till thrones were put in place, and the Ancient of Days was seated. . . . The court was seated, and the books were opened" (Daniel 7:9–10). What books are these? John wrote several hundred years later, "I saw the dead, the great and the small, standing before the throne, and books were opened; and another book was opened, which is the book of life; and the dead were judged from the things which were written in the books, according to their deeds" (Revelation 20:12

NASB). There is one Book of Life, but several *other* books as well, and since the dead were judged by what was written in the books, these heavenly volumes are clearly a record of their *deeds*.

In fact, it's not just our actions that are on permanent record, but even our words. Jesus warned, "But I say unto you, that every idle word that men shall speak, they shall give account thereof in the day of judgment" (Matthew 12:36 KJV). Positive words are also recorded, "The LORD listened and heard them; so a book of remembrance was written before Him for those who fear the LORD and who meditate on His name" (Malachi 3:16).

Even our thoughts are known. David writes, "You have searched me, LORD, and you know me. You. . .perceive my thoughts from afar . . . . Before a word is on my tongue you, LORD, know it completely" (Psalm 139:1–2, 4 NIV). Not only does God *know* our every thought, but "the word of God. . .judges the thoughts and attitudes of the heart" (Hebrews 4:12 NIV; see also John 12:48).

▶ God keeps a permanent record of our words and deeds, a separate list from the names in the Lamb's Book of Life.

OUR HEAVENLY BODIES

When we die, our spirit separates from our physical body and goes to Heaven. As we shall see in chapter 7, one day our spirit will be *reunited* with our transformed body, and the New Jerusalem will come down to the earth. Then we'll be able to fully enjoy life in this physical world again. But the question is, "If heavenly objects are made out of solid, otherworldly materials, and we're still only spirits without bodies for now, how will we be able to touch and handle things in Heaven?"

First of all, we must realize that even though our spirits aren't *physically* tangible, they're made out of real spiritual materials that *are* tangible and solid in the spiritual dimension. They can therefore operate in either Hades or Paradise, allowing the departed to interact with, touch, and experience sensory feedback from spiritual objects. Solid objects in the New Jerusalem also have this dimension, so we'll be able to interact with the things of Heaven.

But, clearly, something will be *lacking* in our experience—otherwise there would be no need to have a physical body again. "For we know that when this earthly tent we live in is taken down (that is, when we die and leave this earthly body), we will have a house in heaven, an eternal body made for us by God himself and not by human hands. We grow weary in our present bodies, and we long to put on our heavenly bodies like new clothing. For we will put on heavenly bodies; we will not be spirits without bodies. While we live in these earthly bodies, we groan and sigh, but it's not that we want to die and get rid of these bodies that clothe us. Rather, we want to put on our new bodies so that these dying bodies will be swallowed up by life" (2 Corinthians 5:1–4 NLT).

Very likely, we will need glorified physical bodies, not for Heaven itself, but to exist in for eternity and to interact with a renewed physical world and physical universe. We won't be spending all eternity just in the heavenly city.

ROBES OF RIGHTEOUSNESS

John writes, "I looked, and there before me was a great multitude that no one could count. . .standing before the throne and before the Lamb. They were wearing white robes and were holding palm branches in their hands" (Revelation 7:9 NIV). Referring to the worldwide body of believers as the bride of Christ, John writes, "To her was granted that she should be arrayed in fine linen, clean and white: for the fine linen is the righteousness of saints" (Revelation 19:8 KJV).

The white linen symbolizes God's righteousness, which allows us to enter into Heaven. On our own, we have nothing. "When we display our righteous deeds, they are nothing but filthy rags" (Isaiah 64:6 NLT). Yet "I will greatly rejoice in the LORD, my soul shall be joyful in my God; for He has clothed me with the garments of salvation, He has covered me with the robe of righteousness" (Isaiah 61:10). The Bible says, "Blessed are those who wash their robes, that they

In Heaven, multitudes will be clothed with robes of righteousness, but this doesn't mean that we won't wear other clothing as well. The painting *Paradise*, by Jacopo Tintoretto (1518–1594), shows myriads of souls in front of God's heavenly throne.

may have the right to the tree of life" (Revelation 22:14 NIV). How do people wash their robes? John tells us that "they have washed their robes and made them white in the blood of the Lamb" (Revelation 7:14 NIV).

Despite the obvious layers of symbolism, and the fact that our heavenly clothes will be made of spiritual materials, they're nevertheless tangible and solid within the heavenly dimension. We will, after all, be wearing *some* kind of extraordinary, unearthly clothing in the next life.

When the Bible talks about departed believers in Heaven all "clothed in fine linen, white and clean" (Revelation 19:14 KJV), many Christians believe this is *all* that *anyone* wears in heaven— white robes. Our spirits will be clothed with robes of righteousness, but that doesn't necessarily mean that we'll *also* wear robes on our immortal, physical bodies. We could wear other forms of casual or elegant attire.

THE CROWN OF LIFE

This brings us to our next subject—the heavenly crowns that God has promised to those who love Him. Read the following promises. "Blessed is the man who endures temptation; for. . .he will receive the crown of life which the Lord has promised to those who love Him" (James 1:12).

"Be faithful until death, and I will give you the crown of life" (Revelation 2:10). Some Christians envision these crowns as some kind of heavyset, spiked medieval crowns, but this is a misunderstanding of the Greek word *stephanos*, which is translated as "crown" in the New Testament. It's more accurate to envision the crown of life as a tiara, because *stephanos* actually means "circlet" when it refers to a royal crown (Revelation 6:2).

Usually, however, in the New Testament, *stephanos* refers not to crowns but to laurel wreaths. During the Greek Olympic Games in

▶ A laurel leaf wreath was given to winners of the Greek Olympic Games in Paul's day, and these wreaths were called "crowns" in the New Testament. God promises heavenly crowns of righteousness to those who love Him.

Paul's day, the winners of the races and other events were presented with wreaths of laurel leaves—garlands—that were placed on their heads. This is what Paul means when he describes it as a "perishable crown."

"And everyone who competes for the prize is temperate in all things. Now they do it to obtain a perishable crown, but we for an imperishable crown" (1 Corinthians 9:25). The crown of life is also called the crown of righteousness, and it is given not just to the greatest saints, but to all true Christians. "And now the prize awaits me—the crown of righteousness, which the Lord,

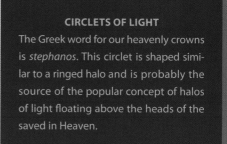

CIRCLETS OF LIGHT

The Greek word for our heavenly crowns is *stephanos*. This circlet is shaped similar to a ringed halo and is probably the source of the popular concept of halos of light floating above the heads of the saved in Heaven.

the righteous Judge, will give me on the day of his return. And the prize is not just for me but for all who eagerly look forward to his appearing" (2 Timothy 4:8 NLT).

Very likely, the luster and glory of our crowns will depend in large measure on how we live our lives for Christ here and now.

DIFFERENT KINDS OF CROWNS

Not only will our crowns be imperishable, but they will be far more glorious than the Greek athletes' temporary laurel crowns. The apostle Peter tells us, "When the Chief Shepherd appears, you will receive the crown of glory that will never fade away" (1 Peter 5:4 NIV). However, some Bible scholars believe that, when Peter talks about the "crown of glory," he is referring to a *separate* crown from the "crown of life." Can someone have more than one crown in Heaven? Jesus does. John describes the King of kings as having many crowns on his head (Revelation 19:12, 16).

In the passage from 1 Peter, the apostle is addressing the elders and shepherds (pastors) who watched over the church and set an example for believers. He says that if they serve Christ well, they will receive the "crown of glory." The crown of life is given to *all* believers, and cannot be lost, but the crown of glory is an award for exceptional service.

Unlike the crown of life, however, it appears that people can lose the crown of glory by not fulfilling what God has called them to do with their lives. Very likely that is what the following verse is referring to: "Hold fast what you have, that no one may take your crown" (Revelation 3:11). If God has given you a job to do and you fail to do it, He will have to find someone else to do that job—and they'll receive your reward.

STARS IN YOUR CROWN

The expression "stars in my crown" is more of a poetic picture than a scriptural doctrine—but there is something to the idea. The clearest representation of this is when John sees a vision of the Church, symbolized as a glorious woman: "There appeared a great wonder in heaven; a woman clothed with the sun, and the moon under her feet, and upon her head a crown of twelve stars" (Revelation 12:1 KJV).

▶ A jeweled crown; the Bible speaks of stars given as rewards for souls won for Him in this life, though this imagery may be more poetic than literal.

The twelve stars on her head symbolize either the twelve tribes of Israel or Jesus' twelve apostles. Yet in Christian hymns, "stars in my crown" refers to rewards that Christ gives us, especially for winning souls to Him. This imagery comes from the book of Daniel: "Those who are wise will shine like the brightness of the heavens, and those who lead many to righteousness, like the stars for ever and ever" (Daniel 12:3 NIV).

In addition, we have Paul's statements that the people he won to Christ were his crown. Paul calls the Christians of Philippi "my brethren dearly beloved and longed for, my joy and crown" (Philippians 4:1 KJV), and he asks the Christians of Thessalonica, "For what is our hope, or joy, or crown of rejoicing? Is it not even you?" (1 Thessalonians 2:19).

Though this could not be called a doctrine per se, it does contain some truth. Certainly we shall be rewarded for serving Christ, even if we don't receive a star-like gem in our crowns for every soul we win.

NEW NAMES AND WHITE STONES

Jesus promises, "To him who overcomes, to him I will give some of the hidden manna, and I will give him a white stone, and a new name written on the stone which no one knows but he who receives it" (Revelation 2:17 NASB). We will not only eat the delicious food of heaven, but each one of us will receive a unique treasure from the Lord—a white stone engraved with God's personal name for us. This name will be known only by the Lord and by the individual to whom it is given. "You will be called by a new name that the mouth of the LORD will bestow" (Isaiah 62:2 NIV).

▶ Jesus will give those who love Him a white stone with a treasured new name engraved on it. Only the recipient and the Lord Himself will know this new name.

We will also have the name of God, the name of the Son of God, and the name of His eternal city on our bodies. Jesus said, "He who overcomes. . .I will write on him the name of My God and the name of the city of My God, the New Jerusalem, which comes down out of heaven from My God. And I will write on him My new name" (Revelation 3:12). Rather than being literally tattooed on our bodies, these names will apparently glow on our spirits. "I looked, and behold, a Lamb standing on Mount Zion, and with Him one hundred and forty-four thousand, having His Father's name written on their foreheads" (Revelation 14:1).

It's unlikely these names will be in script that is physically, visibly engraved on our resurrection bodies, but they'll be emblazoned in letters of light on our spirits.

HEAVENLY HARPS

Something many Christians wonder about is the common belief that we'll all play harps. . .all the time. Though some people actually *like* harp music in moderation, they wouldn't want to listen to it continuously for all eternity. Nor do they particularly look forward to playing

▶ A statue of an angel playing a trumpet; the music in Heaven will be made from harps and trumpets but will sound like nothing we've ever heard in this life.

the harp nonstop. Yet not only do the twenty-four elders around the throne all have harps (Revelation 5:8), but so do a vast multitude of believers: "I heard a voice from heaven, as the voice of many waters, and as the voice of a great thunder: and I heard the voice of harpers harping with their harps" (Revelation 14:2 KJV). "And I saw. . .them that had gotten the victory over the beast. . .stand on the sea of glass, having the harps of God" (Revelation 15:2 KJV).

These "harps of God" could be both literal and symbolic; very likely, they're quite tangible, but like nothing we've ever seen or heard on earth. Also, they may be used only on special occasions, such as at assemblies before God's throne.

There will also be trumpets in Heaven. "For the Lord Himself will descend from heaven. . .with the trumpet of God" (1 Thessalonians 4:16). "I saw the seven angels who stand before God, and to them were given seven trumpets" (Revelation 8:2). Only these two instruments are mentioned, but God Himself inspires the creation of "witty inventions" (Proverbs 8:12 KJV), including musical instruments. So it's safe to assume that there will be many other instruments in Heaven and on the New Earth.

6 | HEAVEN'S COUNTERPART

ALL PEOPLE ARE SINNERS

Some people believe that everyone is basically good, but the Bible tells us, "There is no one on earth who is righteous, no one who does what is right and never sins" (Ecclesiastes 7:20 NIV). Yet there's a prevalent belief that people are basically good. Why is that?

Mankind was created in the image of God (Genesis 1:27), and though we've fallen from that sinless state, we still retain the capacity to care for, nurture, and protect others. We're capable of loving acts, and Jesus pointed out that a greedy tax collector loves those who love him and selfish fathers still provide for their children (Matthew 5:46–47; 7:9–11). But even the good we do is tainted by pride, selfishness, lust, jealousy, greed, and other selfish motivations. "If we say that we have no sin, we deceive ourselves" (1 John 1:8 KJV).

The Bible tells us, "For everyone has sinned; we all fall short of God's glorious standard" (Romans 3:23 NLT). Now, we readily admit that God, to *be* God, must be perfect—and we're also aware that we're *not*. On the other hand, many of us rationalize that, after all, we're only human. We're fallible, weak mortals. We make mistakes, yes; we have selfish motivations at times, yes; but we don't like to consider these things as sins, at least not serious sins.

Although we may do good things, and even attempt to live according to a moral code, our selfish nature constantly asserts itself. We're all guilty of wrong thoughts and actions. With that in mind, we can probably agree that we're sinners.

We must realize, therefore, the destructive end result of sin. Sin may seem like a small, inconsequential thing now, but "sin, when it is full-grown, brings forth death" (James 1:15). As Paul explains, the ultimate wages of sin is death (Romans 6:23). Right now, people may seem to be getting away with sinful habits, but the time of reckoning hasn't yet arrived. When *that* day finally comes, people will find that the wages they have earned amount to death.

GOD'S SOLUTION AND SALVATION

When Adam and Eve disobeyed God and ate the fruit of the tree of the knowledge of good and evil, they gained wisdom at a terrible price: they now knew the difference between good and evil (Genesis 3:6, 22). Afterward, when they disobeyed God, they were *aware* that they were doing wrong—yet still chose it. They were accountable and judged guilty. Just as God had warned, they died spiritually, and we inherited their proclivity to sin. As the Bible states, "The soul who sins shall die" (Ezekiel 18:20).

God, however, longed for His people to repent so that He could forgive them. He therefore allowed them to substitute a sacrificial animal so that they didn't have to die. This act of obedience demonstrated the people's acknowledgment of guilt, repentance, request for forgiveness, and dependence on the mercy of God. "The life of the flesh is in the blood, and I have given it to you. . .to make atonement for your souls" (Leviticus 17:11). "Without the shedding of blood there is no forgiveness of sins" (Hebrews 9:22 RSV). As the blood drained out of the sacrifice, the animal died

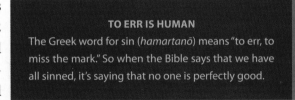

TO ERR IS HUMAN

The Greek word for sin (*hamartanō*) means "to err, to miss the mark." So when the Bible says that we have all sinned, it's saying that no one is perfectly good.

and the price was paid. The blood had made "atonement" for—which means "to cover"—their sins, and God then forgave them.

However, the blood of sacrificial animals could never permanently atone for sin. People kept having to return with a new sacrifice to cover new disobediences. So God made the ultimate sacrifice to forgive *all* of our sins once and for all. He sent His Son, Jesus, to die in our place. Jesus' lifeblood drained out of His body as the ultimate sacrificial offering, and "the blood of Jesus Christ His Son cleanses us from all sin" (1 John 1:7; see also 1 Peter 1:18–19).

▶ Jesus' life was a substitute for our life, bringing salvation for those who believe He died in our place; *The Crucifixion* painted by great Baroque master Jacob Jordaens (1593–1678) in St. Paul's Church depicts the moment that Jesus gave up His life for us.

"But as many as received Him, to them He gave the right to become children of God, to those who believe in His name" (John 1:12). To receive salvation, we must believe that Jesus is the Son of God, that He died on our behalf and was raised from the dead; we must sincerely repent of our sins and trust in Jesus to save us. And He *will* save us. "Whoever believes in the Son has eternal life, but whoever rejects the Son will not see life" (John 3:36 NIV).

Please notice the second half of the verse, however. There is no hope for those who *reject* Christ. What is the end result for those who reject God's offer of forgiveness and salvation? "The Lord Jesus will be revealed from heaven with His mighty angels in flaming fire, dealing out retribution to those who do not know God and to those who do not obey the gospel of our Lord Jesus. These will pay the penalty of eternal destruction, away from the presence of the Lord and from the glory of His power" (2 Thessalonians 1:7–9 NASB).

THE DEVIL AND HELL

Christians often talk about "being saved" and refer to themselves as "the saved," so the question is, "Saved from *what*?" This brings us to the subject of Hell. In stark contrast to the beauties, pleasures, and consolations of Heaven, Hell—particularly the final Hell, the lake of fire—is a place of desolation, misery, and suffering. Jesus tells the wicked, "Depart from me, you who are cursed, into the eternal fire prepared for the devil and his angels" (Matthew 25:41 NIV). This tells us an important fact: Gehenna, the lake of fire, didn't always exist, but was specifically created as a place of punishment for the angels who revolted against God.

UNPOPULAR IN THE POLLS

In 2013, 75 percent of American adults said they believed in God, while only 56 percent believed in the devil. And while 62 percent believed in Heaven, only 53 percent believed in Hell. When specifically asked if they believed in a Hell that was a place of suffering and punishment, even fewer people gave it credence—43 percent. This is a steep drop from 2001, when 71 percent believed in Hell.

Many modern people, while they profess faith in God, disbelieve in the

▶ Pieter Bruegel the Elder's painting *The Fall of the Rebel Angels* (1526); Gehenna, or the lake of fire—a place of misery and suffering—was created for these angels who revolted against God.

existence of an evil being called Satan, or in a destination called Hell. They want a reality that is all positives and no negatives, and this is both unrealistic and dangerous.

For almost all of mankind's existence, there has been a widespread belief in evil spirits or demons. The Bible tells us a great deal about them, and though it's beyond the purpose of this book to do a full study on the subject, we'll benefit from a basic understanding.

As explained in chapter 1, the devil was once a mighty cherub called Lucifer, the morning star. He had an exalted throne and position but became jealous of God and decided that he should rule in Heaven (Isaiah 14:12–15; Ezekiel 28:12–17). He persuaded one-third of God's angels to rebel with him. "And there was war in heaven: Michael and his angels fought against the dragon; and the dragon fought and his angels, and prevailed not; neither was their place found any more in heaven" (Revelation 12:7–8 KJV). The apostle John adds, "His tail drew the third part of the stars of heaven, and did cast them to the earth" (Revelation 12:4 KJV).

Jesus also described Satan's being cast down, saying, "I saw Satan fall like lightning from heaven" (Luke 10:18).

THE DEVIL AND HIS DEMONS

When Lucifer rebelled against God, the highly exalted cherub became "the great dragon. . .that ancient serpent, who is called the Devil and Satan, the deceiver of the whole world" (Revelation 12:9 RSV). He was also called "Beelzebub the prince of the devils" (Matthew 12:24 KJV). The angels who followed Satan were transformed into evil angels, otherwise called demons, devils, evil spirits, or unclean spirits.

There are early references to demons in the Old Testament. The Hebrew word *shed* ("spoiler; destroyer") is translated as "devil." Thus, "they sacrificed unto devils, not to God" (Deuteronomy 32:17 KJV), and "They sacrificed their sons and their daughters unto devils" (Psalm 106:37 KJV). Also, the prophet Isaiah, speaking of desolate ruins, says that "shaggy goats will frolic there" (Isaiah 13:21 NASB). A translators' note informs us that the Hebrew word *sair* can also be translated as "goat demons." Isaiah also writes, "Yes, the night monster will settle there and will find herself a resting place" (Isaiah 34:14 NASB). In this instance, *sair*, which is translated as "night monster," can also be translated as "demon."

Originally, the Greek word *daemon* didn't mean an evil spirit. Plato (429–347 BC) taught that *daemons* were intermediate beings between gods and men—dangerous, though not necessarily evil, spirits. Plato's pupil Xenocrates taught that there were good and evil *daemonion*. Since that time, however, *daemon* almost exclusively refers to evil spirits, whereas good spirits are called angels (*angelos*).

The New Testament makes it clear that demons cause sickness, oppress people, entice us to sin, deceive us, blind us to the truth,

THE DEVIL AND DEMONS
In Greek, when referring to Satan, the word *diabolos* is used; when referring to lesser evil spirits, the word *daimonion* or *daimon* is used.

and lead us to believe and tell lies. Fortunately, Jesus has power over them. "God anointed Jesus of Nazareth with the Holy Ghost and with power: who went about doing good, and healing all that were oppressed of the devil" (Acts 10:38 KJV). "He who sins is of the

▶ *Archangel Michael Hurls the Rebellious Angels into the Abyss*, an oil-on-canvas by Luca Giordano (1632–1705). Jesus has power over all of these demons and will destroy the works of the devil.

devil, for the devil has sinned from the beginning. For this purpose the Son of God was manifested, that He might destroy the works of the devil" (1 John 3:8).

SATAN'S VISITS TO HEAVEN

It may seem incredible to some people that Satan is still allowed access to a place as perfect and holy as Heaven—and even to the throne room of God—yet this is precisely the situation the Bible describes. We must not imagine, however, that the devil goes there as a welcome visitor. Rather, he's only allowed in on official business and is probably watched closely by powerful, well-armed angelic guards.

The Bible tells us that Satan was cast out of Heaven at the beginning of time (Isaiah 14:12–15; Ezekiel 28:13–16), and thus we know that Satan and his angels no longer live there. Yet the book of Job paints a startling picture:

"Now there was a day when the sons of God [angels] came to present themselves before the Lord, and Satan also came among them. . . . The Lord said to Satan, 'Have you considered My servant Job? For there is no one like him on the earth, a blameless and upright man, fearing God and turning away from evil.' Then Satan answered the Lord, 'Does Job fear God for nothing? Have You not made a hedge about him and his house and all that he has, on every side? You have blessed the work of his hands, and his possessions have increased in the land. But put forth Your hand now and touch all that he has; he will surely curse You to Your face.' Then the Lord said to Satan, 'Behold, all that he has is in your power, only do not put forth your hand on him.' So Satan departed from the presence of the Lord" (Job 1:6, 8–12 NASB).

Later in the book of Job, we read, "*Again* there was a day when the sons of God came to present themselves before the Lord, and Satan also came among them to present himself before the Lord" (Job 2:1 NASB, emphasis added). What was the *purpose* of his repeated visits? Job 2:1 says that he arrived "to present himself before the Lord," but for what reason?

▶ Satan appears before God's throne frequently in scripture to accuse believers. Corrado Giaquinto (1703–1765) was an Italian Rococo painter who illustrated this concept in his painting *Satan before the Lord.*

While seeing a vision of the end times, John declared, "Then I heard a loud voice saying in heaven, 'Now. . .the accuser of our brethren, who accused them before our God day and night, has been cast down'" (Revelation 12:10). Note that Satan is "the accuser of our brethren." He accuses God's people of breaking His laws and then demands the right to punish or afflict them.

Notice also how frequently the devil appears before the Lord's throne: He "accused them before our God *day and night.*" This could simply mean that he goes there on a repeated, but irregular, basis (as evidenced by the phrase "now there was a day"), or it could mean that he comes at set times, every day and every night. These activities have been happening since before Job's day in 1600 BC, were still occurring in Jesus' day (Luke 22:31–32), and have continued right up to this present time. They will cease only when Satan is permanently "cast down" to the earth at the beginning of the Tribulation.

JESUS OUR ADVOCATE

The unsaved are largely outside of God's protection, and the devil works freely in their lives. Paul writes, "You formerly walked according to the course of this world, according to the prince of the power of the air, of the spirit that is now working in the sons of disobedience" (Ephesians 2:2–3 NASB). Though Satan also causes trouble for the saved, he must first get permission from God. However, just because God allows Satan to accuse believers and to request permission to harass or attack them, doesn't mean that God always grants those requests. He did in Job's case, but in the case of Joshua the high priest (who lived after the Jewish return from exile), God bluntly refuted Satan's accusations.

"He showed me Joshua the high priest standing before the angel of the LORD, and Satan standing at his right side to accuse him. The LORD said to Satan, 'The LORD rebuke you, Satan! The LORD, who has chosen Jerusalem, rebuke you!'" (Zechariah 3:1–2 NIV). Bear in mind that the angel of the Lord represents the very presence of God Himself. "Now Joshua was dressed in filthy clothes as he stood before the angel" (Zechariah 3:3 NIV). These filthy clothes symbolize his sins, for which Satan was accusing him. Instead of letting the devil attack Joshua, however, "the angel said to those who were standing before him, 'Take off his filthy clothes.' Then he said to Joshua, 'See, I have taken away your sin, and I will put fine garments on you'" (Zechariah 3:4 NIV).

Like Joshua, we, too, have been forgiven of our sins and been clothed in robes of righteousness. As long as we live and walk in the Spirit of Christ, we're protected. At the very least, Satan cannot cancel our salvation. "Who will bring a charge against God's elect? God is the one who justifies; who is the one who condemns? Christ Jesus is He who died, yes, rather who was raised, who is at the right hand of God, who also intercedes for us" (Romans 8:33–34 NASB).

As for this present life, "there is therefore now no condemnation to those who are in Christ Jesus, who do not walk according to the flesh, but according to the Spirit" (Romans 8:1). We're bound to sin at times and to walk without regard to the Holy Spirit, but we can repent, Jesus will intercede for us and advocate for us, and God will forgive us. "These things I write to you, so that you may not sin. And if anyone sins, we have an Advocate with the Father, Jesus Christ the righteous" (1 John 2:1). Thank God for that!

SPIRITS SENT BY GOD

The fact that Satan is allowed access to the courts of Heaven to request permission to bring about judgment or disaster in the lives of God's people might also explain the following enigmatic passages:

After King Saul had stubbornly disobeyed God for years, "the Spirit of the Lord. . .departed from Saul, and an evil [*harmful, injurious*] spirit from the Lord tormented him. Saul's attendants said to him, 'See, an evil spirit from God is tormenting you'" (1 Samuel 16:14–15 NIV). Many Christians are perplexed at the thought of God sending an evil spirit to torment someone, but the concept wasn't unfamiliar to Saul's servants. They even had the confidence to speak candidly

▶ Rembrandt's (1606–1669) painting of Saul and David depicts Saul being tormented by an evil spirit sent by God.

about it to Saul, trusting that he'd understand. And he did.

Many years later, a true prophet named Micaiah told wicked King Ahab, "I saw the LORD sitting on His throne, and all the host of heaven standing by, on His right hand and on His left. And the LORD said, 'Who will persuade Ahab to go up, that he may fall at Ramoth Gilead?' So one spoke in this manner, and another spoke in that manner. Then a spirit came forward and stood before the LORD, and said, 'I will persuade him.' The LORD said to him, 'In what way?' So he said, 'I will go out and be a lying spirit in the mouth of all his prophets.' And the LORD said, 'You shall persuade him, and also prevail. Go out and do so.' Therefore look! The LORD has put a lying spirit in the mouth of all these prophets of yours, and the LORD has declared disaster against you" (1 Kings 22:19–23).

Many people are disturbed by the thought that a holy angel of God would go forth as a "lying spirit," but it's probably more accurate to understand this spirit—and the spirit that tormented Saul—not as an angel, but as a minion of Satan's who was allowed to be present in God's court and was more than willing to do a destructive or deceptive deed. If God granted permission to the devil to afflict Job, a righteous, innocent man, how much more would He give permission to evil spirits to torment a disobedient king, or deceive and destroy an evil king?

This is not meant as a definitive answer; it is merely a suggestion to make sense of these unusual scenes that transpired before God's throne.

AWAITING JUDGMENT IN HADES

While Satan and most of his demons are still loose in the spiritual realms where they fight God's angels and cause misery for mankind, some demons are already awaiting judgment in chains in Tartarus, also known as the abyss or the bottomless pit, a considerable depth below Hades (see "Angels and Titans in Tartarus" and "Spirits in Prison" in chapter 2). Whereas the inhabitants of Paradise are comforted and enjoy the company of wonderful saints of the past, those

▶ A painting by American painter David Howard Hitchcock (1861–1943) titled *Halemaumau, Lake of Fire.* Inhabitants of Hades endure torment, thirst, and isolation, as well as fire emanating up from the lake of fire.

in Hades endure torment in flame and great thirst—and great isolation. Remember, however, that Hades is *not* the final lake of fire.

The lake of fire is "in the neighborhood" of Hades, very likely in the bowels of the earth, at the bottom of a deep abyss or pit far beneath Hades—in what the Bible calls "the lowest hell." From the description given, the hot, choking fumes of Gehenna rise up from the depths into Hades, giving condemned souls a foretaste of what is to come. This concept was mentioned in Moses' day, when God said, "For a fire is kindled in My anger, and shall burn to the lowest hell" (Deuteronomy 32:22).

This "lowest hell" is called "the fiery lake of burning sulfur" in the New International Version and "the lake of fire and brimstone" in the King James Version and New American Standard Bible (Revelation 19:20; 20:10; 21:8). The "hot vapor" is apparently the choking sulphuric smoke rising up from the lake at the bottom of a very deep pit. This imagery appears in Revelation when describing those who receive the mark of the beast: "They will be tormented with burning sulfur. . . . And the smoke of their torment will rise for ever and ever" (Revelation 14:10–11 NIV).

Elsewhere in Revelation, John writes, "He opened the bottomless pit, and smoke arose out of the pit like the smoke of a great furnace" (Revelation 9:2). Jesus mentions this in Matthew 13:42, saying that the angels will cast the unsaved "into the furnace of fire. There will be wailing and gnashing of teeth."

One of the most horrible things about the souls consigned to Hades is that they already feel some of the fire issuing up the pit from the lake of fire below. As we see from the story of the rich man in Hades, they dwell in a netherworld rendered utterly parched and waterless by the flames and heat of Gehenna. Even a single drop of water would be a welcome relief. As bad as this is, they know that one day they'll be cast into a much *worse* place, and thus "are struck with a fearful expectation of a future judgment" (see sidebar below). This thought echoes Hebrews 10:27, which speaks of "a certain fearful expectation of judgment, and fiery indignation which will devour the adversaries."

THE DISCOURSE CONCERNING HADES

The *Discourse to the Greeks concerning Hades* states: "Now those angels that are set over these souls, drag them into the neighborhood of hell itself; who, when they are hard by it, continually hear the noise of it, and do not stand clear of the hot vapor itself; but. . .they are struck with a fearful expectation of a future judgment, and in effect punished thereby. . . . In this region, there is a certain place set apart, as a lake of unquenchable fire, wherein we suppose no one hath hitherto been cast; but it is prepared for a day afore-determined by God. . ."

THE GREAT WHITE THRONE JUDGMENT

Remember, no one is in the lake of fire at the present time. But there will be a final judgment of the unsaved at the *end* of the Millennium. "Then I saw a great white throne and Him who sat upon it. . . . And I saw the dead, the great and the small, standing before the throne, and books were opened; and another book was opened, which is the book of life; and the dead were judged from the things which were written in the books, according to their deeds. . . . Then death and Hades were thrown into the lake of fire. This is the second death, the lake of fire. And if anyone's name was not found written in the book of life, he was thrown into the lake of fire" (Revelation 20:11–12, 14–15 NASB).

The Book of Life will be opened, and a search will be made to see if people's names are found written there. If they're not, those

▶ Angels and unsaved human beings will be judged by God at the Great White Throne, at which time their punishment will be determined. This judgment is illustrated by Fra Angelico in his painting *The Last Judgment*.

people are destined for the lake of fire. But first, they're judged from the things written about them in the *other* books—not only their deeds but also their words and their very thoughts. "But the cowardly, the unbelieving, the vile, the murderers, the sexually immoral, those who practice magic arts, the idolaters and all liars— they will be consigned to the fiery lake of burning sulfur. This is the second death" (Revelation 21:8 NIV).

At this judgment, there will be public trials, both of unsaved people and of fallen angels. Apart from the records of sins in God's books, people will stand up and give testimony at the final judgment. Jesus said, "The Queen of the South will rise at the judgment with the people of this generation and condemn them, for she came from the ends of the earth to listen to Solomon's wisdom; and now something greater than Solomon is here. The men of Nineveh will stand up at the judgment with this generation and condemn it, for they repented at the preaching of Jonah; and now something greater than Jonah is here" (Luke 11:31–32 NIV).

In 1 Corinthians 6:3, Paul asks an amazing question: "Do you not know that we shall judge angels?" He clearly has fallen angels in mind here, because they are the only angels that await judgment (2 Peter 2:4; Jude 1:6). The fact that *we* (Christians) will be doing the judging could indicate that we will stand up and testify as individual demons appear before God, declaring how much evil they caused in our lives.

Why are both fallen angels and unsaved humans judged before being cast into Hell? To determine the severity of their punishment there. This brings us to the next question: What is Hell like?

WHAT IS HELL LIKE?

Many people believe that the graphic descriptions of Hell in the Bible shouldn't be taken literally. But then, what do they think Hell *is* like? They usually can't venture an opinion. Some would suggest that the unsaved are disembodied spirits floating in space, tormented with remorse. Or they visualize these lost souls living some kind of shadowy life, doing many of the same empty things they do now, but eternally separated from God. However, there's every indication that Hell is a tangible location filled with literal suffering.

▶ Modern-day Gehenna, or the Valley of Hinnom near the Old City in Jerusalem, where idolaters would cast their children into the flames while worshipping demonic idols.

Jesus said that Hell was a place where "their worm does not die, and the fire is not quenched" (Mark 9:44). *Gehenna* comes from *ge-Hinnom* (the Valley of Hinnom), where, in centuries past, idolaters cast their children into the flames while worshipping demonic idols (2 Chronicles 28:3). Later, godly Jews destroyed the idols (2 Kings 23:10) and turned the valley into a garbage dump, a place filled with burning trash and rotting, worm-riddled refuse. The bodies of executed criminals were often burned there—hence the imagery of Isaiah 66:24.

If that were the worst description of what Hell is like, it would be bad enough. But John further describes Gehenna as a "lake of fire" (Revelation 20:15 KJV), into which the wicked will be cast. The New International Version calls it a "fiery lake of burning sulfur" (Revelation 19:20; 21:8 NIV), and hardly anything smells as foul as sulfuric smoke. Elsewhere, the scriptures say, "On the wicked he will rain fiery coals and burning sulfur; a scorching wind will be their lot" (Psalm 11:6 NIV). David says of the wicked, "Let burning coals fall upon them; let them be cast into the fire; into deep pits" (Psalm 140:10).

It is commonly believed that Gehenna is synonymous with "the fiery lake of burning sulfur" (Revelation 19:20 NIV), and there is no real reason to doubt this. John writes that the wicked "shall be tormented with fire and brimstone," and that "the smoke of their torment ascends forever and ever" (Revelation 14:10–11). Many Christians take this imagery quite literally.

Hades, the state into which the unsaved dead initially descend, is a place where souls are "in agony in this fire" (Luke 16:24 NIV); but as we've already shown, Hades is only a foretaste of the full force of the final punishment. Though Gehenna is a place of great suffering, the agony in Hades is still tolerable enough to allow rational thinking and remorse, even compassion. The rich man there was sincerely concerned for his five living brothers. Even after he was told it was too late to alleviate *his* suffering, he was desperate that his brothers not suffer a similar fate (Luke 16:27–30). For the first time in his life, perhaps, the rich man was deeply moved with love and pity, concerned about the suffering of others. But it was too late.

The apocryphal Apocalypse of Zephaniah, written a century before the time of Jesus, says that Abraham and Isaac and Jacob regularly cried out to the Lord, "We pray unto Thee on account of those who are in all these torments so that Thou might have mercy on all of them" (Apocalypse of Zephaniah 11:3). The idea here is that after a period of suffering, the unrighteous will be released. However, you'll notice in Jesus' parable in Luke 16 that the rich man never asks Abraham to help *release* him from Hades—nor does Abraham offer any hope that he could be, or pray that he would be, released.

The former rich man knew that he *deserved* his suffering and that "the judgments of the LORD are true and righteous altogether" (Psalm 19:9 KJV). Abraham gently but firmly tells him, "Son, remember that in your lifetime you received your good things, while Lazarus received bad things, but now he is comforted here and you are in agony" (Luke 16:25 NIV), and it's clear that the rich man doesn't dispute that this is fair.

So, although the living often loudly protest the "injustice" of Hell, *those actually there* are convinced that what they're suffering is right and just. In this they have the attitude of the redeemed, who freely admit that they deserve Hell. The difference is that the saved have accepted God's gift of salvation and have thus been *spared* such suffering.

THE DEVIL DOESN'T RULE HELL

Jesus called Satan "the prince of this world" (John 14:30 NIV), and Paul refers to him as "the ruler of the kingdom of the air" (Ephesians 2:2 NIV)—that is, of the spiritual heavens in the atmosphere surrounding the earth. "For our struggle is not against flesh and blood, but against the rulers, against the authorities, against the powers of this dark world and against the spiritual forces of evil in the heavenly realms" (Ephesians 6:12 NIV).

Despite the fact that God has allowed Satan to have authority over

▶ Demons are terrified to go to the abyss, where monsters torment spirits trapped there. This tapestry from Angers, France, depicts the Beast who arises out of the pit/abyss (Revelation 13:1; 17:8).

the heavenly realms of this dark, fallen world, the devil is *not* the ruler of Hell. When Satan goes to Gehenna, it will be for *punishment*, not to exercise authority. The idea that the devil and his demons are in charge of the suffering of the unsaved in the lake of fire is a common one, but it is false. Jesus said that "the devil and his angels. . .will go away into everlasting punishment" (Matthew 25:41, 46). John adds, "Then the devil. . .was thrown into the fiery lake of burning sulfur, joining the beast and the false prophet. There they will be tormented day and night forever and ever" (Revelation 20:10 NLT).

But what about Hades, under the earth, where the unsaved are consigned until the Day of Judgment? Do the demons rule that? Some people who claim to have been taken to Hell report seeing demons bite and scratch souls, or devour their flesh, or hack them apart—only to see them restored to be mutilated again and again. However, in His only description of Hades, Jesus says absolutely nothing of such graphic things. The only suffering the former rich man endures is in flames *designed by God*.

We know that demons try to torment and possess the living, and it appears that they're *also* allowed to attack unsaved souls when they first leave their physical bodies and enter the evil spiritual realm that Satan rules (Ephesians 2:2). But the Bible doesn't say that these demons continue to torment human spirits once they reach the region of Hades. In fact, scripture indicates that this is *not* the case.

Jesus said, "When an unclean spirit goes out of a man, he goes through dry places, seeking rest; and finding none, he says, 'I will return to my house from which I came'" (Luke 11:24). From the plural form of the word *places*, it's apparent that Satan's kingdom is the exact opposite of a lush, well-watered paradise, and is a desolate region, an endless expanse of "dry places." The demons who seek rest there find none. If they *already* feel discomfort in such a realm, why would they descend into Hades, where it's not only arid but divine fire torments those who are there?

We also know that the devil doesn't rule over the abyss—the bottomless pit. Locust-like monsters with scorpion stings (which will one day torment wicked people) swarm there (Revelation 9:2–6). "They had as king over them the angel of the bottomless pit, whose name in Hebrew is Abaddon" (Revelation 9:11). John also writes, "I saw an angel coming down out of heaven, having the key to the Abyss and holding in his hand a great chain. He seized. . .Satan, and bound him for a thousand years" (Revelation 20:1–2 NIV). The abyss (also known as Tartarus) is God's prison house, ruled by an angel of God, and it's there that God—not Satan—chains demons awaiting judgment (2 Peter 2:4; Jude 1:6).

> **DEMONS IN GEHENNA**
> The devil and his demons will be tormented in the lake of fire. They won't be tormenting people there.

The locust-like monsters inhabiting the abyss, when temporarily released, will torment the wicked on earth; but apparently they're normally confined to the abyss, where they torment the wicked spirits who are chained there and can't escape. This is precisely why demons are terrified of going there. "And they begged Jesus repeatedly not to order them to go into the Abyss" (Luke 8:31 NIV).

EVERLASTING CONSCIOUS TORMENT

The belief that the unsaved will suffer eternal, conscious torment in Hell (Gehenna) has been held by the majority of Christians for the past two thousand years. This is also the doctrine that many people, including many believers, have had trouble with for centuries. A number of verses substantiate this view, however. The following are the strongest examples.

First of all, Jesus warned that the unrighteous would be "cast into hell fire—where 'their worm does not die and the fire is not quenched'" (Mark 9:47–48). He also warned, "He [the King, Jesus] will also say to those on the left hand, 'Depart from Me, you cursed, into the everlasting fire prepared for the devil and his angels. . . . And these will go away into everlasting punishment" (Matthew 25:41, 46). John writes that the wicked "will be tormented with fire and brimstone in the presence of the holy angels and in the presence of the Lamb. And the smoke of their torment goes up *forever and ever*; they have no rest day and night" (Revelation 14:10–11 NASB, emphasis added). For many Christians, these three passages are conclusive proof that not only will people suffer conscious torment in Hell, but this suffering will last for all eternity.

In addition, in every passage related to punishment in Hell where the Greek word *aionios* ("agelong") is translated as "eternal" (Matthew 18:8; 25:41, 46; 2 Thessalonians 1:9; Hebrews 6:2; Jude 1:7), it seems to refer to an endless duration of suffering.

Jesus said, "These will go away into everlasting punishment, but the righteous into eternal life" (Matthew 25:46). Those who argue that punishment in Hell is *not* eternal

---

THE ETERNITY OF HELL

The preacher Jonathan Edwards firmly believed in everlasting punishment. In his sermon "The Eternity of Hell Torments," he stated: "If the evil of sin be infinite, as the punishment is, then it is manifest that the punishment is no more than proportionable to the sin punished, and is no more than sin deserves. . . . Whence it follows that if it be suitable that there should be infinite hatred of sin in God, as I have shown it is, it is suitable that he should execute an infinite punishment on it."[12]

must explain why, in the same breath, Jesus said that the righteous would inherit eternal life. If the punishment of the unsaved isn't eternal, how can life for the saved be eternal?

Hell is so terrible, and the punishment of the unrighteous so inescapable, that Jesus said of Judas, "Woe to that man. . . . It would have been good for that man if he had not been born" (Matthew 26:24).

Although God is love, He is also holy and enforces justice, and must therefore punish sin. God is a loving God and He is merciful, but He's also all-knowing and just. If the rich man

▶ Jesus described the everlasting torment waiting for those who are in rebellion against Him as smoke that rises forever and ever.

in Hades couldn't dispute that his suffering there was fair, very possibly those who will be punished in Gehenna will admit the same.

ANNIHILATION OF BODY AND SOUL

A second traditional interpretation of Hell is called *annihilation*. It states that the unsaved indeed go to Hell, where they suffer for their sins, but that this period of suffering is limited, ending when the flames of Hell bring about the complete destruction (annihilation) of the sinner—at which point the person simply ceases to be. Adherents of this belief state that the term "the second death" is not a figurative expression that *actually* means "eternal suffering," but is literally a *death*, an end of existence. Since the lake of fire is where the unsaved are consumed, "the lake of fire is the second death" (Revelation 20:14 NIV).

Christians who believe in annihilation quote the following passages as proof: "These, as natural brute beasts, made to be taken and destroyed. . .shall utterly perish" (2 Peter 2:12 KJV). "These will pay the penalty of eternal destruction" (2 Thessalonians 1:9 NASB). Also,

Jesus said we are to "fear Him who is able to *destroy* both soul and body in hell" (Matthew 10:28, emphasis added).

According to this view, not everyone is destined to exist eternally. Only those who trust in Christ to save them "will not perish but have eternal life" (John 3:16 NLT). Immortality is a unique gift of God. "Christ Jesus. . .has destroyed death and has brought life and immortality to light through the gospel" (2 Timothy 1:10 NIV). As for the wicked, "Behold, the day is coming, burning like an oven, and all the proud, yes, all who do wickedly will be stubble. And the day which is coming shall burn them up. . .they shall be ashes under the soles of your feet" (Malachi 4:1, 3). "But the worthless, every one of them will be thrust away like thorns. . .and they will be completely burned with fire" (2 Samuel 23:6–7 NASB; see also Hebrews 6:8).

Also, the following verses indicate a limit to suffering in Hell. Jesus described the punishment that God exacts: "His master was angry, and delivered him to the torturers *until* he should pay all that was due to him" (Matthew 18:34, emphasis added). Jesus also said, "That slave who knew his master's will and did not get ready or act in accord with his will, will receive many lashes, but the one who did not know it, and committed deeds worthy of a flogging, will receive but few" (Luke 12:47–48 NASB). The idea is that the punishment, whether of short or long duration, will have a limit; it won't be eternal.

When Jesus said that sinners would be "cast into hell fire—where 'their worm does not die and the fire is not quenched'" (Mark 9:47–48), He was quoting Isaiah 66:24, which speaks about dead bodies (corpses) burning up outside Jerusalem. Tied to this image was the concept that these corpses would eventually be reduced to ashes under the feet of the righteous.

When John says in Revelation 14:10–11 that "the smoke of their torment goes up forever and ever; and they have no rest day and night," he echoes Isaiah, who writes, "Edom's streams will be turned into pitch, her dust into burning sulfur; her land will become blazing pitch! It will not be quenched night or day; its smoke will rise forever" (Isaiah 34:9–10 NIV). The Edomites were indeed judged and no longer exist as a people, yet their land didn't literally burn forever. Its smoke didn't literally rise forever.

For these reasons, Christians who believe in annihilation conclude that the punishment God metes out matches the crime and has a limit—and ends when the unsaved are consumed.

▶ *The Last Judgment*—a 17th-century icon from Lipie (historic museum in Sanok, Poland), depicts the unsaved souls in Hell in the lower right corner. Some Christians believe unsaved souls will eventually be completely destroyed, ceasing to exist.

LIMITED SUFFERING, AND THEN RELEASE

A number of Christians believe that all people will eventually come to faith in Christ and go to Heaven, but many will do so only after they've suffered in Hell. After they've paid the full penalty for their sins and are sufficiently penitent and purified, they're released and proceed to Heaven. This theory essentially views the lake of fire as a severe version of Purgatory. In the Catholic view, purgatory is a state in which Christians who committed sins are purified before being allowed into Heaven.

Many modern Jews believe that people will suffer in Hell for a maximum of one year. This belief is based on Isaiah 66:23–24, which says, "It shall come to pass that from one New Moon to another. . . all flesh shall. . .go forth and look upon the corpses of the men who have transgressed against Me. For their worm does not die, and their fire is not quenched." The expression "one New Moon to another" is thought to refer to the twelve months of a year. If you wonder how someone gets that interpretation from this verse, you're not alone.

This is the reason, however, that many Jews mourn for departed loved ones for twelve months. However, they recite the *Kaddish* (the mourner's prayer) daily for only eleven months: they want to make sure they grieve for the full period that it might take for their loved ones to be purified; on the other hand, it is considered inappropriate to assume that a family member was bad enough to suffer in Hell for the *full* year.

In addition, as evidence that most souls suffer in Hell for a time but are then brought back up and allowed to enter Paradise, some will cite this passage: "The Lord kills and makes alive; He brings down to Sheol and raises up" (1 Samuel 2:6 NASB). They envision souls being dipped in Hell then brought back up. This verse, however, in all likelihood describes the promised bodily resurrection from the dead.

Another passage quoted in support of the doctrine of limited suffering is Zechariah 13:9: "I will bring the one-third through the fire, will refine them as silver is refined, and test them as gold is tested. They will call on My name, and I will answer them. I will say, 'This is

My people'; and each one will say, 'The LORD is my God.'" However, verse 9 must be understood in light of verse 8, which says, "'It shall come to pass in all the land,' says the LORD, 'that two-thirds in it shall be cut off and die, but one-third shall be left in it.'" Proponents of this view don't believe that two-thirds of all people will *perish* in Hell, and that the remaining one-third, who *do* survive, will all have to endure hellfire.

Although the limited-suffering view is interesting, the scriptures used to support it are few, vague, and (as we've seen in the last example) actually contradictory.

FIGURATIVE, SYMBOLIC INTERPRETATIONS

Other Christians, who believe that never-ending torment in a lake of fire and burning sulfur is inconsistent with the fact that "God is love" (1 John 4:8), understand this imagery to be symbolic. Billy Graham, for example, said that he thought the fire was a burning thirst for God that can never be quenched. He added, "I think that hell. . .is separation from God forever." In other words, people who reject the truth do not go to Heaven, and then they later regret their decision for all eternity.

The Bible, however, warns that Hell is not simply an unpleasant but tolerable state of separation from God; instead, it is a place where—as Jesus said—soul and body are *destroyed* (Matthew 10:28). "You will make them as a fiery oven in the time of your anger; the LORD will swallow them up in His wrath, and fire will devour them" (Psalm 21:9 NASB). Evoking the image of this fiery fate, Jesus warned, "So it will be at the end of the age. The angels will come forth, separate the wicked from among the just, and cast them into the furnace of fire. There will be wailing and gnashing of teeth" (Matthew 13:49–50). Though perhaps it might be argued that "wailing and gnashing of teeth" are simply an expression of deep regret, in all probability they represent something more intense.

Whatever Hell is like, however long or short it lasts, whether it involves eternal conscious suffering or eventual annihilation, whether its suffering is intolerable or barely tolerable, the point is still the same: *People don't have to go there!* God has made a way for humanity to be saved and to live in Heaven forever—and that way is open to us if we accept Jesus' sacrifice as payment for our sins.

C. S. LEWIS AND PURGATORY

C. S. Lewis, the late Christian apologist, is often criticized for his statements in *Letters to Malcolm* where he affirms, "I believe in Purgatory,"[13] not as a hope for those who have rejected faith in Christ in this life, but as a place where Christians willingly choose to go before entering into the presence of God. He adds that "our souls demand Purgatory,"[14] and indicates that the process of purification involves suffering.

THE STATE OF PURGATORY

Purgatory, according to Catholic doctrine, is a temporary, intermediate state after death, in which those destined to receive salvation are purified in order that they may attain the holiness necessary to enter God's presence. Only those who die in a "state of grace" (relationship with God) go through Purgatory. Serious, *mortal sins* cannot be forgiven, but *venial* (forgivable) *sins* can. Such sins are "burned away" in Purgatory. Notwithstanding Dante's description of Purgatory in *The Divine Comedy*, officially Purgatory was seen as a purifying inner fire, not as a place.

Catholics and some Orthodox Christians believe in praying for souls in Purgatory. So did some ancient Jews. In 2 Maccabees 12:42–46, Judas Maccabee is said to have prayed for God to forgive the sins of fallen Jewish fighters: "They turned to prayer, beseeching that the sin which had been committed might be wholly blotted out. . . . Therefore [Judas] made atonement for the dead, that they might be delivered from their sin" (2 Maccabees 12:42, 45 RSV). Few Protestants, however, accept the book of 2 Maccabees as canonical, and thus find no scriptural basis for a belief in Purgatory.

The heavenly fire that Paul tells us will one day burn away all our worthless works (1 Corinthians 3:11–15) should not be construed as referring to Purgatory, as some theologians have suggested. Paul writes, "If anyone's work is burned, he will suffer loss; but he himself will be saved, yet so as through fire" (1 Corinthians 3:15). The writer of Hebrews states, "Our God is a consuming fire" (Hebrews 12:29 KJV), which implies that, most likely, entering the presence of the Lord, when we'll be required to give an account of our lives (Matthew 12:36; 2 Corinthians 5:10), involves passing through this fire.

We *will* experience a measure of suffering and sorrow when we

▶ *The Last Judgment* by Viktor Vasnetsov (1848–1926) shows what looks to be the idea of Purgatory. This doctrine purports there is an intermediate state after death where people are purified in order that they may attain the holiness necessary to enter God's presence.

realize how many opportunities or years we've wasted, and how many of our dead works will be consumed in God's holy fire—and we *will* emerge purified; but this is not a prolonged process. On two different occasions, John says that "God shall wipe away all tears from [our] eyes" in Heaven (Revelation 7:17; 21:4 KJV); and perhaps this is one reason we have tears (see chapter 7, "The Judgment Seat of Christ"). We are therefore advised to "abide in Him, so that when He appears, we may have confidence and not shrink away from Him in shame at His coming" (1 John 2:28 NASB).

CHRISTIAN UNIVERSALISM

Universalism is the belief that all people are saved and destined for Heaven, regardless of what religion they follow, what god they believe in, or even how wicked they are in this life. This is clearly wishful thinking. Jesus said, "I am the way, the truth, and the life. No one comes to the Father except through Me" (John 14:6). Christian universalism acknowledges that faith in Christ is essential, but also states that *everyone* will eventually believe in the Son of God and be saved, because God is merciful.

> **THE APPEAL OF UNIVERSALISM**
>
> The view that all people will be saved doesn't arise because a large number of scriptures compel us to believe it. The passages that support universalism are few and far between, and people generally arrive at this conclusion because they refuse to believe that God would allow anyone to suffer in Hell.

Christian Universalists often quote verses such as: "God our Savior . . .desires all men to be saved and to come to the knowledge of the truth" (1 Timothy 2:3–4), and "Your Father in heaven is not willing that any of these little ones should perish" (Matthew 18:14 NIV). According to this view, no one goes to Hell when they die; everyone is given another chance after death, and everyone accepts it. They encounter Jesus, "the true light that enlightens every man" (John 1:9 RSV); are overwhelmed with His love, acceptance, and forgiveness; choose life; and are saved.

As appealing as this doctrine is, it has major weaknesses in that it ignores scores of scriptures (including the words of Christ Himself) that describe people going to Hell. Mind you, some Christian Universalists believe that the wicked *will* suffer at least temporary pain of separation from God, just long enough to come to their senses, receive His grace, and *then* enter Heaven.

THOSE WHO NEVER HEARD THE GOSPEL

For those who believe that all unsaved people go to Hell, the question arises, "What about the millions upon millions of people down through the ages who never *heard* the Gospel and never had a *chance* to either accept or reject Jesus? Will they be eternally condemned as well?"

Many people say, "Yes, they will." This view is based, in part, on Paul's statement that *all* humanity is without excuse because God has supplied ample witness, even in His creation. "The wrath of God is being revealed from heaven against all the godlessness and wickedness of people. . . . For since the creation of the world God's invisible qualities—his eternal power and divine nature—have been clearly

▶ Giovanni Paolo Pannini's (1692–1765) painting *The Apostle Paul Preaching on the Ruins*. Paul was fulfilling Jesus' commission to go into the world and preach the Good News to everyone.

seen, being understood from what has been made, so that people are without excuse" (Romans 1:18, 20 NIV).

However, even those who believe in eternal, conscious torment trust that those who never heard the Gospel will be judged less harshly than those who heard and rejected it. Jesus said, "If anyone will not welcome you or listen to your words. . .it will be more bearable for Sodom and Gomorrah on the day of judgment than for that town" (Matthew 10:14–15 NIV; see also Matthew 11:20–24). It therefore seems that such people will be better able to *tolerate* or *endure* the punishment they receive.

Another scripture also brings out this principle: "That slave who knew his master's will and did not get ready or act in accord with his will, will receive many lashes, but the one who did not know it, and committed deeds worthy of a flogging, will receive but few" (Luke 12:47–48 NASB).

However, if God has made an exception for those who never hear the Gospel, and gives them an opportunity after death to hear the Gospel, we're not aware of it, because scripture is silent on the subject. Rather than wishfully stating, "*Surely* God will have mercy on them," we must obey Christ's great commission: "Go into all the world and preach the Good News to everyone" (Mark 16:15 NLT). Paul writes, "How then shall they call on him in whom they have not believed? and how shall they believe in him of whom they have not heard? and how shall they hear without a preacher? And how shall they preach, except they be sent?" (Romans 10:14–15 KJV). We must all bear witness to our faith, as well as praying for and supporting missionaries.

THE MARK OF THE BEAST AND DAMNATION

In Revelation, a mighty angel shouts, "If anyone worships the beast [the Antichrist] and his image, and receives a mark on his forehead or on his hand. . .he will be tormented with fire and brimstone in the presence of the holy angels and in the presence of the Lamb. And the smoke of their torment goes up forever and ever; they have no

William Blake's (1757–1827) painting *The Number of the Beast Is 666* graphically illustrates the evil associated with taking the mark of the beast, indicating rebellion against God.

rest day and night, those who worship the beast and his image, and whoever receives the mark of his name" (Revelation 14:9–11 NASB).

People will receive the mark on their right hand or forehead—a tangible seal of a fully informed decision—so it's very dangerous theology to teach that people can worship the Antichrist and receive his mark (to buy food and live) because "they can always repent and be delivered afterward." Receiving the mark of the beast appears to be an irreversible decision. But the question is, why? If simply a world ruler and his image were involved, those who worship him could wake up and repent. After all, multitudes of pagans in the early days of the church prayed to idols and worshipped the Roman emperors as gods; but when they turned to the truth, they were forgiven and saved.

Some think that worshipping the Antichrist and receiving his mark causes a person to be possessed by a demon—but demons can be driven out and their victims redeemed by the blood of the Lamb. Consider Mary Magdalene, out of whom Jesus drove seven demons (Luke 8:2). There must be something *more* that makes receiving the mark of the beast so final.

Although the mark of the beast will be widely advertised as a new, efficient means of financial transaction, no one will receive it ignorantly, thinking that it's merely an improved financial system. That's because the Antichrist's open hatred of God will *also* be widely known. "The beast. . .opened its mouth to blaspheme God, and to slander his name and his dwelling place and those who live in heaven. It was given power to wage war against God's holy people and to conquer them." Yet, despite the beast's raw hatred for God, "all inhabitants of the earth will worship the beast—all whose names have not been written in the Lamb's book of life" (Revelation 13:6, 8 NIV).

Jesus prophesied, "This gospel of the kingdom shall be preached in *all* the world. . .and *then* shall the end come" (Matthew 24:14 KJV, emphasis added). By the time the mark of the beast is ready to be implemented, the *entire world* will have heard a clear presentation of the Gospel and will have either received it or rejected it. People will have made their choice. Only *then* will the mark of the beast appear. And "if we sin willfully after we have received the knowledge of the truth, there no longer remains a sacrifice for sins, but a certain fearful expectation of judgment, and fiery indignation which will devour the adversaries" (Hebrews 10:26–27).

HOW CAN WE ENJOY HEAVEN?

Some people wonder how the redeemed can experience peace (let alone joy) in Heaven, knowing that billions of eternal souls are wailing and gnashing their teeth in Hell at that very moment. Many reason that the saved must be completely unaware of the suffering of those in Hell. They note that God declares, "I create new heavens and a new earth; and the former shall not be remembered or come to mind" (Isaiah 65:17). Others suggest that we'll remember those in Hell, but the *pain* of such knowledge will be absent. "You will surely forget your trouble, recalling it only as waters gone by" (Job 11:16 NIV). But this refers to our own *past* troubles—not the ongoing suffering of others.

This question mainly troubles those who believe in eternal, conscious torment in Hell. For those who believe in annihilation, it's not an issue. After a period of suffering for their sins, the condemned would be no more. However, what if, while perishing, they saw what the rich man saw when in Hades? What if his experience wasn't unique, but a *common* event?

"Being in torments in Hades, he lifted up his eyes and saw Abraham afar off, and Lazarus in his bosom" (Luke 16:23). What if the perishing pass into oblivion with the full knowledge that they *could have* had a wonderful, everlasting life in Paradise? What if they're given a prolonged look into Heaven and realize the full extent of the joy of the saved? They'd realize too late what a terrible mistake they'd made, choosing death and nonexistence instead of eternal life.

There are two instances in the Bible of God's wiping away tears from the eyes of the saved. The *first* is when the redeemed are

▶ After being bound for a thousand years in the Bottomless Plt, Satan will be cast into the Lake of Fire.

newly arrived in Heaven, *before* the final judgment of the unsaved (Revelation 7:17). From the immediate context (see Revelation 7:14–16), it's evident that the redeemed are being comforted over their own earthly sorrows, suffering, and personal failures.

But the *second* instance occurs immediately *after* the unsaved are cast into the lake of fire (Revelation 20:11–15). Then "'He will wipe every tear from their eyes. There will be no more death' or mourning or crying or pain, for the old order of things has passed away" (Revelation 21:4 NIV). From an annihilationist viewpoint, perhaps the saved will initially mourn those who were lost, but then will be comforted when there is "no more death. . .or pain" and the suffering of the unsaved has come to an end.

THE DEMONS' ETERNAL TORMENTS

Some people who believe in Christian universalism argue that for God to truly "reconcile *all things* to Himself. . .whether things on earth or things in heaven" (Colossians 1:20, emphasis added), He must eventually purge and restore even the devil and his demons.

Most Christians, however, believe that this is stretching things way too far—that regardless of whatever mercy God extends to people, Satan and his angels have given themselves over so completely to evil that they're incorrigible and irredeemable. Whatever punishment humans receive—whether eternal torment, limited suffering and release, or annihilation—the evil spirits will suffer eternally. After all, Jesus clearly stated that "the everlasting fire [was] prepared for the devil and his angels" (Matthew 25:41).

But before the demons are cast into the lake of fire, they will be consigned to the abyss (bottomless pit) for a thousand years. After the battle of Armageddon, John observes in Revelation, a mighty angel "seized. . .Satan, and bound him for a thousand years. He threw him into the Abyss, and locked and sealed it over him, to keep him from deceiving the nations anymore until the thousand years were ended" (Revelation 20:2–3 NIV). Although this verse refers only to Satan being bound there, we can be certain that his demons are *with* him, because the purpose of this confinement is "to keep him from deceiving the nations." If only the devil were locked away, but not his hosts, they'd continue deceiving people. But that doesn't happen.

The demons will be locked up in the abyss, the place they so greatly feared, and will be tormented there. Then, at the end of the millennium, they'll go out to deceive the nations one last time. "Then the devil, who had deceived them, was thrown into the fiery lake of burning sulfur, joining the beast and the false prophet. There they will be tormented day and night forever and ever" (Revelation 20:10 NLT). Again, the passage in Revelation only mentions Satan being cast into Gehenna, but his demons are cast in with him. In Matthew 25:41, Jesus Himself says that this will be the case.

These torments have not yet begun. When Jesus confronts the

▶ Satan, as drawn by Gustave Doré (1832–1883) in John Milton's *Paradise Lost*; this shows Satan in anguish over being cast out of Heaven.

demon-possessed man in Matthew 8, the demons cry out, "What have we to do with You, Jesus, You Son of God? Have You come here to torment us *before the time*?" (Matthew 8:29, emphasis added). No, they're not in Hell yet, but "the Lord. . .sees that [the wicked one's] day is coming" (Psalm 37:13).

HELL AS "OUTER DARKNESS"

It's commonly believed that Gehenna, the lake of fire, is in the center of the earth. The reasoning goes like this: Since Hades is itself under the earth, and there's evidence that the "lowest hell" is at the bottom of the bottomless pit, far below Hades, that would put the lake of fire a great depth in the earth—in or near the earth's center. The fact that scientists tell us that our planet's iron core is as hot as the surface of the sun only seems to confirm this.

However, we read in Isaiah, "'All mankind will come and bow down before me,' says the LORD. 'And they will go out and look on the dead bodies of those who rebelled against me; the worms that eat them will not die, the fire that burns them will not be quenched" (Isaiah 66:23–24 NIV). It appears, from a casual reading at least, that after worshipping God in the New Jerusalem, the saved will step outside the gates and see the burning bodies of the wicked right there—just as, in Bible times, Jerusalem's garbage dump (the Valley of Hinnom) was just outside the Dung Gate, south of the city.

> **PARADISE LOST**
>
> In *Paradise Lost*, John Milton mentions the outer darkness when he describes Satan and his demons cast into "a Dungeon horrible, on all sides round as one great Furnace flam'd, yet from those flames no light, but rather darkness visible serv'd onely to discover sights of woe, regions of sorrow, doleful shades, where peace and rest can never dwell, hope never comes."[15]

This would seem to locate Hell just outside the city walls, on the *surface* of the otherwise paradisiacal New Earth. Furthermore, John tells us that the wicked "will be tormented with fire and brimstone in the presence of the holy angels and in the presence of the Lamb" (Revelation 14:10 NASB). Because the Lamb (Jesus) and the angels dwell in the New Jerusalem, does being punished *in their presence* imply physical proximity? Not necessarily. Remember that when the rich man was in Hades, "he lifted up his eyes and saw Abraham afar off" (Luke 16:23). For his part, Abraham was able to look *down* into Hades, even though it was "afar off."

So, although the lake of fire is somewhere outside the heavenly city, it's in an unspecified location and an unspecified distance away. However, it doesn't necessarily have to be located in the center of the earth. Remember that Gehenna isn't a physical location; it's a spiritual place, and its flames are spiritual—completely unrelated to the heat of the earth's core. The point is this: Wherever Hell is situated, even if it's far beneath the earth's surface, Jesus and the angels will be able to look upon it as if it was right in their presence. And believers will also be able to "go out" to look upon Gehenna and consider the fate of the rebels.

Jesus referred to Hell as "outer darkness," saying, "The sons of the kingdom will be cast out into the outer darkness; in that place there will be weeping and gnashing of teeth" (Matthew 8:12 NASB; see also

▶ Thomas Eakins's (1844–1916) painting of the crucifixion; Jesus' blood shed on the cross cleanses all who believe in Him from sin.

Matthew 22:13; 25:30).

Jude describes Gehenna as being in "the blackness of darkness forever" (Jude 1:13). Despite the flames, it's an extremely dark place. Apparently, the fires of Hell don't give off visible light.

AVOIDING HELL

You may have a hopeful doctrine of Hell, staking your future on the prospect of eventually being released after relatively minor suffering or merely a time of sincere regret; but don't count on it. You may disbelieve in Hell entirely and insist that God is too loving to allow anyone to suffer in the afterlife, that everyone goes to Heaven. But John tells us that the glorious promise of eternal life has a warning attached: "Whoever believes in the Son has eternal life, but whoever rejects the Son will not see life, for God's wrath remains on them" (John 3:36 NIV).

God has provided a way for you to be saved from Hell, and it's found in the person of Jesus Christ. It doesn't matter what kind of life you've lived, because "the blood of Jesus Christ His Son cleanses us from *all* sin" (1 John 1:7, emphasis added). "Though your sins are as scarlet, they will be as white as snow; though they are red like crimson, they will be like wool" (Isaiah 1:18 NASB).

If you've never surrendered your life to God, you can do so right now. Receive Jesus into your heart by sincerely repeating this prayer: "Dear God, I acknowledge that I'm a sinner. I've lived selfishly, I've lied, and I've hurt others. I know that I can't save myself, so I thank You that Your Son died on the cross for my sins. I ask You to send Your Holy Spirit into my heart. I receive Jesus now as my Lord and Savior. Dear God, forgive my sins and give me eternal life. You promised that "whoever calls on the name of the Lord shall be saved," so I thank You for hearing me and answering this prayer. Help me now to live for You by the power of Your Spirit. In Jesus' name, I pray. Amen."

If you prayed these words sincerely and in faith, you're now saved and are no longer destined for Hell. Your name is written in the Book of Life in Heaven. Rejoice!

7 | NEW BODIES AND A NEW EARTH

OUR RESURRECTION BODIES

When we as Christians die, our spirit separates from our body and goes directly to Heaven. As long as we exist in that state, we're a spirit without a body. But God doesn't intend for us to remain that way forever. Just as He resurrected Jesus from the dead, He will raise up our physical bodies as well. "If the Spirit of Him who raised Jesus from the dead dwells in you, He who raised Christ from the dead will also give life to your mortal bodies through His Spirit who dwells in you" (Romans 8:11). "The Lord Jesus Christ. . .will transform our lowly bodies so that they will be like his glorious body" (Philippians 3:20–21 NIV).

Some people mistakenly believe we receive our resurrection bodies the instant we go to Heaven, but this isn't the case. The resurrection from the dead happens on the day of Christ's second coming, which is still a future event. Those who have died will return with Christ at that time, and their bodies will rise as glorified supernatural bodies and reunite with their spirits. Then those of us who are physically alive at that time will be transformed and caught up into the air to join Jesus and the other saints.

"The Lord himself shall descend from heaven with a shout, with the voice of the archangel, and with the trump of God: and the dead in Christ shall rise first: Then we which are alive and remain shall be caught up together with them in the clouds, to meet the Lord in the air" (1 Thessalonians 4:16–17 KJV). Paul writes, "We will all be changed, in a moment, in the twinkling of an eye, at the last trumpet; for the trumpet will sound, and the dead will be raised imperishable, and we will be changed" (1 Corinthians 15:51–52 NASB).

Jesus said, "If your right eye causes you to sin, pluck it out and cast it from you; for it is more profitable for you that one of your members perish, than for your whole body to be cast into hell" (Matthew 5:29). He said to do the same with your right hand. Some people fear that Jesus was advising self-mutilation, and envision individuals in Heaven with missing eyes and hands—just grateful to have escaped Hell. First, Jesus was speaking in hyperbole; and even if we were to do such a thing, our resurrected bodies would be complete.

Although our natural, physical bodies are now perishable and weak, they will become glorious, powerful, eternal bodies. "So will it be with the resurrection of the dead. The body that is sown is

▶ A stained glass window titled *Resurrection of the Dead*, by an unknown artist, showing an angel blowing a trumpet; it will be the trumpet call of God that will cause the dead in Christ to rise first.

perishable, it is raised imperishable; it is sown in dishonor, it is raised in glory; it is sown in weakness, it is raised in power; it is sown a natural body, it is raised a spiritual body" (1 Corinthians 15:42–44 NIV).

In Heaven, the blind will see, the deaf will hear, those presently bound to wheelchairs will leap for joy, the lepers will glow with radiant health, and the mentally challenged will engage in lively intellectual discussions. Those incapacitated by the ravages of old age will enjoy eternal youth, and those presently sick and weak "shall run, and not be weary; and they shall walk, and not faint" (Isaiah 40:31 KJV).

But though our bodies will instantly be made *immortal* at the resurrection, it seems that they won't receive the full measure of glory due them until we're individually rewarded by Christ. As we'll see, this may happen immediately following the Rapture.

WHEN THE MORTAL BECOMES IMMORTAL

Paul tells us, "Now I say this, brethren, that flesh and blood cannot inherit the kingdom of God; nor does the perishable inherit the imperishable. Behold. . .the dead will be raised imperishable, and we will be changed. For this perishable must put on the imperishable, and this mortal must put on immortality. But when this perishable will have put on the imperishable, and this mortal will have put on immortality, then will come about the saying that is written, 'Death is swallowed up in victory'" (1 Corinthians 15:50–55 NASB).

Though the Jehovah's Witnesses teach that Jesus wasn't resurrected in the same earthly body, but was given a new "spiritual" body, we can be certain that God will not dispose of our mortal bodies. Paul states clearly in 1 Corinthians 15:13–17 that if we don't believe that Jesus resurrected in His same physical body, our faith is useless and we're still in our sins.

God won't get rid of our mortal, physical bodies. Rather, He will *add* extra, spiritual, immortal dimensions to them. "For we who are in this tent [body] groan, being burdened, not because we want to be *un*clothed, but *further* clothed, that mortality may be swallowed up

▶ The water of life may flow through our glorified eternal bodies.

by life" (2 Corinthians 5:4, emphasis added).

Paul said that "flesh and blood cannot inherit the kingdom of God" (1 Corinthians 15:50). In our present physical bodies, "the life of the flesh is in the blood" (Leviticus 17:11). But when Jesus appeared in His resurrection body, He told His disciples, "Behold My hands and My feet, that it is I Myself. Handle Me and see, for a spirit does not have *flesh and bones* as you see I have" (Luke 24:39, emphasis added). Jesus didn't say he had "flesh and blood," but "flesh and bones." His new immortal body no longer had blood but had been transformed. His body now lived by the power of the Spirit. And our eternal bodies shall be the same.

We may ask, "What will fill our veins then, if not blood? What will our hearts pump?" Though the Bible doesn't specifically address this point, we can ask a question in return: "What if, instead of blood flowing through our veins, the *water of life* flows through us, and gives our bodies life?" Jesus stated, "But those who drink the water I give will never be thirsty again. It becomes a fresh, bubbling spring within them, giving them eternal life" (John 4:14 NLT). Plasma, the liquid that carries our blood cells, is 90 percent water. This water may very well be replaced by the water of life. Also, the average adult human body is 55 percent water. Will our eternal bodies be half natural water? Not likely. But they might be 55 percent *water of life*. Now, *there's* a thought to get excited about!

THE JUDGMENT SEAT OF CHRIST

Believers must one day appear before the Judgment Seat of Christ to give an account of their lives—both their words and their deeds. (This judgment of the saved occurs one thousand years before the Great White Throne judgment of the unsaved.) Jesus warned, "I say to you that for every idle word men may speak, they will give account of it in the day of judgment" (Matthew 12:36), and Paul tells us, "Remember, we will all stand before the judgment seat of God. . . . Yes, each of us will give a personal account to God" (Romans 14:10, 12 NLT).

We will not only be required to give an *account* of how we lived our lives on this earth, but we'll then be rewarded in proportion to the good we have done, or suffer loss for the wrong we have done, or the good we failed to do. "For we must all appear before the judgment seat of Christ, so that each of us may receive what is due us for the things done while in the body, whether good or bad" (2 Corinthians 5:10 NIV).

▶ A statue of Lady Justice, representing fairness. At the Judgment Seat of Christ, those who have trusted Jesus as their Savior will receive loving and fair judgment and will be granted their rewards.

This judgment is not to determine whether we'll go to Heaven or to Hell. Our eternal destination was decided the day we trusted Christ to save us. We will enter Heaven because our names are already written in the Lamb's Book of Life. Remember, this judgment is *not* the same as the judgment of the unsaved that happens at the end of the Millennium (Revelation 20:11–15), when God will determine the punishment of the unsaved. The Judgment Seat of Christ is where we, the redeemed, will appear before Him who saved us. This judgment will determine *how much* we're rewarded. It will be a very loving and fair judgment—but it will be thorough. As Paul writes: "For no other foundation can anyone lay than that which is laid, which is Jesus Christ. Now if anyone builds on this foundation with gold, silver, precious stones, wood, hay, straw, each one's work will become clear; for the Day will declare it, because it will be revealed by fire; and the fire will test each one's work, of what sort it is. If anyone's work which he has built on it endures, he will receive a reward. If anyone's work is burned, he will suffer loss; but he himself will be saved, yet so as through fire" (1 Corinthians 3:11–15).

> **THE BEMA**
>
> The Greek word translated as "judgment seat" is *bema*. In the ancient Greek Olympic Games, the bema was *not* a tribunal that judged someone guilty or innocent and decided punishments. Rather, it was where the judges sat and awarded crowns (laurel wreaths) to the winners of various events. Those who appeared before the bema were those who had already been recognized as winning the race.

Even if we live futile lives, doing little for Christ, our salvation remains secure. But what a terrible, needless loss to see years of selfish ambition and self-seeking works burned away. Nevertheless, we are forgiven and remain in Christ's love.

Some people worry that these sessions will be open to all Heaven, that multitudes will witness a public airing of our secret sins and failings, to our utter embarrassment. They draw that conclusion from the passage where Jesus says, "There is nothing covered that will not be revealed, nor hidden that will not be known. Therefore whatever you have spoken in the dark will be heard in the light, and what you have spoken in the ear in inner rooms will be proclaimed on the housetops" (Luke 12:2–3).

But Jesus was referring to the hypocrisy of the Pharisees, so this passage is most likely referring to the very public trials of the unsaved at the Great White Throne judgment (see chapter 6), not to our personal appearances before Christ, which are apparently private.

WHEN WILL WE APPEAR BEFORE THE JUDGMENT SEAT?

Many Christians imagine that they will appear before the Judgment Seat of Christ (to give an account of their lives) shortly after death, sometime soon after arriving in Heaven. The scripture used to back this view is Hebrews 9:27, which says, "It is appointed for men to die once, but after this the judgment." However, it should be pointed out that this verse merely indicates that judgment comes after death. How *long* after is not stipulated.

Probably the most compelling reason for believing that we will face the Judgment Seat of Christ shortly after death is that this view is corroborated by the "life review" that many people report after a near-death experience (NDE). People who have nearly died, or who died and were brought back to life, commonly report that they encountered a "being of light" and experienced an almost-instantaneous review of their entire lives in great detail. This "life review" is typically loving and nonjudgmental, and thus has a positive influence on a person's behavior and choices from then on. Some Christians theorize that this corresponds to our appearance before Christ.

However, we should be cautious about accepting descriptions of NDEs as authoritative in determining Christian

> **DIFFERENT KINDS OF REWARDS**
> Though the body of every believer will be made immortal in the resurrection, the exact nature of the rewards at the Judgment Seat of Christ seem to include: (a) the beauty and power of our heavenly body; (b) the amount of God's glory and light that we radiate; (c) the glory of the crowns we receive; (d) our proximity to God; (e) the privileges and responsibilities we're given; and (f) the beauty and grandeur of our heavenly mansions.

doctrine. Though many elements of NDEs seem to confirm scriptural teaching, other elements frequently contradict it. It is commonly noted that people's cultural backgrounds often heavily influence what they experience, leading to the conclusion that NDEs are, after all, subjective experiences. Also, people sometimes experience "life reviews" merely as a result of threatening circumstances or stress-filled times when they aren't even in danger of dying.

When we look to scripture to inform us about the timing of the Judgment Seat of Christ, the evidence points to a time shortly after the rapture and resurrection of all the saints—which is still a future event. Luke 14:13–14, for example, states clearly that we will be rewarded at the resurrection. In 2 Timothy 4:8, Paul speaks of "the crown of righteousness, which the Lord, the righteous Judge, will give to me on that Day." What is "that Day"? Paul adds that Jesus will judge and award us *after* His second coming. "Therefore judge nothing before the appointed time; wait *until the Lord comes*. He will. . .expose the motives of the heart. *At that time* each will receive their praise from God" (1 Corinthians 4:5 NIV, emphasis added).

We've already looked at several of these rewards in chapter 4. Now let's look at how a life spent serving God affects us personally.

FACES GLOWING LIKE THE SUN

When our bodies are transformed at the resurrection, they'll be made immortal. Not long afterward, each of us will appear before Christ to be rewarded. To the extent that we have borne the image of the Son of God in our lives, we'll radiate His glory. As much as we have striven to reflect Christ in this life, we'll emanate His glory in the next. David prayed, "And let the beauty of the LORD our God be upon us" (Psalm 90:17). So what will we look like?

When Jesus stood on a mountain with Peter, James, and John, His "appearance was transformed so that his face shone like the sun, and his clothes became as white as light" (Matthew 17:2 NLT). Years later, when the apostle John saw Jesus in Heaven in His glorified, resurrected body, he described Him this way: "The hair on his head was white like

▶ An image of the transfiguration of the Lord, showing Jesus' face glowing; since we will be like Him, with glorified bodies, God's Spirit may cause us to glow as we reflect His glory as well.

wool, as white as snow, and his eyes were like blazing fire. His feet were like bronze glowing in a furnace, and his voice was like the sound of rushing waters. . . . His face was like the sun shining in all its brilliance" (Revelation 1:14–16 NIV).

John also tells us, "We know that when Christ appears, we shall be like him, for we shall see him as he is" (1 John 3:2 NIV). The Lord's face shone like the sun, and so will ours—to a lesser degree, of course. Jesus Himself, said, "Then shall the righteous shine forth as the sun in the kingdom of their Father" (Matthew 13:43 KJV).

After spending forty days and nights in the presence of God, the skin of Moses' face glowed with the glory of the Lord (Exodus 34:28–30). Many Christians believe that this same thing will happen to us when we get our resurrection bodies. We can be full of the Holy Spirit now, even here on earth in our physical bodies (Acts 6:15), but in Heaven, God's Spirit within us will cause us to literally glow. Moses and Elijah "appeared in glorious splendor" (Luke 9:30 NIV), and so will we, in direct proportion to our relationship with God.

POWERS LIKE ANGELS

Jesus said, "At the resurrection people will neither marry nor be given in marriage; they will be like the angels in heaven" (Matthew 22:30 NIV). By the strictest interpretation, Jesus was saying only that we will be "like the angels" in that we won't marry. But we may be like the angels in *other* ways as well. Psalm 8:4–5 says, "What is man that You are mindful of him. . . . For You have made him a little lower than the angels." But one day, like the angels, we will have glorious, eternal bodies. So will we have *more* powers than we now have?

When crowds in Sodom mobbed Lot's house, two angels struck them blind (Genesis 19:1–11). When Daniel was thrown in the lions' den, angels prevented the lions from attacking him (Daniel 6:16–22). When the apostles were thrown in prison, an angel miraculously opened the prison doors (Acts 5:17–25). Another angel made chains snap open and caused a locked iron gate to swing open without even touching it (Acts 12:5–11). The Angel of God caused fire to rise out

▶ *The Liberation of Saint Peter* by Bartlome Esteban Murillo (1617–1682). When we have our glorified bodies, we may have God's power to perform miracles, as did the angels who opened prison doors and caused chains to snap.

of a rock and consume an offering (Judges 6:20–21).

When we have our new bodies, will we still be required to pray to God for every miracle, or will we be trusted with a measure of angelic power? If we're walking into a house with our arms full, can we simply nod at a door and cause it to open? Will we be able to will a campfire to ignite? This isn't referring to raising a staff and causing the Red Sea to part, or striking an entire crowd blind like the angels did, but smaller miracles. The Bible isn't clear, but it's reasonable to conclude that if we have new eternal bodies glowing with the presence of God's Spirit, we'll also have access to God's power to perform at least small, necessary miracles. Exactly what kind of miracles remains to be seen, however.

OUTSTANDING HEAVENLY POWERS

Some people take the notion of enhanced abilities quite a bit further, thinking that when we have our new bodies, we'll have the power to call things into existence at will. Just as God "calls into being things that were not" (Romans 4:17 NIV), it's argued that, as exalted sons and daughters of God, we, too, will have such powers. Well. . .*God* is certainly able to do outstanding miracles of resurrection and regeneration, but *we* may have to continue to depend on Him to perform such miracles.

Some men in the Bible were able to perform outstanding miracles even during their physical lifetimes. Moses, Elijah, and Elisha come to mind. Moses was able to morph a common shepherd's staff into an Egyptian cobra by the power of God (Exodus 4:2–4). Perhaps he will have the same faith and gifts in Heaven— or even more pronounced. But remember, Moses didn't do such miracles by his own will or his own power, and certainly not for his convenience or amusement. These miracles happened because *God* willed them to.

▶ God's power allowed Moses to turn his common staff into a cobra in front of Pharaoh, illustrated here in *Moses and Aaron before Pharaoh* by Benjamin West (1738–1820).

Also, not everyone has the same gifts of God's Spirit, and our glorified resurrection bodies won't all be equal. Every star in the universe is different, and we'll likewise have varying degrees of glory and power. Speaking about our resurrection bodies, Paul said, "There is one glory of the sun, another glory of the moon, and another glory of the stars; for one star differs from another star in glory" (1 Corinthians 15:41).

> **SCI-FI OR HEAVENLY REALITY?**
> Some people think that in Heaven we'll be able to simply make things appear—like speaking to a *Star Trek* replicator (food synthesizer) and asking for our favorite Vulcan dessert to materialize. These kinds of miracles are God's department, however.

Perhaps this is part of our eternal reward. The closer we are to God now, the more time we spend in His presence, the more glory and power will be imparted to us. Of course, our heavenly rewards won't just be determined by time we spent in prayer, but by how we lived after we rose from our knees. God gives His Spirit to those who *obey* Him (Acts 5:32). So although there will be snakes on the New Earth (Isaiah 65:25), don't necessarily expect to be able to snap your fingers and turn them into walking sticks.

THE MARRIAGE SUPPER OF THE LAMB

There will be a great feast in Heaven after we've all arrived there. This feast is called the marriage supper of the Lamb. All genuine Christians will be present at this gathering, and we'll be truly blessed to be there. "Blessed are they which are called unto the marriage supper of the Lamb" (Revelation 19:9 KJV).

The church, the entire body of believers worldwide, is the bride of Christ. Right now we're betrothed to Christ—engaged to be married. Paul writes, "For I have betrothed you to one husband, that I may present you as a chaste virgin to Christ" (2 Corinthians 11:2). One day, the wedding will happen in Heaven. "'Let us be glad and rejoice and give Him glory, for the marriage of the Lamb has come, and His wife has made herself ready.' And to her it was granted to be arrayed in fine linen, clean and bright" (Revelation 19:7–8).

That this marriage is symbolic of spiritual union is obvious. In the same book, John also describes the celestial city as the bride of Christ. "Then I, John, saw the holy city, New Jerusalem, coming down out of heaven from God, prepared as a bride adorned for her husband" (Revelation 21:2). "Then one of the seven angels. . .came and said to me, 'Come with me! I will show you the bride, the wife of the Lamb.' So he. . .showed me the holy city, Jerusalem, descending out of heaven from God" (Revelation 21:9–10 NLT).

▶ A picture of a large banquet table, ready for guests to arrive; Jesus, too, is preparing a feast to bless those who trust Him.

God compares us to these eternal, heavenly abodes—His city, His temple—because just as He dwells in these places, so He dwells in our hearts. But our marriage to the Son of God will nevertheless be a joyous, incomparable event and will set the stage for our eternal happiness and rapturous joy in Heaven and on the heavenly New Earth forever.

A GREAT WORLDWIDE EARTHQUAKE

Meanwhile, *before* the earth is transformed into a paradise where we'll live forever, it will go through some cataclysmic changes. When the wrath of God is poured out in the end time, numerous plagues and famines will strike the earth, but none of these comes close to the utter devastation of the final bowl of wrath: "Then the seventh angel poured out his bowl. . .and there was a great earthquake, such a mighty and great earthquake as had not occurred since men

▶ The final bowl of wrath spoken of in the book of Revelation will include devastating earthquakes, more powerful than man has ever experienced.

were on the earth. Now the great city was divided into three parts, and the cities of the nations fell. . . . Then every island fled away, and the mountains were not found. And great hail from heaven fell upon men, each hailstone about the weight of a talent [75 pounds]" (Revelation 16:17–20). Imagine an earthquake so severe that entire mountain ranges are displaced, islands crumble and sink under the waves, and every one of man's cities around the globe is reduced to heaps of rubble. This will truly be the end of civilization as we know it.

Even the city of Jerusalem will not be spared. When Christ returns, "the Mount of Olives will split apart, making a wide valley running from east to west. Half the mountain will move toward the north and half toward the south" (Zechariah 14:4 NLT). Jerusalem, which is directly west of the Mount of Olives, will be split in two and shaken to its foundations. The Wailing Wall will crumble. Everything about Jerusalem that endeared it to people will collapse.

Surprisingly, untold millions of people (perhaps those in remote regions who never received the mark of the beast) will survive the cataclysm, but the entire planet will be in ruins and unrecognizable.

HAILSTONES FROM HEAVEN

With this major disruption of the earth's tectonic plates also comes unprecedented volcanic activity, resulting in seventy-five-pound blocks of burning pumice falling like hail on the world (Revelation 16:21). Either that, or the largest meteor shower in history engulfs the world.

It's small wonder that at the *end* of the Millennium, a thousand years after this, God will create a New Heaven and a New Earth.

THE KINGDOM OF CHRIST

But first, God will institute the reign of Christ on earth. Jesus will rule over the natural, flesh-and-blood nations of the earth, over the people who have not received the mark of the beast and who managed to survive the wrath of God. The Bible says, however, that "all inhabitants of the earth will worship the beast—all whose names have not been written in the Lamb's book of life, the Lamb who was

▶ The kingdom of Christ will be marked by world peace, or *God's shalom*, which means "completion." Jesus will rule this kingdom with justice and righteousness.

slain from the creation of the world" (Revelation 13:8 NIV). Does this mean that all the unsaved of the world will receive the mark of the beast? If that were true, then no one would survive into the Millennium and submit to Christ's rule.

Then who are these people over whom Christ rules in the Millennium, whose descendants later rebel and attack Jerusalem (Revelation 20:7–9)? In the New International Version, the translators' note to Revelation 13:8 says that it can also be translated as follows: "All inhabitants of the earth will worship the beast—all whose names have not been written from the creation of the world in the book of life belonging to the Lamb who was slain." These people hadn't made a decision for Christ before the Rapture, or they would've been taken up; but apparently they received Him afterward, because their names *were* written in the Book of Life. God knew that they would eventually choose Him. But multitudes of their descendants after them *won't* choose Christ and will later rebel.

> **THE MILLENNIUM**
> The thousand-year reign of Christ on earth is called the Millennium, from the Greek words *mille* (thousand) and *ennium* (years).

At first, when the Millennium begins, there will be a tremendous amount of reconstruction to do. The entire planet will have been destroyed—a combination of man's pollution and wars, and God's judgment on the wicked. After some time, however, the earth will become a paradise, despite the rubble and debris.

The still-mortal inhabitants of the earth will marry and repopulate the world, live in their own nations, speak their own languages, and follow many of their own customs. However, they all will have to acknowledge the rule of Christ. The Son of God will rule visibly, in person, over the entire world, and we will serve as His vice-regents, governing nations, provinces, districts, and cities. "I saw thrones, and they sat on them, and judgment was committed to them. . . . And they lived and reigned with Christ for a thousand years" (Revelation 20:4).

There will be world peace under the just rule of Christ and His saints. "And he shall judge among the nations, and shall rebuke many people: and they shall beat their swords into plowshares, and their spears into pruninghooks: nation shall not lift up sword against nation, neither shall they learn war any more" (Isaiah 2:4 KJV). But as the centuries roll on, their descendants will become discontent with Christ's firm rule and will rebel. "Though the wicked is shown favor, he does not learn righteousness; he deals unjustly in the land of uprightness, and does not perceive the majesty of the LORD" (Isaiah 26:10 NASB).

REMAKING HEAVEN AND EARTH

John describes how, at the end of the Millennium, Satan will be released from prison, deceive the nations, and gather them for war. But just as they surround Jerusalem and are about to overwhelm it, "fire [will come] down from heaven and devou[r] them" (Revelation 20:9 NASB). This fire will be global in scope and its heat will be intense. It will dissolve the entire earth and vaporize its oceans and atmosphere: "The day of the Lord will come. . .in the which the heavens shall pass away with a great noise, and the elements shall melt with fervent heat, the earth also and the works that are therein shall be burned up" (2 Peter 3:10 KJV).

As a result, John writes, "I saw a new heaven and a new earth, for the old heaven and the old earth had disappeared. And the sea was also gone" (Revelation 21:1 NLT). This is in fulfillment of an ancient prophecy in which God declares, "Behold, I create new heavens and a new earth; and the former shall not be remembered or come to mind" (Isaiah 65:17). God also states that the new creation will last forever, saying that "the new heavens and the new earth which I make will endure before Me" (Isaiah 66:22 NASB). This tells us that the physical matter of this world will take on eternal qualities.

Some people think that when scripture says the old heavens disappear and God creates new heavens, it means He will totally dissolve and then re-create the entire known universe. This is unlikely. Our own Milky Way galaxy is immense, and it is only one of some 170,000,000,000 galaxies that God created. There's no reason to start all over again with the entire universe. There's not even any need to change our galaxy. The only heavenly body that needs to be changed is planet Earth—and that's only because the eternal city of God will rest on it.

The sun will *also* need to be made eternal because God intended that it exist in unending partnership with the earth. Otherwise, scientists say that if things continue at the present rate, our sun will

▶ A view of planet Earth, the moon, and the sun. One day, Jesus will create a new Heaven and Earth, when physical material will also have spiritual characteristics.

eventually expand in size to a red giant so that in a billion years, it will evaporate Earth's oceans and burn up our atmosphere; by about five billion years, the sun will expand out beyond the orbit of Venus, and the entire planet Earth will be vaporized. So God will have to stabilize our sun and continually replenish its fuel so that it can endure indefinitely.

Some people theorize that our sun and moon will be removed, because scripture says, "The city does not need the sun or the moon to shine on it, for the glory of God gives it light, and the Lamb is its lamp" (Revelation 21:23 NIV). No, the *city itself* won't need the sun or moon to shine on it, but the *rest* of Earth's surface—especially the opposite side of the globe away from the city's glow—will con-

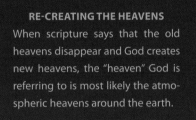

RE-CREATING THE HEAVENS
When scripture says that the old heavens disappear and God creates new heavens, the "heaven" God is referring to is most likely the atmospheric heavens around the earth.

tinue to need sunlight. Also, the Bible states that humanity will fear God "as long as the sun and moon endure, throughout all generations" (Psalm 72:5). If the sun and moon no longer exist, that would imply that God's people would then cease worshipping and revering Him. That simply isn't about to happen.

JESUS AND THE NEW CREATION

At the beginning of time, God created the entire physical universe through His Son. "All things were made through Him, and without Him nothing was made that was made" (John 1:3). Jesus is the One "through whom also He made the worlds" (Hebrews 1:2). Therefore, when God the Father melts the old earth and transforms it into a new world, Jesus will also be involved, exerting His creative power.

The old world was badly polluted by mankind, and all lands and islands and mountains will have become heaps of rubble in the great earthquake. But just as God will resurrect our mortal, earthly bodies and they will recognizably be us—only much better and eternal—so He will also restore the earth to its original state. The Mount of

This beautiful image of Tuscany, Italy, which features a rural sunset landscape, cypress trees, a green field, sunlight, and clouds, is only a shadow of what God has planned for the New Earth.

Olives, which was split in two, will be restored, and the ancient city of Jerusalem that crumbled in the massive earthquake will be rebuilt.

Many things will be different, however. The Bible says that "there was no more sea" (Revelation 21:1 KJV) on the New Earth. Many Christians believe that the oceans that now cover three-quarters of the earth's surface will no longer exist. One view is that there will be so many redeemed people that the former continents won't be large enough for all of them. So when God remakes the surface of the earth, there will be mountains and plenty of rolling hills, and the planet will be dotted with rivers and lakes, including large bodies of water—but no more vast oceans.

As for the climate of the New Earth, many people envision a balmy, temperate environment from pole to pole with the polar ice caps gone, no more desolate deserts, and the entire planet like the Garden of Eden. This is quite possible. After all, God is the God of all creation, and Earth is His special treasure. So He will spare no trouble in making it the most wonderful paradise in the entire universe. The New Earth will continue to experience changing seasons and variations in weather, however, from summer rains to snowfall in winter in the mountains and higher latitudes. All these things are good, and there's no need to discontinue them.

THE NEW JERUSALEM ON EARTH

Right now, the abode of God, the New Jerusalem, is in the spiritual dimension somewhere above the earth. Paul calls it "the Jerusalem above" (Galatians 4:26). When our entire world has been renewed and transformed into a paradise, God's city will emerge from the heavenly dimension and descend. "'Sing and rejoice, O daughter of Zion! For behold, I am coming and I will dwell in your midst,' says the Lord" (Zechariah 2:10). "I saw the Holy City, the new Jerusalem, coming down out of heaven. . .'God's dwelling place is now among the people, and he will dwell with them'" (Revelation 21:2–3 NIV).

The reason that the New Jerusalem doesn't descend now is that not only is our present world inhabited by unregenerated people but also the planet itself is only physical, a weak shadow of what it needs to be. God's city is made out of eternal materials, but the earth is temporal. God will therefore remake the planet out of eternal materials. Only then will it be fit for God's city. In that day, it will truly be Heaven on earth.

PLANTS AND ANIMALS OF PARADISE

The New Earth will be filled with a profusion of plant life—from dazzlingly beautiful meadows of flowers, to awe-inspiring redwoods towering along misty coasts, to tropical rain forests dripping with moisture, to bamboo groves creaking in the breeze. In the midst of all

▶ A photograph of four horses. In Heaven, there will be numerous herds of horses—some that are ordinary and some that will fly.

this vegetation will be millions of animals. After all, we'll enjoy seeing butterflies fluttering among blossoming cherry trees, peacocks displaying their plumage amid banks of flowers, and deer gracefully darting across sun-dappled lawns. God created both flora *and* fauna in His original Earth, and His New Earth will be even more inspiring and glorious.

The Bible tells us that there will be animals such as wolves, sheep, cattle, bears, leopards, cobras, etc., when Jesus rules the earth (Isaiah 11:1–9). This is commonly thought to be during the Millennium; but at the *end* of the Millennium, God will dissolve the old world. So will all these animals be gone forever? No, there will be animals on the New Earth as well. God told the prophet Isaiah: "Look! I am creating new heavens and a new earth. . . . The wolf and the lamb will feed together. The lion will eat hay like a cow. But the snakes will eat dust" (Isaiah 65:17, 25 NLT).

Imagine! Packs of timber wolves will run through dark forests and moonlit glades in Paradise. Prides of lions will loll in the shade of acacias and baobabs in wide savannas. Pandas will munch bamboo shoots on fog-shrouded mountains. Playful bottlenose dolphins and singing blue whales will surge through watery depths. Magnificent jaguars may even roam freely down the golden streets of God's city. Why not? After all, "they shall not hurt nor destroy in all my holy mountain, saith the LORD" (Isaiah 65:25 KJV).

Furthermore, there will be vast herds of white horses in Heaven (Revelation 19:11, 14). However, these horses aren't ordinary horses; they will be able to fly through the air. This doesn't mean there won't be ordinary horses in Heaven. There will. But they will exist side by side with supernatural horses.

Many people also believe that their beloved pets go to Heaven when they die. This view seems to be particularly prevalent among dog owners. Dogs aren't specifically mentioned in Paradise, but we can safely assume that if even wolves are there, dogs will be, too. A few people think that dogs won't be allowed inside the holy city because Revelation says, "Outside are the dogs. . .and everyone who loves and practices falsehood" (Revelation 22:15 NIV). However, this verse isn't talking about literal dogs, but about unworthy people (see Psalm 22:16; Matthew 7:6).

A LAKESIDE, WOODLAND HEAVEN

When describing the heavenly city, John writes: "The nations of those who are saved shall walk in its light, and the kings of the earth bring their glory and honor into it. Its gates shall not be shut at all by day (there shall be no night there). And they shall bring the glory and the honor of the nations into it" (Revelation 21:24–26).

However, if the saved live *inside* the heavenly city, then who are these people living *outside* the city, who bring the best of their produce and goods into the city? They're obviously redeemed believers,

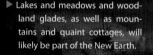

Lakes and meadows and woodland glades, as well as mountains and quaint cottages, will likely be part of the New Earth.

too, because those whose names weren't found in the Book of Life went to Hell at the end of the Millennium. So what are the saved doing *outside* the city? There is a very plausible explanation for this passage.

Though many people, when they think of Heaven, are enthralled by descriptions of a shining city of transparent gold, they nevertheless long to be surrounded by the beauty of nature. They'll be immensely thankful for a mansion inside the New Jerusalem, and enjoy fellowship with saints of all ages, but at times they'll also long for a "country house," to be surrounded by peaceful nature—lakes and meadows and woodland glades—with deer and birds and other peaceful creatures. They dream of a bit of acreage with a cottage where they can putter in a garden, walk their dog, and chat leisurely.

Is this too much to ask for? Is it out of the question? Such people are definitely going to get their wish. They'll enjoy the best of both worlds—life in the transcendently beautiful city of God, *and* life in the Eden-like tranquil countryside outside the city. And apparently they'll be growing fruit and other food, which they'll then bring into the city. Even though we'll be immortal, we'll still eat food, so someone will need to grow this food. Scripture indicates that this will indeed be the case.

It's unlikely that there will be sprawling cities on the New Earth. We'll have all the ultramodern conveniences of city life we need in the New Jerusalem. Instead, the surface of the earth will likely be dotted with cottages and cozy villages, the occasional hamlet or small town, not to mention luxurious lodges and resorts on all the millions of lakes.

KINGS AND QUEENS OF EARTH

Also, the fact that there will still be kings ruling over the nations of the world shows that we'll still rule and reign with Christ *after* the Millennium. The Bible tells us that we'll serve God for eternity (Revelation 22:3), and "serving" means *doing* something.

Besides the throne of God, the thrones of the archangels, and the thrones of the twenty-four elders, there will be other thrones in God's kingdom. These won't all be *inside* the heavenly city, but also on the renewed earth outside. John writes, "I saw thrones, and they sat on them, and judgment was committed to them" (Revelation 20:4). Even *after* the Millennium,

> ### CASTLES, CHATEAUS, AND MANORS
> Since there will be kings and queens on the earth, and since God delights to honor His obedient servants in the kingdom of Heaven, it seems probable that they'll dwell in castles at least as beautiful as the famous Hohenzollern and Wernigerode and Neuschwanstein castles in Germany, nestled atop green hills, their beauty and grandeur visible for many miles. For the governors of provinces, there may be palaces as stunning as the Château de Fontainebleau in France; and for the rulers of districts, great manor houses more luxurious than any found in the English countryside.

▶ Those who have served God faithfully in this life will be trusted with authority and power in God's coming kingdom; some will rule as kings and queens. Neuschwanstein, a fairy-tale castle near Munich in Bavaria, helps us imagine where those kings and queens might dwell.

saints will rule for all eternity: "His servants shall worship him; they shall see his face. . . . And they shall reign for ever and ever" (Revelation 22:3–5 RSV). "Then the sovereignty. . .of all the kingdoms under heaven will be handed over to the holy people of the Most High" (Daniel 7:27 NIV).

Those who served Christ faithfully and well on earth will be trusted with positions of great power and authority in the kingdom to come. Some will rule as kings and queens over entire nations, others will govern provinces, others will administer districts, still others will be in charge of cities. In the parable of the talents, Jesus said, "Well done, good servant; because you were faithful in a very little, have authority over ten cities" (Luke 19:17).

We will have perfect bodies and greatly enhanced minds in our new lives, but we won't automatically know everything. We will still look to those who are leaders in their particular fields of expertise for advice and counsel. And we'll humbly acknowledge the authority of the wise rulers God has set over us.

REST FROM OUR LABORS

Some people have the idea that we'll do absolutely *nothing* in Heaven. When speaking of the afterlife, Job said, "There the weary are at rest" (Job 3:17). Of course, the departed spirits rested in Sheol because they were *unable* to do anything. That's why Solomon advised, "Whatever your hand finds to do, do it with all your might; for there is no activity. . .in Sheol where you are going" (Ecclesiastes 9:10 NASB). But Heaven is a far different matter.

Mind you, *rest* in Heaven is also stated as a blessing. John heard a voice saying, "Blessed are those who die in the Lord from now on. Yes, says the Spirit, they are blessed indeed, for they will rest from their hard work; for their good deeds follow them!" (Revelation

14:13 NLT). However, the idea is *not* that we will do nothing for all eternity; that we'll simply put our minds in neutral and coast forever. Our weary toil on earth will be over, but we'll still actively, joyfully serve God.

Hard labor was part of the curse: God told Adam, "Cursed is the ground because of you; in toil you will eat of it all the days of your life. . . . By the sweat of your face you will eat bread" (Genesis 3:17, 19 NASB). But in Heaven and the New Earth, we'll enjoy our labor: "There shall be no more curse: but. . .[God's] servants shall serve him" (Revelation 22:3 KJV).

John also says of the saved in Heaven: "I looked, and there before me was a great multitude that no one could count, from every nation,

▶ A farmer walking through a golden wheat field in Heaven—
work will be a joy and no longer a curse.

tribe, people and language. . . .They are before the throne of God and serve him day and night in his temple" (Revelation 7:9, 15 NIV). Apparently there's plenty for *everyone* to do serving God, both in the eternal city and on the New Earth.

ACTIVITIES ON THE NEW EARTH

What will we do in Paradise—besides praising God, ruling the nations, strolling through nature, feasting, and talking? Many people may be surprised to learn that we'll do some very down-to-earth things: for example, people will farm the land, working on everything from strawberry farms to rice paddies to banana plantations to plum orchards. Others will distill apple cider, produce maple syrup, and tend honeybees. And if farmers are producing all kinds of food, there will be millions more people engaged in cooking stews, baking cakes and pastries, preparing fruit salads, and even inventing tasty new culinary delights.

> **THE EARTH'S GLORY AND HONOR**
> If "the kings of the earth bring their *glory* and *honor*" into the heavenly city, this cannot refer only to garden produce, but will include all the rare and beautiful treasures of the earth.

Very likely, people who have a talent for it will be employed in mining, supplying the gems for stone cutters and jewelers to make rare treasures. Other people will be involved in forestry, producing the timber for carpenters and woodworkers to craft sturdy houses and carve beautiful furniture. Still others will grow cotton and flax and weave the cloth for skilled seamstresses and clothing designers.

For recreation, we'll probably do a multitude of pleasurable and exciting things, such as sailing on clipper ships, drifting in hot-air balloons above lakes and fields, skiing down snow-covered mountains, riding horses through the surf of tropical beaches, swimming among coral reefs with millions of colorful fish, spending an afternoon with a herd of once-extinct brontotheres, etc. The sky's the limit.

We'll do things we never thought of in our wildest imaginations. Perhaps we'll take a paddlewheel down a mighty river with Mozart, discussing classical music. Maybe we'll join Abraham and Isaac for a discussion on a hardy breed of sheep for the newly terraformed Mars. Perhaps we'll discuss theology with David Livingstone while wrestling with gorillas in the Rwenzori Mountains. Maybe we'll tend gardens of gigantic vegetables in Antarctica's six months of summer while discussing literature with Tolkien.

And after we've done what we *most* wished to do, we'll be able to move on to *new* horizons and new opportunities and experiences.

MAKING UP FOR LOSSES ON EARTH

Jesus repeatedly told us to refrain from selfish pursuits of fame, pleasure, and riches and to "seek first the kingdom of God and His righteousness" (Matthew 6:33). He told us to give freely to those who ask, to "do good, and lend, hoping for nothing in return." Then He added a promise: "Your reward will be great" (Luke 6:35). He was aware that these teachings ran contrary to our natural tendencies, which is why He promised to reward us in His kingdom for whatever sacrifices we made in this life.

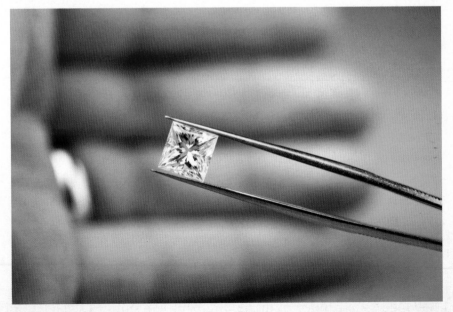

▶ Though earthly riches may be beautiful, like this diamond, riches in Heaven are not fleeting. God desires to give us much greater gifts in eternity.

Many of us, though we know Jesus' teachings, struggle to obey them. We're often tempted to ignore them as we strive to succeed, get ahead, and gain our share of what this world has to offer. But Jesus challenged us: "If any man will come after me, let him deny himself, and take up his cross daily, and follow me. For whosoever will save his life shall lose it: but whosoever will lose his life for my sake, the same shall save it" (Luke 9:23–24 KJV).

If we focus on our present life by seeking riches, fame, and pleasure, we may enjoy the fleeting rewards this world has to offer, but miss the much greater rewards God wishes to give us in eternity. But if we live unselfishly, love our enemies, forgive those who offend us or fail to return our belongings or money, God will more than make these things up to us. He promised, "Look, I am coming soon! My reward is with me, and I will give to each person according to what they have done" (Revelation 22:12 NIV).

The Lord will say in that day, "Well done, good and faithful servant; you have been faithful over a few things, I will make you ruler over many things. Enter into the joy of your Lord" (Matthew 25:23). What does it mean to "enter into the *joy* of your lord"? It means that it gives God great joy to bless you with the lavish riches of His kingdom. Jesus said, "It is your Father's good pleasure to give you the kingdom" (Luke 12:32).

This doesn't just apply to our deliberately choosing an unselfish lifestyle. It also means patiently and cheerfully enduring circumstances we wouldn't normally choose. Perhaps we weren't blessed with a loving family, a happy childhood, or a blissful marriage. Maybe we've had to endure a job we didn't enjoy, or constantly struggled with finances, doing without things—such as new clothes, vacations, or dining out—that others enjoyed. Perhaps we were born with a physical handicap that greatly limited what we could do.

Perhaps life's obligations prevented us from following our most cherished dreams. Perhaps much of the good we set out to do with such high hopes ended in disappointment. We suffered setbacks or devastating losses, and as old age and infirmity approached, instead of retiring with a sense of contentment and accomplishment, we carried the pain of broken relationships and the sorrow of half-finished dreams. Is God able to restore *these* things as well? Or have our dreams died permanently?

Consider this: There were millions of slaves in the Roman Empire, and multitudes of these embraced the Christian faith. . .but continued living as slaves, often for harsh pagan masters. What hope did they have of living out *any* of their dreams or even of devoting their time to "serving Christ"? Yet Paul said to them, "Whatever you do, do it heartily, as to the Lord and not to men, knowing that from the Lord you will receive the reward of the inheritance; for you serve the Lord Christ" (Colossians 3:23–24).

God sees the heart. He is aware if we love Him and "serve the Lord Christ" to the best of our abilities, however limited we feel our efforts are. The good news is that if our heart's desires—unfulfilled in this life—are pleasing to God, we'll be able to pick them up in the kingdom of God with renewed youth, joy, freedom, and inspiration, and complete them. Or perhaps God will transform and redirect our inspirations and passions and launch us into something similar yet different—and more rewarding and enjoyable.

NEW BODIES AND TRANSPORTATION

As for transportation, though many people in that day may enjoy traveling long distances in camel caravans for the sheer fun of it, or lumbering along leisurely atop elephants, or traveling down country roads in horse-drawn buggies, there will also be faster means of getting around. After all, we won't necessarily want to spend six months traveling to the New Jerusalem for a banquet. This is especially true for those who will travel often between the heavenly city and a farm on the opposite side of the globe.

So although there won't be internal combustion engines spewing out pollution, there will likely be modern transportation. Some people believe that we won't actually *need* any modes of transportation, that we'll be able to disappear from one location and reappear in a

▶ Transportation in God's future kingdom will likely include modern transportation.

distant place simply by thinking ourselves there. They point to the fact that after Jesus received His eternal body, He was able to suddenly appear in a locked room, to the amazement of His disciples (John 20:19; Luke 24:36–37). They also point to the time when Philip vanished from the Gaza Road and reappeared in Azotus, miles to the north (Acts 8:39–40)—and this was *before* he was resurrected!

Taking this to its logical conclusion, they envision our being able to travel from Earth to distant planets in the blink of an eye. While this is a possibility, it seems more likely that we'll one day (not necessarily immediately) use fantastic spaceships to traverse the vast gulfs of space. Also, even if we *will* be able to blink in and out of places at will, there are issues such as privacy and permission. Would you simply be able to teleport yourself into Moses' mansion without invitation or warning—interrupting his banquet with Adam and Elijah? It hardly seems likely.

Some people also imagine they'll be able to fly like angels once they receive their new bodies. Again, while this is certainly not impossible, the evidence for it is thin. And though Jesus ascended bodily to Heaven (Acts 1:9), this may well have been an exceptional case.

TECHNOLOGY ON HEAVEN AND EARTH

Though some people might actually *enjoy* spending weeks handcrafting a wooden armchair with simple tools, many of us won't hesitate to employ the latest, cutting-edge equipment to mine for treasures deep in the earth, and use lasers to cut gems. And though we may live in chalets or cottages, these dwellings may have all the latest technology for cooking, cleaning, and communication.

The entire city of the heavenly Jerusalem will be a showcase of unearthly architecture and supernatural beauty—but embedded in it will be unimaginably advanced technology. The New Earth will be similar. Though most of the planet will appear to be a profusion of natural beauty—hills and valleys, lakes and rivers, forests and fields, peaceful cottages and castles—it may well be filled with unobtrusive, hidden—even miraculous—technology.

And besides the slow, natural modes of transportation, there will most likely be shimmering, sleek electric vehicles, including flying cars even better than those presently being produced. In fact, there may be huge transport vehicles with antigravity drives capable of carrying tons of fresh produce rapidly from the far corners of the globe to the heavenly city. If the only food available to the city will be what's grown in its immediate vicinity, it simply won't be sufficient for the city's population. Just because mankind hasn't invented something yet, doesn't mean that God won't inspire us to invent it in the near future.

> **AMAZING FUTURE INVENTIONS**
>
> After a thousand years, people with eternal bodies and brilliant, inquisitive minds will be able to uncover many of the amazing secrets of God's universe. "It is the glory of God to conceal a matter; to search out a matter is the glory of kings" (Proverbs 25:2 NIV). God delights to give us the wisdom to "find out knowledge of witty inventions" (Proverbs 8:12 KJV).

This same principle applies when it comes to interstellar travel. There'll probably be no need for us to travel to other star systems during the first few hundred to a thousand years. We'll be far too busy exploring the New Jerusalem and enjoying life on the New Earth. But when the day comes that we *do* want to explore the far-flung stars and head out to new, habitable planets, we'll surely have come up with the technology by that time to do so—even if God leaves it entirely up to us to make the technological breakthroughs.

DYNAMIC, IMMORTAL ANIMALS

Jesus said there will be no marriage in God's future kingdom. He explained, "Those who are considered worthy of taking part in the age to come and in the resurrection from the dead will neither marry nor be given in marriage" (Luke 20:35 NIV). Since God intends for men and women to have sex only within a marriage relationship, the fact that there's no marriage implies that there will be no further pro-creation of the human race.

▶ A white-tailed deer fawn in a field of flowers; animals will exist in Heaven and will be immortal like people.

By extension, because the animals of the New Earth will *also* be eternal, this may imply that they'll also no longer procreate. If they *did* keep reproducing, yet no animals died to make room for them, the earth would eventually become overcrowded. So creation will, in a sense, become static. But it won't be boring. Although every facet of life will continue existing throughout all time, they'll have extra dimensions to them that will continually make them new.

However, the Bible doesn't actually *say* that animals will cease reproducing, so it's possible they won't. After all, what's cuter than brand-new, playful tiger cubs—or even kittens or fawns? One possibility might be that as animals continue to increase and fill the earth with their offspring, these new animals will eventually be taken as man's companions to other worlds throughout our galaxy—where they'll continue to "be fruitful, and multiply" (Genesis 1:22 KJV). They may fill the trillions of habitable planets that scientists estimate exist in our universe.

ETERNALLY LEARNING IN HEAVEN

Some people suspect that Heaven will be boring. They ask, "If we know *everything* there is to know the instant we arrive there, what will be left to learn?" But gaining knowledge in Heaven will be an ongoing process. Though our ability to learn will be greatly enhanced and accelerated, scripture is clear that arriving in Heaven doesn't confer total wisdom upon us.

The apostle John writes, "I saw underneath the altar the souls of those who had been slain because of the word of God. . .and they cried out with a loud voice, saying, 'How long, O Lord, holy and true, will You refrain from judging and avenging our blood on those who dwell on the earth?' And. . .they were told that they should rest for a little while longer, until the number of their fellow servants and their brethren who were to be killed even as they had been, would be completed also" (Revelation 6:9–11 NASB). These martyrs were in Heaven. In fact, they were at the altar of incense before the very throne of God. Yet they didn't know the answer to their most pressing question. So they

NO INSTANT OMNISCIENCE
People get the idea that we'll become instantly omniscient from Paul's statement, "Now I know in part, but then I will know fully just as I also have been fully known" (1 Corinthians 13:12 NASB). But "to know fully" comes from the Greek word *epiginosko*, which means "to know extensively," not to know all things like God does.

asked about it. And notice that even when God answered them, He didn't give them a precise date or a full answer. He told them only as much as they needed to know at the time.

Also, consider this promise: Jesus says, "I will give him a white stone, and a new name written on the stone which no one knows but he who receives it" (Revelation 2:17 NASB). There will be things— such as the secret names of billions of other believers—that we won't know, even in Heaven. Even the angels, who are much wiser than human beings and have been in Heaven for untold ages, don't know everything. "The angel of the LORD said, 'LORD Almighty, how long will you withhold mercy from Jerusalem and from the towns of Judah, which you have been angry with these seventy years?' So the LORD spoke kind and comforting words to the angel" (Zechariah 1:12–13 NIV).

Regarding certain future events, Jesus said, "No one knows the day or hour when these things will happen, not even the angels in heaven" (Matthew 24:36 NLT). Peter tells us that there are "things which angels desire to look into" (1 Peter 1:12). This displays a curiosity and a thirst for learning, and if even the angels have this attribute, we, too—who have this trait in *this* life—will continue learning throughout all eternity.

LIBRARIES, 3D TVS, AND HOLODECKS

God is meticulous about keeping records and has several exhaustive volumes in Heaven, so it stands to reason that there will be immense libraries in the New Jerusalem—possibly even with exact replicas of ancient books re-created for our benefit. Vast libraries may have rooms whose walls are covered with books. If you enjoy reading, you'll be in Heaven. . .literally! We may even be able to acquire copies of volumes we treasure the most, to add to our personal libraries in our heavenly mansions.

Our homes may also house enormous 3D televisions, on which we can watch documentaries on the lives of famous men and women of God. Why should they repeatedly tell their stories to one person after another, down through endless ages, without even the benefit of visual aids? How much better to create realistic 3D documentaries that millions of believers can watch at their leisure. And for real hands-on learning, there may be even more exciting options!

In the *Star Trek* series, the crews of the starships sometimes entered holodecks (holographic environment simulators), whether for entertainment or for educational and training purposes. Wouldn't it be fascinating to enter Bible worlds of the past, walk among tangible, physical people and witness and experience re-created events—experiencing the sights, sounds, and even smells? And what if you could hear the original foreign languages, but instantly understand them with cutting-edge technology?

Imagine spending a day exploring the ark of Noah, filled with endless cages of animals. Imagine walking with Jonah through the mighty city of Nineveh. Imagine sitting on the Areopagus listening to Paul give his Mars' Hill sermon. Imagine spending an entire *month* traveling and camping out with Jesus and His disciples as they tour Galilee. You would truly understand the Bible for the first time. Talk about questions being answered!

> **AMAZING MEMORIES IN ETERNITY**
> We will have far clearer, better-functioning minds, and mental blocks that once hindered us will be no more. This will likely include having *total recall*, the ability to remember literally everything we learn. Only a few people today possess this unusual ability, but in Heaven it will likely be standard issue.

You would also be able to step into re-created history. You could experience the most pivotal events of all time and learn what really happened and why. How about listening to D. L. Moody preach to crowds in Chicago during the 1800s? And what about exploring the humble homestead of your godly ancestors? How about looking in on key moments of your own life, with the added benefit of seeing into the spiritual world and watching angels strengthen and comfort you, answer your prayers, and guide you? "All that I know now is partial and incomplete, but then I will know everything completely" (1 Corinthians 13:12 NLT).

BEYOND HEAVEN ON EARTH

We'll have forever and ever to worship God, ask Him questions, learn whatever we wish to learn, and talk with fascinating saints of God from ages past. We'll also get the opportunity to do everything on earth that we missed doing in this lifetime. During this entire time, the Bible tells us, we'll continue to serve God, world without end. But surely, many people reason, even after we do every conceivable thing we could imagine doing on this earth, the day will come when we'll look for *new* horizons, *new* worlds to explore.

Here is where many Christians let their imaginations run wild with even more exciting possibilities. When they think of "new worlds to explore," they think of new worlds *literally*. Why not? When God created our sun, "he made the stars also" (Genesis 1:16 KJV). Astronomers estimate that there are 170 billion galaxies in the universe, with each galaxy containing 10 million to 100 billion stars. That's a *lot* of stars!

Recently, scientists have discovered something that they've suspected all along—that our sun is not the only star with planets. They have detected many hundreds of planets orbiting nearby stars, and calculate that our galaxy has some 50 billion planets, of which 500 million are within the habitable zone of their star. Think of that! Some 500 million planets in our galaxy alone can potentially support a dizzying variety of life! There's obviously no need to worry that we'll run out of things to do and see and rule over in eternity.

Some Christians note that God created habitable planets like Earth for the express purpose of being inhabited (Isaiah 45:18). But whether life exists elsewhere or not, whether alien worlds are teeming with exotic flora and fauna, we simply can't say. Christians such as C. S. Lewis believed this was possible, and he wrote about it in *Religion and Rocketry*. Although this is a fascinating topic, it's beyond the scope of this book. If such life does exist, remember that it was God (through Christ) who created it: "All things were made through Him, and without Him nothing was made that was made" (John 1:3).

A compilation of elements from various NASA images of planets over a breathtaking galaxy; there are unimaginable new worlds to explore beyond Heaven and Earth.

And, as already noted, there may not have to be new, never-before-seen kinds of *alien* life on these worlds for them to have life. As humans explore these new worlds, they may take the animals of Earth to these far-flung planets to start new Eden-like paradises. We may even bring back the dinosaurs from extinction and dedicate entire planets to them as vast game reserves.

Our future is definitely not going to be boring. We'll have all of eternity to explore Heaven and the vastness of God's creation.

WE ARE FOREIGNERS AND NOMADS

After describing a long list of Bible heroes who lived and died before Jesus' day, the writer of Hebrews says: "These all died in faith, not having received the promises, but having seen them afar off, and were persuaded of them, and embraced them, and confessed that they were strangers and pilgrims on the earth. For they that say such things declare plainly that they seek a country" (Hebrews 11:13–14 KJV).

What does it mean to be "strangers and pilgrims on the earth"? The New Living Translation puts it this way: "They agreed that they were foreigners and nomads here on earth." In other words, not "strangers" in the sense of a fellow citizen you haven't been introduced to, but a foreigner—someone who stands out as different and doesn't fit into established society. And not only a foreigner, but a rootless nomad, someone having no certain dwelling place. In a very real sense, we *are* nomads in this world.

This may not seem to describe millions of Christians who are settled securely with a thirty-year mortgage, but God has the

> **TEMPORARY TENANTS**
>
> Even though the Lord promised the land of Canaan to the Israelites and they lived on the land and farmed it, they never truly *owned* it because their lives were so short that they were like flickering shadows passing over it. God made it clear who *really* owned the land and what this meant: "The land must never be sold on a permanent basis, for the land belongs to me. You are only foreigners and tenant farmers working for me" (Leviticus 25:23 NLT).

long view. We're shortsighted.

King Solomon, master of a kingdom that stretched from Egypt to the Euphrates River, sitting on his throne in all his splendor and glory, nevertheless declared: "Vanity of vanities, saith the Preacher, vanity of vanities; all is vanity. What profit hath a man of all his labour which he taketh under the sun? One generation passeth away, and another generation cometh: but the earth abideth for ever" (Ecclesiastes 1:2–4 KJV). Even Job, the long-lived, immensely wealthy landowner, complained, "My life is but a breath" (Job 7:7 NIV). Job bemoaned his lot, saying: "How frail is humanity! How short is life, how full of trouble! We blossom like a flower and then wither. Like a passing shadow, we quickly disappear" (Job 14:1–2 NLT).

Despite the fact that we presently live in this world, we're not here long. We pass like a shadow over the land and we're gone. Our ultimate home, our final forwarding address, is Heaven. That's why the Bible cautions us to not love this present world too much or allow ourselves to become too attached to it. Yes, we may love our country

▶ Camel caravan on a nomadic trip through a sand desert. Those who follow Jesus are like wandering nomads in this world; our true dwelling place is with God.

now and feel allegiance to it, but when it comes down to it, we're foreigners, nomads, and migrant workers traveling through this world on our way to an eternal destination. We must love Heaven far more.

MOTIVATION TO LIVE GODLY LIVES

Not only are our lives on earth fleeting shadows, but this entire present earth is transitory and soon to pass away. "On that day, he will set the heavens on fire, and the elements will melt away in the flames. But we are looking forward to the new heavens and new earth he has promised" (2 Peter 3:12–13 NLT). What does this mean for us?

"Since everything around us is going to be destroyed like this, what holy and godly lives you should live, looking forward to the day of God. . . . And so, dear friends, while you are waiting for these things to happen, make every effort to be found living peaceful lives that are pure and blameless in his sight" (2 Peter 3:11–12, 14 NLT).

Jesus said, "Don't store up treasures here on earth. . . . Store your treasures in heaven. . . . Wherever your treasure is, there your heart . . .will also be" (Matthew 6:19–21 NLT). And Paul writes, "Since you

▶ The Bible, seen in the image above, is the only truth that will help people live in this temporary, evil world with God's wisdom, righteousness, and pure devotion.

have been raised to new life with Christ, set your sights on the realities of heaven" (Colossians 3:1 NLT).

However, God knows that it's often difficult for our thoughts to be filled with Heaven when we're just starting to make our mark in life. It's easier for those who are older, who have grown weary of what this world has to offer, to have a clearer perspective. But many young people are just as disillusioned with the dog-eat-dog worldly systems and long for something better. "But now they desire a better country, that is, an heavenly: wherefore God is not ashamed to be called their God: for he hath prepared for them a city" (Hebrews 11:16 KJV).

The better country we desire is the paradisiacal New Earth, and the city that God has prepared for us is "the Holy City, the new Jerusalem" (Revelation 21:2 NIV). The New Jerusalem is the capital of the kingdom of Heaven, both now and when the heavenly city appears on the New Earth. Knowing that our ultimate loyalties are to the kingdom of God should cause us to live according to the laws of His kingdom, as citizens of Heaven, in the here and now. "We should live in this evil world with wisdom, righteousness, and devotion to God" (Titus 2:12 NLT).

This knowledge will help us love our neighbors, even when they're difficult, and obey Christ's commands, even when they're not convenient. In so doing, we will store up treasures in Heaven. Therefore put your trust in "Him who is able to keep you from stumbling, and to present you faultless before the presence of His glory with exceeding joy" (Jude 1:24).

ENDNOTES

1. Randy Alcorn, *Heaven* (Wheaton, IL: Tyndale House, 2004), 178.

2. Homer, *The Odyssey*, trans. Samuel Butler (El Paso: Norte Press, 2005), 465.

3. *Praying Together*, copyright © 1988 English Language Liturgical Consultation, 2; www.englishtexts.org/praying.pdf.

4. *The Catechism of the Catholic Church*, section 2, chapter 2, article 5, paragraph 1:633,635; www.vatican.va/archive/ENG0015/_index.htm.

5. Mark Galli, "Incredible Journeys: What to Make of Visits to Heaven," *Christianity Today*, December 21, 2012; www.christianitytoday.com/ct/2012/december/incredible-journeys.html.

6. Eben Alexander III, *Proof of Heaven: A Neurosurgeon's Journey into the Afterlife* (New York: Simon & Schuster, 2012), 41.

7. Donald S. Whitney, "*Proof of Heaven*: A Review," Center for Biblical Spirituality; http://biblicalspirituality.org/wp-content/uploads/2013/01/Proof-of-Heaven-1.pdf.

8. Eusebius, *The History of the Church*, III:39.

9. Alcorn, *Heaven*, 51–63.

10. J. R. R. Tolkien, *The Silmarillion* (New York: Random House, 1977), 19.

11. Jonathan Edwards, "The Eternity of Hell Torments"; www.jonathan-edwards.org/Eternity.html.

12. C. S. Lewis, *Letters to Malcolm: Chiefly on Prayer* (New York: Harcourt Brace Jovanovich, 1964), 108.

13. Ibid.

14. John Milton, *Paradise Lost* (1674), book 1, lines 61–66.

ART CREDITS

ABOUT THE AUTHOR

Ed Strauss is a freelance writer living in British Columbia, Canada. Ed has written more than thirty books and has a passion for biblical apologetics. Besides writing for Barbour Publishing, he has been published by Zondervan, Tyndale, Moody, and Focus on the Family.